Robb Walsh

Are You Really Going to Eat That?

Robb Walsh is the restaurant critic for the *Houston Press*, an occasional commentator for NPR's *Weekend Edition*, the former food columnist for *Natural History* magazine, and the former editor in chief of *Chile Pepper* magazine. He is the author of *Legends of Texas Barbecue Cookbook* and *The Tex-Mex Cookbook: A History in Recipes and Photos*, and the co-author of several other cooking and travel books. He lives in Houston, Texas.

Also by Robb Walsh

Legends of Texas Barbecue Cookbook:
Recipes and Recollections from the Pit Bosses

A Cowboy in the Kitchen:
Recipes from Reata and Texas West of the Pecos
(with Grady Spears and James Evans)

Nuevo Tex-Mex:
Festive New Recipes from Just North of the Border
(with David Garrido)

Traveling Jamaica with Knife, Fork & Spoon:
A Righteous Guide to Jamaican Cookery
(with Jay McCarthy)

The Tex-Mex Cookbook:
A History in Recipes and Photos

Are You
Really Going
to Eat That?

Are You Really Going to Eat That?

Reflections of a
Culinary Thrill Seeker

Robb Walsh

Anchor Books
A Division of Random House, Inc.
New York

FIRST ANCHOR BOOKS EDITION, NOVEMBER 2004

Copyright © 2003 by Robb Walsh

All rights reserved under International and Pan-American Copyright Conventions.
Published in the United States by Anchor Books, a division of Random House, Inc.,
New York, and simultaneously in Canada by Random House of Canada Limited,
Toronto. *Are You Really Going to Eat That?* was originally published in hardcover in the
United States by Counterpoint, a member of the Perseus Books Group, in 2003.

Anchor Books and colophon are registered trademarks of Random House, Inc.

The Cataloging-in-Publication Data is on file at the Library of Congress.

Anchor ISBN: 1-4000-7716-8

Author photograph © Will van Overbeek

www.anchorbooks.com

Printed in the United States of America
10 9 8 7 6 5 4 3 2 1

In memory of my father:
R. J. Walsh

Contents

Acknowledgments

Thanks to my dear friends Tim Carman and Lisa Gray for helping to put this book together. Thanks to Anna Ossenfort for setting it straight. Thanks to David McCormick and Nina Collins for selling it and to Dawn Seferian for buying it.

Thanks to the *Houston Press* for a real job with dental insurance. And thanks to my editors Lauren Kern and Margaret Downing and *New Times* editors Christine Brennan and Mike Lacey for their support.

Thanks to *American Way* for the places I saw. And thanks to Dana Joseph, Jill Becker, John Ostdick, and Elaine Srnka for their editing help. Thanks to *Natural History* for the Ivory Tower perspective. Thanks to my editors there, Richard Milner and Bruce Stutz.

Thanks to Louis Black at the *Austin Chronicle* for "throwing the baby in the swimming pool." Thanks to Jim Shahin for mentoring me, even though I turned my back on him. Thanks to Marion Winik for the chutzpah lessons. Thanks to Robert Bryce for beer, commiseration, and hot tips. And thanks to Pableaux Johnson for the sanctuary on Bayou Teche.

Thanks to Kelly Klaasmeyer for holding me close. Thanks to my fellow members of the Walsh pack, Scott, David, Gordon,

Ricky, and Mike for always being there with a helping hand or a swift kick in the ass. Thanks to Mom for her prayers and *holupki*. And thanks to my daughters, Katie and Julia Walsh, for being happy in little houses.

Introduction

I have never been a picky eater. Sure, I have preferences. I like the toasted grasshoppers in Oaxaca better than the salt-cured *gusanos* (although, in truth, the caterpillars taste a lot like sun-dried tomatoes). Ants are bitter, if you ask me, but ant egg soup is very delicate. And I'll never forget the steamed fish I had with a Laotian sauce made from the *mang da* beetle; the male insect's musk gland gives it an aroma that bears a striking resemblance to blue cheese.

Don't worry. You won't see any stories about eating bugs in this book. In the end, I didn't find the subject all that interesting. But in the early 1990s, the bugs, the armadillos, and all the other weird stuff I was eating led me to an endeavor that has kept me busy ever since: to explore the world—its cultures, its history, and its emotions—through food.

National Public Radio's Liane Hansen once called me "the Indiana Jones of food writers," and I've tried to live up to the title. In this book, you'll read my reporting on food and culture from improbable locations—including a durian plantation in Thailand, a fishing boat off the coast of Chile, and the kitchen of Darrington penitentiary in Texas.

I've always experienced the world through food. My maternal grandmother was born in the Carpathian Mountains between

Slovakia and Poland. She spoke English just fine, but she was more comfortable in pastry than in conversation. She was affectionate, but she expressed that affection best through cooking. When she came to visit, we bought her a twenty-five-pound sack of flour, and she spent her entire vacation in the kitchen. I'd come home from school to find the aromas of Ruthenia hanging in the air. We'd carve up a huge slab of *pagachi*, a sauerkraut-and-bacon-stuffed flatbread, for dinner while a fresh batch of sweetened poppy-seed strudel cooled on the rack. Grandma never said a thing about her former homeland to us, and yet I feel as if my five brothers and I all came to know the old country intimately.

My mom inherited Grandma's delicious yet sublimated way of expressing affection, along with her whole Eastern European repertoire. But as a member of the assimilationist second generation, Mom moved beyond the confines of Slavic fare. She clipped articles from magazines and experimented with suburban recipe swapping. Tuna noodle casseroles, American dishes that employed cream of mushroom soup, and European "gourmet" creations like beef burgundy, chicken cacciatore, and stuffed pork all appeared on our dinner table (though never with quite the frequency of sauerkraut).

My dad returned from the Korean War when I was two, and he promptly went to work in the food business. During most of my youth, he was a salesman in the restaurant and institutions division of General Foods Corporation. Eating out was part of his job. I used to visit restaurants with him when I went along on sales trips. Though Dad came from a meat-and-potatoes Irish background, he prided himself on the food knowledge he acquired working with chefs. Conveniently, at about the time I entered college, he went to work for Gallo Brothers. The firm was never known for great wines, but the position nevertheless required my father to take a crash course in viniculture and enology. Dad happily held forth on the subject whenever we popped a cork.

I started cooking as a teenager. As I was the oldest of six sons, it fell to me to cook dinner for my brothers when Mom and Dad left for the weekend. And I took a great interest. Soon I was reading the only cookbook in the house and trying my own recipes.

Dad was a hunter and regularly stocked the freezer with deer, pheasant, and other game. Mom had no interest in cooking such exotica, so it just sat there until the annual freezer cleaning, when she threw it all away. When I learned that wild game was treasured by gourmets, I got her permission to cook with the stuff. At age sixteen, I attempted pheasant under glass. (My brothers opted for pizza that night.)

Every fall, Dad and I went to Packard's Hunting Camp in Maine for a weekend of deer hunting. After sampling Mrs. Packard's venison mincemeat pie one year, I decided we should try making some. The recipe in Mom's cookbook was quite complicated. It called for a lot of apples and apple cider.

I had recently gotten my driver's license. We lived in Connecticut, a state dotted with apple orchards and cider mills. New England apple farmers could argue for hours on end about the varieties of apples and what they were best suited for or about the superiority of one cider mill over the others.

These comparisons fascinated me. And so I turned the project of gathering ingredients for our mincemeat into a nearly month-long affair that required me to drive all over the state in Mom's station wagon, sampling apples and ciders and talking to farmers. The apple tour was a lot more interesting than the resulting pie filling.

The mincemeat was tasty, but it was much richer than the bottled stuff most people are used to. One slice of pie was more than most people could handle—especially after Thanksgiving or Christmas dinner. The recipe made several gallons of the stuff. Minus about three pies' worth, it all ended up in the freezer. I never made mincemeat again, but ever since, I have been traveling around, talking to farmers and comparing edibles.

In Austin, Texas, where I went to college, I drove my motorcycle to the most unusual restaurants, barbecue joints, catfish shacks, and tamale stands that I could find. Then I dropped out of college for a couple of years and worked in Denmark, where I drove another motorcycle around Jutland looking for the definitive version of Danish village inn favorites. My Danish girlfriends taught me to debate the merits of rye bread, herring, Danish bacon, and Danish cheese in the native language. I ended up graduating from the University of Texas with a degree in Scandinavian studies.

I was the first person on either side of my family to get a college degree. I wanted to pursue a career as a writer, but my folks thought that was crazy. I ended up taking a job, fresh out of college, as an advertising copywriter. A few years later, I had my own small agency in Hartford, Connecticut. I was sleeping with a very attractive restaurant professional—and so was a caterer named David Glass. One day, she took me to his house to recover something she had left there. Glass wasn't home, but in his kitchen were huge cauldrons of veal stock, and the whole place smelled of chocolate.

My interest in the woman was short-lived, as was his. But I never forgot Glass's kitchen, and after the woman moved away, I hired Glass to cater a holiday dinner for a few clients. In the course of planning it, he taught me a new way to think about food.

Glass had just returned from an apprenticeship in the kitchen of the Archestrate restaurant in Paris, where the wild man of the nouvelle cuisine, Alain Senderens, was the chef. But in 1980 no one in my circle had heard of the nouvelle cuisine.

From the first course—a salad of lobster meat tossed with pureed mango, which Glass paired with a Raymond Chardonnay—my clients and I were mystified and delighted. After that dinner, I pestered Glass for more information. He told me to buy a cookbook by David Leiderman called *Cooking the Nouvelle Cuisine in America*. The recipes were interesting, but it was the introduction that I found riveting. Leiderman encapsulated the budding school of thought: seasonal indigenous ingredients, a return to the simplicity of regional cooking . . . . The litany has become boring by now, but at the time, it was astonishing.

In 1981 I moved my advertising business to a magnificent house on a hill in Lafayette, California, and David Glass became a regular houseguest. The East Bay was the cradle of the new American cooking, and like a lot of other Northern Californians, I became a foodie. My new wife and I spent weekends driving around the state, visiting farms and fishing docks. I carried a cast-iron skillet and a chef's knife in my car at all times, so that I could cook anywhere. My idea of a great dinner was a bottle of wine, a loaf of sourdough, and some fresh mussels pulled off the rocks at the beach.

We moved back to Austin to start a family in 1985. No one in Texas seemed to have noticed that in California, Mark Miller was creating a new, Southwestern cuisine, and I considered it my job to inform the state. I sent feature articles to anyone I thought might print them. Nothing happened.

Some years later, a couple of paragraphs from one story ended up in the *Austin Chronicle*, a freewheeling alternative weekly. I called the *Chronicle*'s editor, Louis Black, to ask about payment. He said that he'd send me $10, but what he really needed were short restaurant reviews. The conversation lasted twenty seconds. I was elated.

Thus began my food-writing career. I think I got $20 for each short review. As time went by, the reviews grew longer, and I began to range farther afield. Soon I was writing about food without even mentioning restaurants.

I wrote a lot about chile peppers—growing them, eating them, and cooking with them and how to tell them apart. I wrote about their psychotropic effects. I quoted Andrew Weil, not yet a natural-health guru, who compared the high from eating peppers to that from marijuana and cocaine. Soon I was known as a scribe of the chile-head tribe.

I traveled to Oaxaca to find what Austin writer Jean Andrews, author of *Peppers: The Domesticated Capsicums*, claimed was the hottest pepper in the world. I went to the Caribbean to find obscure salsas. In 1991 I founded the *Austin Chronicle* Hot Sauce Festival, which is still one of the biggest hot sauce competitions in the country. I had found my niche.

But chile eating and associated thrill seeking slowly segued into other forms of food adventures. The search for obscure peppers led me to the mysterious culture of Mexico and begat a fascination with Mesoamerican history. I became a culinary explorer—looking for the lost recipes of the Zapotecs, Mayans, and Aztecs. I spent vacations exploring Mesoamerican ruins and asking archeologists about pottery shards and ancient cooking vessels.

Eventually, I began writing food stories for *American Way*, the in-flight magazine of American Airlines. My frequent research trips to Latin America, France, and the Caribbean didn't help my standing with either my wife or my boss. In 1994 I was laid off from my advertising job, and my wife filed for divorce. With little left to lose, I decided to make my freelance food writing a full-time career.

It was the job I'd always wished for: flying around the world writing about interesting food. *American Way* and *Natural History* picked up the tab on most of my travels. Unfortunately, I'd forgotten to wish that this career would pay a lot. Five years later, in 1999, I was flat broke. So when I was offered a desk job as the editor of *Chile Pepper Magazine*, I had to take it. My traveling days were over.

Are You Really Going to Eat That? Reflections of a Culinary Thrill Seeker is a collection of forty of my favorite stories with twenty accompanying recipes. The first two sections—"A Chowhound on the Scent" and "I'll Have What He's Having"—were written during the five years that I traveled the globe in search of food thrills. With these early pieces, I discovered that weird food isn't all that interesting unless somebody interesting eats it, or somebody eats it for an interesting reason.

As I matured as a writer, I found that interesting people also live in places with reliable phone service. In the middle sections of the book titled "Chicken-Fried Soul" and "Those Cranky Europeans," I eat my way across the American South and Europe trying my best to understand as much as I digest.

I miss my traveling days sometimes, but all that roaming around also taught me how to enjoy staying in one place. In "Indiana Jones in the Suburbs," I've collected a few pieces from my recent writings for the *Houston Press*. Maybe I'm just getting old, but these days I find the markets and restaurants in my hometown almost as exotic as those I've seen abroad. And thanks to the concentration of immigrants here, I can talk to Cambodian farmers, Vietnamese shrimpers, African cooks, and people from every state in Mexico without leaving the city limits. Finding an herb I've never heard of or a vegetable I've never eaten has always been exciting—but it's even more exciting when it's right in my own backyard.

That brings us to the last section, "You Are What You Eat." Yes, I'm still fascinated by exotic edibles, but experience has finally taught me that the simplest foods trigger the most profound experiences. I can honestly say that I changed the day I shared bread with a dead man.

That story and the others in the last section recount my most personal food experiences. They bring the voyage full circle. What started as a search for weird things to eat slowly morphed into the study of how cultures express themselves through food. And that quest led me to better understand myself.

The stories assembled here are also an attempt to explain an odd career and to understand how someone becomes so utterly obsessed with food. It's a popular subject when my brothers and I get together. (Most of them are almost as bad as I am.)

Maybe it has something to do with the elemental sort of love my grandmother and my mom invested in every meal. They put into their cooking what they couldn't say in words. Now I spend my mealtimes trying to get all that emotion and meaning back out.

This much I know: in times of great emotion, I always crave sauerkraut.

Part ONE

A Chowhound on the Scent

Hot Sauce Safari

The little house looks like it's about to slip off the side of the cliff into the thicket of banana plants and herb gardens below. Knocking on the door, I am greeted by reggae on the radio and several loud, simultaneous conversations. "Come in," somebody finally hollers over the din. "It's open!"

Inside, seven women are sitting around a kitchen table, cleaning herbs and laughing. Out the window behind them, I can see the green squares of hundreds of garden plots covering the steep slopes of Trinidad's Paramin Hills. Stacked along the wall is the treasure I've traveled thousands of miles to find: cases upon cases of Genuine Paramin Pepper Sauce.

Hillary Boisson is the Paramin Women's Group's unofficial leader. She is scrutinizing my T-shirt, trying to find some clue as to what this large sunburned American wants in her clubhouse kitchen. The T-shirt reads "Austin Hot Sauce Contest, Fourth Annual." It was in my role as head judge of that contest that I had my first encounter with Caribbean-style pepper sauces. Over the years, the contest has turned into one of the world's largest, with more than three hundred hot sauces entered every year.

For the past few years, Caribbean-style hot sauces made with habaneros and Scotch bonnet peppers have been running away with the show. Instead of the jalapeño, tomatoes, onions, and

3

garlic used to make Mexican-style hot sauces, these vibrant Caribbean salsas are made with various combinations of Scotch bonnets, papaya, mango, or pineapple and seasoned with fresh herbs, ginger, allspice, or mustard. They taste sensational.

After I got hooked, I started looking for Caribbean pepper sauces in the supermarket, but I found that there weren't many to choose from. The most exotic sauces, like Dragon's Breath, Apocalyptic Hot Sauce, and Voodoo Jerk Slather, are made in small batches and sold by mail order through pepper-cult publications like *Chile Pepper Magazine* and the *Mo Hotta Mo Betta* catalog.

And the most sought-after of all are the local sauces made in minuscule quantities. If the stuff couldn't be mailed to me, I decided, I'd just have to go to the source. So I'm on a hot sauce safari, island-hopping in the Caribbean for three weeks now, stalking elusive pepper sauces. To find this particular little salsa factory, I had to brave the treacherous switchbacks of the nearly vertical one-lane road in an overheating truck. The Paramin Women's Group is suitably impressed.

"The Paramin Women's Group has been meeting for twenty-six years," member Veronica Romany tells me. "We used to make handicrafts: baskets, crocheting, that kind of thing. But you know, we grow the best herbs and peppers here in Paramin, so for the last year, we've been bottling pepper sauce."

I buy a bottle of Genuine Paramin Pepper Sauce and open it on the spot. I dip my little finger into the bottle and taste it, much to the amusement of the Paramin Women's Group. Their pepper sauce is unique among bottled sauces, but I can't identify the source of its strong herbal taste and aroma.

"That's shadow benny," Veronica giggles.

"Shadow benny?" I ask, dumbfounded.

"Here, this stuff," she says leading me to a tub filled with the dark green herb. I put my nose into it and sniff; the aroma is a pungent slap in the face.

Shadow benny proves to be a variety of the herb called *cu-lantro* in Latin America. Seldom seen in the United States, it is a distant cousin to cilantro. The thick-leafed herb has an even stronger flavor than cilantro. In Trinidadian cooking, shadow benny is used in intensely flavored dishes because it tends to overpower almost any other taste. But it is just the herb to stand up to the full fury of Trinidad's congo peppers.

Congo peppers and their Caribbean cousins, the Scotch bonnet and the habanero, are members of the pepper species *Capsicum chinense*; they are the hottest peppers in the world. But while they may be the most incendiary peppers under the sun, they are also among the tastiest. Their distinctive fruitiness, with hints of apricot, peach, and citrus, is the main flavor of this new breed of hot sauce that has set the world on fire.

I ask the Paramin Women's Group if they can ship their hot sauce to the United States. They have never done it before, and they are a little unclear on the technicalities. Looking around the kitchen, I realize that one order from a supermarket would wipe out the world's entire supply of Genuine Paramin Pepper Sauce.

The only shelves you'll find these bottles on are inside the refrigerators of the pepper sauce cognoscenti.

Other bottles I'd like to see in my refrigerator are the underground classics from Virgin Fire. Bob Kennedy's hot sauce line includes a tangy, sweet sauce called Pineapple Sizzle and a ferocious liquid lava known as Dragon's Breath. Kennedy brews his secret concoctions on the eccentric island of St. John in the U.S. Virgin Islands.

Bumping around the island's dirt roads in his Jeep, Kennedy gives me a tour on the way to his pepper farm. Two-thirds of St. John is national parkland, he explains, and the rest is inhabited by self-professed oddballs. Stopping at a beach along the way, Kennedy points to the bumper sticker on a parked Jeep: "St. John U.S.V.I. We're all here because we're not all there."

In the kitchen of his ramshackle hilltop duplex overlooking St. John and the island of Tortola, across the water, Kennedy cooks up Virgin Fire sauces thirty gallons at a time. He reluctantly agrees to part with one of the increasingly hard-to-find bottles of his legendary Pineapple Sizzle.

"The drought this year has ruined us," complains Kennedy. "Water was so scarce that at one point they were bringing water trucks over on the ferry from St. Thomas." The water–poor Virgin Islands are a tough place to make pepper sauces. The tour of Kennedy's garden is a requiem. Inadequate rainfall has killed the peppers and the fruit trees that once supplied his raw ingredients. The cost of trucked-in water makes irrigation impossible.

"We had to pull out of the *Mo Hotta Mo Betta* catalog because we just couldn't keep up with the orders anymore," Kennedy admits ruefully. He hates the idea of leaving St. John, but he is determined to pack up his operation and relocate to Puerto Rico, where he will have a constant supply of peppers and access to a bottling plant. He predicts that he will soon be able to supply all the Pineapple Sizzle and Dragon's Breath anybody could want.

Across the bay on the more populous island of St. Thomas, Richard Reiher is having the same problems with the pepper supply at his Virgin Island Herb and Pepper Company. But somehow Reiher has managed to scrounge up enough peppers to keep up with the demand.

Over a cold beer at the Normandie Bar, the oldest watering hole on St. Thomas, in picturesque Frenchtown, Reiher hands me a bottle of his most popular sauce, but he stops me before I can taste it. Apocalyptic Hot Sauce is an insanely hot mixture of pure peppers and vinegar; it's recommended for cooking, he says, not eating out of the bottle. But Reiher makes two other sauces that taste great straight out of the bottle. His Peppered Ginger Hot Sauce has a wonderful gingery burn, and his Curry Garlic

Hot Sauce tastes like a fiery Indian curry. These two are hard to come by, and I happily stuff a couple of bottles into my pockets.

Reiher and two other cottage hot sauce companies on St. Thomas, Heat Wave and Uncle Willie's, do a steady business selling hot sauce to the endless stream of tourists disembarking from cruise ships in Charlotte Amalie's harbor every day.

But according to Reiher, the real hot sauce action is elsewhere. "The islands with the most water have the best peppers," he says. "Haiti, Trinidad, Jamaica, and Dominica."

It's been said that if Columbus ever returned to the West Indies, Dominica is the only place he'd recognize. The nature island, as it's often called because of its unspoiled landscape, is tucked away in the Lesser Antilles between the French-speaking islands of Guadeloupe and Martinique; it is often confused with Haiti's neighbor, the Dominican Republic.

Tourists are invisible in Dominica. There's only a tiny trickle of visitors to begin with, and nearly all the backpacking nature lovers disappear into Dominica's vast unexplored rain forest as soon as they arrive. The island's 365 rivers feature spectacular waterfalls, some of which were only recently discovered when a hurricane blew away the dense vegetation that surrounded them.

But as Richard Reiher suggests, this bounty of fresh water makes Dominica a great place to grow things. And peppers are one of the island's main crops. They call the pepper variety here *piment bonda ma jack*. (The name is an off-color Creole joke about Mrs. Jacque's behind.) The pepper with the racy name looks and tastes a lot like the congo pepper of Trinidad.

Since 1944, Parry W. Bello & Co. Ltd. in the tiny village of Castle Comfort has purchased the lion's share of the island's pepper crop and turned it into one of the Caribbean's most popular hot sauces. The bullet-shaped shaker bottle containing Bello's Special Pepper Sauce can be found on almost any island in the Caribbean. The vinegary orange stuff tastes a little like a fruity version of Tabasco sauce.

Bello's hot sauce has more of a mass-produced commercial flavor than most of my favorites, so I'm not expecting much when I stop by the factory. Michael Fagan, son of the owners of the company, gives me a tour of the enormous pepper-crushing operation, and Justin Adonis, the head pepper buyer, shows me the latest crop of peppers. Michael, whose dark skin and distinctively sharp nose make him look part Amerindian, was born and raised in New York and recently returned to Dominica to handle the company's marketing.

My impressions of Bello hot sauce take a drastic change for the better when I sit down with Fagan and taste another hot sauce Bello makes. Working with a British food marketing company called Enco, Bello has developed a delicious, thick, chunky, and extremely hot sauce, made with peppers, papaya, onions, vinegar, and other spices, called West Indian Pepper Sauce. It's currently the United Kingdom's top-selling hot sauce.

Luckily for us, Bello markets this same product under its own label in the United States. The chunky British formula is simply called Bello Hot Pepper Sauce. This thick, fruity, naturally aged tonsil-torcher has already been discovered by the chile cult through the *Mo Hotta Mo Betta* catalog.

In Bello's research labs, quality control director Allan Phillip shows me a bottle of a new, dark-yellow, mustard-turmeric-based formula that Bello has just perfected. Michael Fagan hopes to sell this and his other hot sauces in the United States someday. Unlike the little hot sauce companies that struggle to ship mail-order customers a couple of bottles at a time, Bello could easily ship a container full of hot sauce to your front door tomorrow.

But they've already got a little competition in the U.S. market—from a fried-chicken chain, of all things. Trinidad Habañero Pepper Sauce is made by Trinidad's Royal Castle chicken chain, famous for its fried chicken but even better known for the sensational hot sauce it uses as a marinade and condiment. Trinidad Habañero Pepper Sauce is currently sold in thirty-five states and is featured on the tables of the Planet Hollywood chain. (The Spanish word *habanero* isn't used in Trinidad, but it's so well known in the United States that many pepper sauce producers use it as a generic name for Scotch bonnets, congo peppers, and all the other cultivars of the *Capsicum chinense* family.)

Royal Castle's owner, American-born Marie Permenter, was well aware of the pent-up demand for exotic hot sauces in the United States. With plenty of sauce in inventory, she decided to try her hand at the export business.

With her American accent and genteel manner, Permenter seems like an unlikely hot sauce magnate. But every month the orders increase for Trinidad Habañero Pepper Sauce, a hot green condiment made with congo peppers and pungent herbs unique to Trinidad. Nowadays, the peppers and herbs are shipped to a processing plant in Florida, where the onions, garlic, ginger, and the sauce's other ingredients are added just before bottling. Unlike many sauces that are simply hot, Trinidad Habañero Pepper Sauce beautifully balances the heat of the peppers with fresh herbs and spices. Though shipped in relatively large quantities, it still tastes homemade.

Like her neighbors the Paramin Women's Group, Marie Permenter of Royal Castle gets all her herbs from the farmers who work the tiny mountain plots in the Paramin Hills, where the slopes are so steep that tractors are useless and irrigation impossible. It's an impractical place for farming, but during the wet season, rain falls on the hills every day. And according to Permenter, the quality of the herbs and peppers grown on these steep slopes, with pure jungle rainwater, under the hot Trinidadian sun, is the secret of a truly great hot sauce.

Driving down a narrow island road at sunset on the last day of my hot sauce safari, I stop to watch a couple of farmers returning from their herb plots a few hundred feet below. They look like ants crawling up a green patchwork curtain, proof of the trouble people will go to to make a better hot sauce.

In the past three weeks, I've met some people who already run vast multinational hot sauce empires, some whose sauces may soon catch fire, and some talented home chefs and women's clubs who are happy to make hot sauces for a tiny audience of friends and fanatics. There's a place under the sun for all of them, I think, smiling as I caress what will soon become the only bottle of Genuine Paramin Pepper Sauce in the United States.

Caution: Extremely Hot!

Island-hopping in search of new pepper sauces, I found wild combinations everywhere. In St. John, I ate a salsa made from the fruit of the night-blooming cereus. In Guadeloupe, I ate French-style pepper sauce made with shallots and parsley. In Jamaica, fresh ginger was my favorite hot sauce ingredient, and in Trinidad, I learned about herb-flavored hot sauce.

Here are a few of the best recipes I picked up on the trip. Enjoy, but be careful—all of these concoctions are very hot!

Papaya Pepper Sauce

8–12 Scotch bonnet peppers, stemmed and seeded
2 ripe papayas, skinned and seeded
6 carrots, diced
2 onions, diced
2 chayote squash, peeled and diced
12 allspice berries
10 peppercorns
4 sprigs of thyme, stems removed

1 ounce fresh ginger, finely diced
1/2 cup sugar
1/4 cup cane vinegar
1 tablespoon oil

Heat the oil in a skillet. Sauté onions until clear, then add carrots, squash, allspice berries, peppercorns, thyme, and ginger. Cook 5 minutes, stirring constantly. Add the papayas, sugar, and peppers. When the sugar becomes syrupy, add vinegar and cook until carrots are soft (about 5–10 more minutes). Blend and strain into a bottle.
    Yields 3–4 cups

Mango Salsa

2 ripe mangoes, peeled, seeded, and chopped
3 tablespoons chopped fresh mint
1/2 red onion, minced
Juice of 2 limes
Juice of 1 orange
1/2 Scotch bonnet pepper, seeded, stemmed,
    and minced very fine
1/2 teaspoon salt
1 teaspoon fresh ginger juice

Squeeze the ginger juice by placing fresh ginger in a garlic press. Blend all the ingredients together in a glass bowl and chill. Serve with grilled seafood.

Sauce Piment de Guadeloupe

1/4 pound Scotch bonnet or habanero peppers
2 onions, minced

    1 cup shallots, minced
    3 cloves garlic, minced
    1 cup champagne vinegar
    1 cup virgin olive oil
    Salt and pepper to taste

Combine all ingredients (or as they say in Guadeloupe, *mixer le tout*). Store in a sealed bottle in the refrigerator.

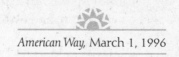

One Night in Trinidad

There is no twilight in the tropics. There is sunset and then a sudden darkness at 6 P.M. On a street that runs alongside the vast green cricket fields and gardens of Queen's Park Savannah, near the center of Port of Spain, the coconut seller is packing up; I am just in time. I pay him, and he picks a green coconut out of the ice chest, raises it up in one hand, then swings his machete with a violent flash, cleanly hacking off the top. Then he hands it to me with a toothy smile.

As the light fades, my camera hangs uselessly around my neck. I had spent the afternoon taking pictures in the Royal Botanic Gardens of Trinidad and Tobago across the street. But now, as I sit on a bench and wait for oysters, the camera can't capture the things I am seeing: a Rastaman carrying his boom box on his shoulder; a laughing gaggle of children in pale-blue school uniforms; a black man sleeping in the roots of a flowering tree with the last flames of an orange sunset behind him.

I was told that at nightfall, the coconut men are replaced by oyster sellers who work under the eerie lights of the oil lamps called *flambeaux*. But the only light now comes from the street-lights, and I'm beginning to suspect that the oystermen will never show up. I question a woman passing by. As near as I can understand from my halting grasp of Creole patois, there has been some kind of public health scare and oysters are outlawed for the time being.

This is a bitter disappointment. I am here to write the Trinidadian chapter of a cookbook about hot and spicy food. Everyone who knows anything about Trinidad has told me to be sure not to miss the oyster sellers around the park, as they are famous for their homemade hot sauce. Even the Trinidadian writer V. S. Naipaul mentions the oyster sellers in his seminal novel *A House for Mr. Biswas*. The main character, sick of bland vegetarian food, storms out of the Hindu household where he is living and comes here to the park to eat oysters in hot sauce. He eats too many and ends up with a severe stomachache.

I, conversely, have no oysters and the beginnings of a migraine. I am sulking as I walk back to my hotel, feeling like a tourist with my camera banging against my chest. How can I pretend to write about Trinidadian food when I can't even sample the famous oysters in hot sauce? I moan to myself. What am I doing here? How can a foreigner pretend to be an expert on Trinidad's cuisine based on the fleeting impressions of a five-day visit?

Later, back at my hotel, I am comforted by another book by V. S. Naipaul. In *A Way in the World*, Naipaul writes about the foreign travel writers who have come to Trinidad on cruise ships over the years and written accounts of the place based on their overnight stays. I expected Naipaul to lambaste this sort of Instamatic expertise as an insult to Trinidadians, but instead he welcomes it.

He compares the travel writers to Columbus, who named this island Trinidad (Spanish for "trinity") because of three low hills that he spotted while still far out at sea. In the book, Naipaul's character sits on a cliff Columbus named "the galley." From the sea, this cliff evidently resembles a sailing ship, but Naipaul's character can't see the resemblance from his vantage point. He realizes that Columbus saw the island in a way that people who live here can't see for themselves. Naipaul's point is that sometimes it takes an outsider, someone not connected to the tiny details of everyday life, to see the whole.

I try to feel comforted by this as I head for the hotel bar, but I still feel something is missing from my mission. Taste cannot be experienced from a distance. To a fellow hotel guest, a telephone executive from Toronto, I complain that while I have sampled the food in the restaurants and food stalls of Port of Spain, traveled to a pepper farm in Cunupia, and walked the plots of the herb farmers of the Paramin Hills, I still haven't had a plate of curry.

What I need is to visit an Indo-Trinidadian home to eat the famous West Indian version of curry, I tell him. I'm thinking of asking an Indian taxi driver to take me home so I can pay his wife to cook me dinner. Or maybe I should start chatting up the barmaid.

As the telephone executive and I drink our rum, an acquaintance of his quietly sits down with us. Sue is a woman from Texas who runs a boutique in the hotel lobby. "My last night in Trinidad, and still no curry," I lament as I lay my head on the bar dramatically.

"Funny you should say that," Sue says. "I'm going to dinner at an Indian family's home tonight. Come along if you want; they won't mind." I'm shocked by the offer but accept on the spot before she can change her mind. As I quickly shower and shave, I smile at myself in the mirror, marveling at the magic way this invitation materialized.

"Savitri is a very good cook," Sue tells me as we wait in the hotel lobby for our ride. "She comes from a well-known family here. She's V. S. Naipaul's sister. Do you know the writer V. S. Naipaul?"

I am too stunned to reply. Were I a Naipaul character myself, I would take a coincidence like this as some kind of mystical sign.

Naipaul's beautiful books about the Hindus of Trinidad are an insight into the enigma of Caribbean culture. The descendants of the humble Indian workers who came here to tend the sugar cane plantations of the wealthy Europeans have inherited Trinidad from their former masters. The world they created here is an accident; the temporary existence they endured while waiting to go home to India has become their permanent culture.

The Hindi language, the caste system, and most of the complicated rituals of their religion were abandoned as impractical in the early days of plantation life. But the mystical outlook on life still remains.

Some Trinidadians seem to embrace a sort of patois Hinduism, Indian superstitions blended with the fables of other cultures. Driving to Savitri's home through the suburbs of Port of Spain, I wonder at the sight of Hindu prayer flags flying on high bamboo poles in the garden of a house festooned with Christmas lights. When I point out the oddity to our driver, I am told that here in Trinidad images of Hindu gods and Santa Claus coexist peacefully in the same living rooms.

In the sumptuous home of Savitri and Melvin Akal in the affluent suburb of Valsayn Park, the Hindu statues watch over an impressive modern art collection. While most of the guests sip cocktails on the patio beside the swimming pool, I follow Savitri Akal around in the kitchen.

"We are only having roti," Mrs. Akal apologizes as she works on her dinner. Roti is an Indian flatbread, but in Trinidad the word means more than bread. In the thousands of roti shops all over the island, when you ask for a roti, you get a large piece of flatbread rolled around a combination of curry and other fillings.

To her, it's only roti. To me, it's Christmas morning in Hindu heaven.

As she shapes the dough balls, Mrs. Akal explains about the many varieties of roti bread. *Puri* means "filled," she says, *dahl* means "yellow split peas," so *dahl puri* roti is "filled with yellow split peas." The explanation makes sense as I recall the kitchen of the famous Patraj Roti shop. I had watched the women there making roti by stuffing a handful of yellow paste into the center of the dough ball and then rolling the whole thing out, painting it with clarified butter and cooking it on a griddle. The result is a flatbread with the wonderful texture of mashed yellow peas running through it.

"You can also make *aloo puri* [potato-filled] roti," says Mrs. Akal. "And then there's *paratha* roti, which has a flaky crust, and *sada* roti, which means 'plain roti.' *Dosti* roti means 'double roti'; that's the kind I'm making now."

To make the *dosti* roti, she paints one dough ball with the clarified butter called ghee in Indian cookery and then sandwiches another dough ball on top of it. She then rolls the combined dough balls out thin. I am hard-pressed to see what effect the sandwich operation is having since now she has just a thin pancake of dough, but once she throws it onto the circular electric griddle, I understand.

As the dough cooks, it begins to separate along the edge. Inserting her spatula into the separation, Mrs. Akal splits the halves apart to form two extremely thin pieces of bread. She paints the halves with ghee and, when they are cooked through, folds them twice and puts them in a basket lined with a napkin to keep them warm.

When all the guests have arrived, Mrs. Akal spreads out her little roti supper on a buffet table. We start with *saheena*, an appetizer made by rolling dasheen leaf around a yellow-pea filling; and *cachourie*, a dish of split peas with onion and saffron fried into cakes. The wonderfully crunchy fried cakes are served with Mrs. Akal's fiery homemade condiments. Her *kuchela* is a relish of grated green mango mixed with hot peppers and spices. The green mango isn't sweet; the mixture tastes like a hot, crunchy cole slaw. Her tamarind chutney is a chocolate-colored mixture of hot peppers and sweet tamarind with the seeds still in it. And these are just the hors d'oeuvres.

The dinner course consists of fried okra; tomato *chokha*, a dish of roasted tomatoes sautéed with onion, garlic, cumin, and pepper; steamed pumpkin; spinach with garlic and onion; curried green mango; curried potato and string beans; curry chicken; *dahl*, the yellow-split-pea puree that is served over rice, cucumber, and yogurt; and, of course, roti. The chicken curry is excellent—juicy pieces of chicken still on the bone in a spicy deep-yellow sauce.

Alongside the curry, Mrs. Akal puts a dish containing a simple mash of local hot peppers and vinegar. "It's not really a hot sauce," she explains. "It's just preserved hot peppers to add to other things." This mash, designed to preserve fresh peppers for year-round use, is the genesis of all Caribbean hot sauces. "I might add mustard and onions for one kind of dinner and fruit and ginger for another," Mrs. Akal says. Tonight, the pepper mash is on the table to add to the curry. In Trinidad, curries are generally very mild, so the pepper mash is served on the side for diners who like their food hotter.

The guest of honor arrives, and I am drawn still further into the mystical mélange of Naipaul's Trinidad. The eagerly awaited celebrity turns out to be a famous Trinidadian psychic named Sean Haribance. The other diners gather around Mr. Haribance with an intensity bordering on devotion. This is no parlor game. The company assembled here is quite certain that Mr. Haribance can see their futures.

The competition for his attention gives me the opportunity to wipe out the rest of the buffet table and monopolize our hostess with endless cooking questions. But once everyone else has had their palms examined, they insist that I sit down and have a reading done too. I have all the recipes I need, so I oblige.

After examining my palm and my driver's license, Mr. Haribance tells me that I am a very bright man and a good writer. (I like him so far.) I will have a long and productive literary career. Whatever endeavors I've begun in the last six years will last me the rest of my life. And, finally, my cookbook will be a huge success.

Do I believe in psychic phenomena? Well, not ordinarily. But then a few hours ago I was trudging home from Queen's Park Savannah wishing for a taste of the real Trinidad. Then some genie, hearing my wish, whisked me off to this amazing dinner party, where I've learned the art of roti and the science of curry at the knee of V. S. Naipaul's sister.

So maybe I need to reconsider my skepticism. Besides, I could use the royalties.

Mrs. Akal's Dosti Roti

Pulling the two halves of a *dosti* roti apart takes a little practice, but this is still the most practical recipe for home use because it's the easiest way to make the roti very thin.

1 cup all-purpose flour
1 cup whole-wheat flour
1/4 teaspoon salt
1 teaspoon baking powder
1/4 cup clarified butter
1 cup warm water

Put the dry ingredients in the bowl of a food processor. Add 1-1/2 tablespoons clarified butter, blend with a dough hook until well mixed. Add the water a little at a time until a soft dough forms. Continue kneading with the dough hook for 30 seconds.

Divide the dough into balls. The size of the dough ball depends on your griddle. Trinidadian cooks have large round electric griddles for making roti, so they can make roti as large as 9 inches across. If you are using a pancake griddle, you will probably have to settle for 5-inch roti. This recipe makes six 9-inch roti or ten 5-inch roti.

Put the balls on a floured pastry board and flatten into disks. Brush clarified butter on top of one disk and then press another disk on top of it. Roll the combined disks out to a diameter of 5 to 6 inches.

Heat the griddle until water droplets will dance on it. Brush the griddle lightly with clarified butter and put the roti on. Brush the top of the roti with clarified butter and turn it. Continue cooking until the roti bubbles and a seam opens along the edge. Insert a wooden paddle into the seam and gently separate the two halves. Brush the inner side of each half with clarified butter and finish cooking until nicely browned.

Fold the roti and place in a basket covered with a napkin. Serve immediately with fillings and condiments.

Variations

Sada roti: Plain roti is made the same way without the doubling step. This results in a thicker roti bread.

Puri roti: Stuffed roti is a little tricky. At the Patraj Roti shop, the women who rolled the roti were very adept at stuffing the pea filling into the dough ball, forming the dough around the filling and rolling the whole thing out so that the filling stayed in the middle. My own attempts often send the filling squirting across the kitchen. Chilling the dough and the filling helps, but some of the filling is bound to leak out anyway.

For 5-inch stuffed roti, use less than a teaspoon of filling. Make a ball of the chilled filling mixture and press it into the dough ball, gathering the dough around it. Roll out carefully and cook as above, except do not separate it into halves.

Ghee (Clarified Butter)

You can cook Indian food with vegetable oil, but the taste of clarified butter is superior and it's really not very hard to make. The absence of the milk solids allows you to heat this butter to much higher temperatures.

1 stick of unsalted butter

Melt the butter in a small heavy saucepan over low heat. Remove it from heat and allow it to settle for 5 minutes. Skim the foam from the top. Pour or spoon the clear yellow oil into a container. (This is the clarified butter.) Discard the milk solids in the bottom of the pan.

Dahl

This yellow-pea puree is the Indo-Trinidadian equivalent of Latin America's beans. It is served over rice as a main dish, wrapped in dasheen leaves to make the appetizer *saheena*, and stuffed into dough to make *dahl puri* roti.

    1 cup dried split yellow peas
    2 scallions, minced
    1 teaspoon turmeric
    1/2 teaspoon ground black pepper
    Salt to taste

Sort and wash the peas, cover with water, and soak for two hours. Pour off the water, rinse the peas, and put them in a pot. Cover with 3 cups of water and add all the remaining ingredients except the salt. Bring to a boil and reduce the heat. Simmer covered for 40 minutes, stirring occasionally.

When the peas are soft, turn the heat to high and stir often for 10 minutes until the peas thicken. Put the peas through a sieve or food mill to make a smooth puree. Add salt to taste.

Curry Powder

In Trinidad, Chief, Rajah, Turban, and Indi are the most popular curry powders. While many cooks are content to use these, the most particular make their own. By starting with seeds and roasting and grinding them yourself, you get a much richer flavor. If you can't find all of the ingredients in seed form, add the powders after roasting and grinding the seeds. You may omit one or two ingredients and still have a good curry powder. If you omit the turmeric, which gives curry its characteristic yellow color, the mixture is called a *masala*.

4 parts coriander seed
3 parts fenugreek seed
2 parts cumin seed
2 parts mustard seed
2 parts fennel seed
2 parts star anise and/or aniseed (optional)
5 parts turmeric powder

Place the seeds in a dry 12-inch sauté pan, place over medium heat, and cook until the spices just begin to smoke and smell aromatic, about 4 minutes. Then grind the spices into a fine powder using a coffee grinder. Add the powdered ingredients and mix well.

Curry Chicken

In Trinidad, the Hindus don't eat beef and the Muslims don't eat pork. So as a result, everybody eats a whole lot of chicken. This curry tastes best with a yard bird, or a range-fed chicken. You can find canned coconut milk in the ethnic section of most supermarkets, but be sure you don't mistakenly pick up the sweetened coconut cream, which is for tropical drinks.

Two 3-pound chickens, cut into 10 pieces each
Juice of one lime
1/2 cup ghee
3 cloves garlic, minced
3 scallions, chopped
1/2 teaspoon black pepper, freshly ground
2 tablespoons curry powder
3 sprigs thyme
1 ounce fresh ginger, peeled and finely diced

1 cup coconut milk
1 cho-cho (also known as mirliton or chayote squash),
   peeled and diced into 1-inch pieces
2 carrots, sliced
1 potato, peeled and diced in 1-inch pieces

Sear the chicken in the hot pan with 1/2 cup ghee and the garlic, then remove. Pour the lime juice over it and set aside.

In a casserole, heat the remaining ghee. Add the scallions, pepper, curry, thyme, and ginger and cook until the scallions are bright green. Add the chicken and simmer, covered over low heat for about 10 minutes. Add the coconut milk, cho-cho, carrots, and potato. Continue to cook for 30–40 minutes, covered. Serve with hot sauce on the side.

Serves 6

The Ultimate Cup of Coffee

Tucked into a secluded notch of Jamaica's Blue Mountains is the home of an English-born coffee planter named Alex Twyman. The "Coffee Renegade," as he is known, lives in simple metal-roofed house at 4,200 feet. It's a long way to go for a cup of coffee.

Like a lot of Americans, I've become very particular about my coffee lately. In the last twenty years, we have become a nation of coffee connoisseurs. Buying coffee has become almost as complicated as buying wine. We don't pick up a pound of coffee anymore; we choose from Kona blend, Kenya AA, Costa Rica, or aged Sumatra.

But beyond these exotic coffees, another has always held more mystique: Jamaican Blue Mountain. While a pound of some other rare beans will run you from $6 to $14 at your local coffee shop, Jamaican Blue Mountain coffee sells for up to $35! In Tokyo, it sells for $60. It's by far the most expensive coffee in the world.

I love coffee. But I'd never considered paying $35 a pound for it. Then one day, standing in line at the coffee shop staring at that magical name, I broke down and bought a half-pound. It was good coffee all right, light-bodied and surprisingly mild, with a wonderful aroma and none of the acrid aftertaste I often get from other coffees. But it was, after all, only a cup of coffee. I was disappointed.

So I called a few coffee experts to see if I was missing something. "Run-of-the-mill Blue Mountain coffee is overpriced, underroasted, and more of a novelty item than anything," said Dave Olsen, the head coffee buyer for the 265-store Starbucks coffee chain. But at its best, he said, Jamaican Blue Mountain is unforgettable.

"Good Jamaican Blue Mountain coffee has a distinct characteristic; it's lighter and sweeter than other coffee," said Ted Lingle, the executive director of the Specialty Coffee Association of America. "But the problem is getting the real McCoy." Evidently there is an enormous variation in the quality of coffee, even coffee from the same source. If you drink a cup from a good batch, the experts assured me, you'll know why Jamaican Blue Mountain coffee is called the best in the world.

I love a challenge almost as much as I love a good cup of coffee. So I set out for Jamaica determined to drink the ultimate cup of coffee.

The Mavis Bank Central Factory Ltd. is easy to miss. It's hidden in the jungle foliage on a hillside below the mountain road, completely out of view. It was the aroma of roasting coffee that made us realize we had already passed it. So we doubled back until we spotted it below us. It was an old complex of brick buildings centered on a huge patio spread with drying coffee beans.

Mavis Bank is one of four pulperies through which all Blue Mountain coffee must pass. These coffee-processing plants are not allowed to accept coffee from any grower outside the official Blue Mountain area, and Blue Mountain growers cannot sell their coffee anywhere else. This arrangement began after World War II when the Coffee Industry Board of Jamaica was set up to ensure the quality of Blue Mountain coffee.

Norman W. Grant, head of operations at Mavis Bank, took me on a tour of the facility. He explained the process by which the "cherry berries," as the raw coffee fruits are known, are turned into green beans ready for roasting. The highlight of the tour was a cup tasting. Quality control in the coffee business is not a scientific or mechanized process. Samples from each batch of coffee are roasted, ground, and put into a cup with boiling water. Then a trained coffee taster starts slurping.

Actually, "slurping" is putting it mildly. As Grant spun the rotating table with our seven coffee samples, he would use a spoon to move the floating grounds out of the way, and after assessing the bouquet, he would suck back a mouthful of coffee with more force than I ever thought humanly possible. This intense, whistling intake of breath was intended to coat the back of the throat with a fine spray of coffee, Grant explained.

I gave it a try and started coughing. After a few more attempts, I got the hang of it, though I never worked up to the frenzy of Grant's slurp. The seven samples we tried were of vastly different qualities.

The first was very good. The second was magnificent. It had an aroma of fruit and flowers and a pure, sweet taste that instantly explained why Jamaican Blue Mountain coffee is so highly prized. But the five remaining samples were all lackluster by comparison. They tasted flat and boring, yet all seven would end up in some blend of Jamaican Blue Mountain coffee.

Back in Kingston, I talked to a few restaurant owners about my experience at Mavis Bank. Too bad you can't buy just the very best Blue Mountain coffee, I said. An elegant woman quietly took me aside and gave me the name of Alex Twyman. "He's a renegade," she said, "but he has what you're looking for: the best coffee in Jamaica. His aged coffee is just wonderful." Aged coffee? I wondered. But then I remembered seeing "aged Sumatra" at the coffee store. Maybe coffee is more like wine than I thought.

Some days later, I made the tortuous trip back up the mountain to find Twyman. I knocked on his door unannounced, since he doesn't have a phone. He and his wife, Dorothy, were sitting in their modest living room, looking out over the red and silver clouds and the silhouetted mountain peaks. Directly below the living room window, the mountain took a frighteningly steep drop. All along the mountainside, coffee trees reflected the dying sunlight.

London-born Twyman has lived in Jamaica for thirty-five years. He makes a living as a surveyor and is notorious for his independent thinking. "Would you like a cup of coffee?" he asked. As he made a pot, he began to tell me a strange tale of international politics.

"The Japanese make all the money on Jamaican coffee," he told me. They buy 90 percent of the entire crop at $7.50 a pound. The Coffee Industry Board of Jamaica pays the farmers about half that much. Then the Japanese roast the coffee in Tokyo and sell it for $60 a pound. Twyman finds this arrangement crazy. "It's a form of Japanese colonialism," he thundered.

"I'm required by law to sell to the coffee board at whatever price they choose to pay, regardless of the value of the product in the world market," complained Twyman. He feels his plantation produces the very highest-quality beans, and he wants to sell them under his own estate label instead of seeing them blended with lesser beans from other Blue Mountain areas.

The tiny room was beginning to fill with the rich, toasty aroma of fresh coffee. "Because of the microclimate up here, my beans take ten to eleven months to get from the blossom to the picking stage. The average is five months. I get a larger, harder bean because it takes so long to mature," he said.

In the early 1980s Twyman applied for a license to process and roast his own beans and sell them directly to buyers in Japan and the United States. The coffee board refused. That's when the stubborn Englishman started to age his coffee.

"I didn't set out to age my coffee," he said. "It was pure bloody-mindedness. I just told the coffee board to get stuffed." Twyman stopped selling his coffee beans to the board in 1982. He started putting the beans in storage in a warehouse in Kingston, hoping for the day when he would finally get a license to sell it direct.

The intense smell of the coffee was starting to torture me. Twyman went on to explain about aging. He had started to worry about the effects of storage on his coffee beans. So he did a little research, and he discovered that aged coffee was once a highly prized commodity. In both Venezuela and Sumatra, coffee beans aged for five years or more command a premium price. "We discovered that aging enhances the flavor of coffee," Twyman said. "It mellows it."

His wife, Dorothy, came to my rescue. She gently reminded her husband that we were all waiting to taste some. He handed me a cup. Although I usually take cream and sugar, I drank this one black. The fragrance was fruity in the way that fine chocolate can smell fruity. Though it was medium-roasted and strong, the flavor was sweet and round and mellow all the way to the back of my throat. It was a spectacular cup of coffee.

"This is not your everyday cup of coffee," Twyman grinned. "This is the kind of coffee you serve after dinner with your best cognac." And so the mystique of Jamaican Blue Mountain coffee lives on. Yes, coffee really can be *that* good. In fact, Twyman's coffee would be a bargain at $35 a pound. And if he ever gets his way, it may sell someday in your local coffee shop for even more than that.

But for now, Alex Twyman is sitting on tens of thousands of pounds of the finest coffee beans in the world, probably the only aged Blue Mountain coffee in existence. And under Jamaican law he can't sell an ounce of it.

Dorothy returned with the pot. "Anybody for a refill?"

The King of Cabrito

There were fifty hungry people waiting with plates in hand the day I ruined my first *cabrito.* My wife's family and some old friends had flown in for a big barbecue to celebrate the birthdays of our two daughters. Roasted *cabrito* (Spanish for "kid goat") is traditional at family gatherings in South Texas.

My wife and I thought it would be fun to adopt the *cabrito* custom for our barbecue. So I stopped into a Mexican meat market in San Antonio and bought one—whole. When you're used to buying your meat in neat little plastic packages, it's a shock to be handed a twenty-pound dead animal. The skinless legs sticking out of the plastic garbage bag looked pretty strange on the bottom shelf of our refrigerator, too.

The night before the party, I threw the *cabrito* in the huge rented smoker with some briskets and pork roasts and smoked the meat overnight. The next day, we discovered that smoked *cabrito* tastes terrible. Everybody appreciated the other barbecue, and there was plenty of food for all, but I was depressed. My out-of-town friends were teasing me, and the subject was starting to get my goat. So I resolved to find out more about *cabrito* cookery.

Goat was once the basic meat of the poor in Europe; Columbus introduced goats and sheep to the New World in 1493 on his second voyage. The Spanish shepherds who accompanied the flocks raised sheep for wool—but they raised goats for meat, cheese, and milk.

By the 1700s, sheep, goats, and cattle had reached the Spanish missions of northern Mexico and South Texas. There they flourished on the enormous open ranges. By 1765 a royal Spanish census put the combined sheep and goat herd belonging to the San Antonio Mission at 12,000 head. But the distances were so vast and the animals so spread out that the herders began to do their work on horseback. These mounted herdsmen, or vaqueros, began the traditions of the cowboy culture, and they made *cabrito* eating part of it.

But information about the history of *cabrito* proved much easier to find than recipes for it. Both of my favorite Mexican cookbook authors, Rick Bayless and Diana Kennedy, rave about its taste, but neither explains how to cook it. They both agree, however, that the most delicious *cabrito* is found in Monterrey, Mexico.

A year had passed since my barbecue disaster when my wife asked me what I wanted to do for Father's Day.

"Let's go to Monterrey for the weekend," I suggested.

"What's there to do in Monterrey?" she asked.

"It's a leather-producing center," I offered. "You and the girls can go shopping for shoes."

My wife regarded me suspiciously.

"Since when do you plan your travels around our shoe shopping?" she wanted to know.

"Well, I hear they have pretty good *cabrito* down there, and I thought I might pick up a few tips on how to cook it," I said.

My wife winced. She had been dragged along on my culinary research trips before.

"Does that mean we're going to eat nothing but *cabrito* for three days?" she wanted to know.

"There'll be other stuff to eat, too," I promised.

To say that Monterrey has pretty good *cabrito* is like saying that Hawaii has pretty good surfing. Monterrey is the *cabrito* capital of the world. Nowhere else will you find a city so obsessed with goat meat. We had been in town for less than two hours when we sat down to our first *cabrito* feast. It was in one of Monterrey's best restaurants, El Tio, on Hidalgo. My daughters were thrilled to discover that El Tio's dining room is an outdoor patio with live music. They explored the gardens and waterfall while I asked the waiter about the menu item *cabrito al pastor* (*cabrito* "in the style of the shepherd").

In interior Mexico, goat is usually cooked *barbacoa* style— wrapped in avocado or banana leaves and steamed. But that style wouldn't work for the shepherds of north Mexico, who lacked aromatic leaves and were short on water. They came up with an incredibly simple cooking method better suited to the desert: they roasted the kid on a spit over a mesquite fire.

Our waiter escorted me to the open-air kitchen to show me how it's done. In the middle of the brick courtyard, a circular pit held a simple open campfire. Whole kids were skewered on long metal rods that leaned just close enough to the fire to cook the meat and crisp the skin.

Cabrito has a strong gamy aroma, and this is surely part of the reason that it is still usually cooked outdoors. But despite the strong fragrance, the juicy white meat is tender and surprisingly mild. The trick to *cabrito al pastor* is to turn the spitted kid close enough to the fire to crisp the skin but to char the bones as little as possible. Our waiter explained that when ordering *cabrito al pastor* in Monterrey, you should specify which cut you want. There was the *pierna*, the juicy thigh portion; the *paleta*, the dry and crispy shoulder blade; and his personal favorite, the *riñonada*, the lower loin portion near the kidney. I suggested he bring us a big platter with some of each cut.

What a feast. The *cabrito* had all the strong character of meat cooked on an open fire: crunchy skin; juicy, flavorful meat; and the sharp taste and aroma of charcoal. The *riñonada* was my favorite cut, too. The white loin meat along the spine pulled away in long, tender pieces. Attached to the bone were several ribs; I pulled them apart and enjoyed the moist tidbits of meat and the crispy skin covering them. My daughters went for the *piernas*—"drumsticks," they called them. My wife liked the crunchy shoulder pieces. We were as content as the Jack Sprat family.

The next morning I resisted going out for breakfast, rationing everyone to coffee, juice, and toast in the hotel. Afterward, we strolled around the Gran Plaza, Monterrey's multiacre city square. The girls liked the Neptune fountain; I was impressed by the strikingly modern architecture. We sat on a bench for a while and marveled at the sheer blue wall of the Sierra Madre rising abruptly from the desert floor. I pointed out the weird-shaped notch in one mountaintop called Cerro de la Silla, or "Saddle Peak," the symbol of the city of Monterrey.

"What are we going to do today?" my younger daughter asked.

"I know," interrupted her sister. "We're going to eat *cabrito*, aren't we, Daddy?"

"Yes, dear," I assured her, "but only after the ancient shoe-shopping ritual."

I am positive that at least one-third of the Zona Rosa, Monterrey's upscale shopping district, is dedicated to women's shoes. We visited at least five shoe stores, where my wife and daughters tried on endless varieties of boots, high heels, flats, pumps, and sandals. I tried to feign interest when I was asked whether I preferred the coral or the peach, but I'm afraid I wasn't very convincing. How the other members of my family would actually enjoy trying on dozens and dozens of different kinds of shoes baffled me to begin with. When the girls were finally shopped out, we dumped the small mountain of shoe boxes at our hotel. Then we piled into a cab and headed for lunch.

Since we arrived, I had asked every taxi driver, waiter, and shoe salesman where the best *cabrito* in Monterrey was to be found. In a remarkable show of unity, they all had the same answer: El Rey del Cabrito ("The King of Cabrito"). Before you even set foot in the restaurant, you know that El Rey is serious about *cabrito*. Displayed in the front window are twenty or thirty whole kids roasting on spits by the open fire.

"It smells kind of weird in here," my older daughter said as we entered.

She was right. The smell of roasting goat permeated every corner of the huge dining room. El Rey del Cabrito's menu consisted of each of the *cabrito al pastor* cuts we had tried at El Tio, plus *cabrito fritada*, a stewed *cabrito* appetizer; *machitos*, a sausage of *cabrito* liver roasted by the fire; and *cabecita*, the head of the kid. We ordered all of it, except for the head.

It was easy to see why El Rey del Cabrito has become Monterrey's favorite. The portions were enormous, and the prices were much lower than those at fancy restaurants such as El Tio. The *riñonada* featured a huge chunk of juicy meat, perfectly cooked. But the *machitos* were the real shockers. When the sizzling metal platter arrived at the table, I was skeptical—the slices looked alien and unappetizing. They were served on top of a pile of grilled onions.

Suddenly my wife dug into the *machitos* with a passion. She was raving about the universal role of liver and onions in world culture while she washed down slice after slice with a cold Bohemia beer. I figured I'd better try some before they were all gone. The outside was very crunchy; the liver was creamy and rich. While I savored the wonderful but robust combination of flavors, a fork appeared from my wife's side of the table and the last slice of *machitos* was gone.

That afternoon, I took the girls swimming in the hotel pool while my wife rested in the room—she said she was very full. Later, we all went for a stroll in the tiny, tree-shaded Plaza Hidalgo. Then we crossed the street for espresso and ice cream in the elegant lobby of the Hotel Ancira, with its black-and-white checkerboard marble floor. The girls were fascinated by the caged birds and by our waiter, whose name was Reuben. He did a remarkable bird imitation by fluttering his bow tie on his Adam's apple while chirping and whistling. I bought some goat-milk caramel candies at the newsstand to go with our espressos. I was contentedly designing a *cabrito*-cooking backyard fireplace on a napkin when my wife gave me the bad news.

"I can't go to another *cabrito* restaurant tonight," she announced. "If I smell another goat, I'll lose my appetite." The *machitos* had done her in.

So much for Los Cabritos, El Cabritero ("The Cabrito Man"), El Cabrito, and El Pastor. We compromised on El Regio, a restaurant that features a twelve-piece mariachi band, all kinds of regional specialties of northeast Mexico—and *cabrito* that's roasted outside. My wife ordered grilled skirt steak and I tried *cabrito en salsa*, a dish of stewed *cabrito* pieces in a complex roasted tomato and green chile sauce. I added it to my list of *cabrito* cooking ideas.

"I don't know how you can keep eating the same thing at every meal," my wife said, shaking her head.

"What I call thorough research, somebody else might call obsessive eating," I admitted. "But by the same logic, what you call shopping for shoes . . . ."

I stopped when her eyes narrowed.

"Well, maybe that's why we get along so well," I said, recovering. "We're both very thorough."

A Taste of Antiquity

To make *sopa de guias*, the traditional Oaxacan squash soup, you slice some *huiche* squash, then you chop up the small, tender leaves of the squash plant, then you peel the stalks of the plant and chop them like celery. You boil all these in water, add some *chepil*, a mustardy herb that grows wild in the fields, and some slices of corn on the cob. After the mixture has boiled awhile, you add some squash blossoms. The leaves give the broth a spinachlike flavor and color, the stalk retains a little crunch, and the squash and blossoms lend a delicate sweetness. The soup is as delicious as it is astonishing. It tastes like you are eating the entire squash plant and a little of the surrounding field.

"Sometimes the Zapotecs added agave worms to their *sopa de guias,* too," says cooking instructor Susana Trilling, who runs the Seasons of My Heart cooking school in a rural Oaxacan village. Trilling enlists the aid of a local Zapotec woman to teach us how to make a side dish for the *sopa* called *tclayudas.* The name is often used to refer to the distinctive oversized tortilla of Oaxaca, but in this case it applies to a bean-covered variant.

With her black and gray shawl wrapped around her shoulders, the elderly Oaxacan woman kneels on the floor and leans forward to mash the black beans on a metate, a flat stone grinding pedestal with three legs, with a stone rolling pin called a mano. The bean paste is then spread on toasted tortillas and dried in the oven to form a crisp, bean-covered tostada that will keep well for several weeks. Although no one can say how old the recipes for *sopa de guias* and *tclayudas* really are, their ingredients, preparations, and flavors take your imagination back in time to ancient Mesoamerica. In fact, modern Zapotec cooking is so close to its roots that archaeologists are studying it in order to make sense of pottery shards dating from 2,000 years ago.

"The core of Zapotec culture persists to a greater extent than tribes who were conquered and overthrown," says Dr. Marcus Winter, a researcher in the archaeology section of the Oaxacan Regional Center of the Mexican National Institute of Anthropology and History (INAH). The Aztecs, who dominated Mesoamerica at the time of the Conquest, never really overran Oaxaca, although they did make incursions into Zapotec territory in the 1400s. After the Conquest, however, Nahuatl, the Aztec language, became the administrative language of most of Mesoamerica. The Zapotec names for Oaxacan towns and villages were replaced by Nahuatl and Spanish names, and so were the names of Zapotec foods. The *tc* spelling of the word *tclayuda*, for instance, is a tip-off that the word is probably Nahuatl. Among themselves, the Zapotecs use another word for tortillas, a word that sounds like "xhet."

There is no written Zapotec language, but spoken Zapotec is still one of the most widely used languages in Mexico. According to the 1993 Mexican National Census, there were over a million speakers of indigenous languages in the Mexican state of Oaxaca. Two-thirds of that indigenous population is Zapotec. The rough mountainous countryside of Oaxaca discouraged invasions and still provides the isolation that has allowed Zapotec culture to remain largely unaffected by outside influences. But

that's not the only explanation for the unchanging nature of Zapotec food. "A lot of the reason is economic," says Winter. "The
food hasn't changed because this is a region of autoproduc-
tion—people here still eat what they grow."

I meet Dr. Winter in an old convent that now serves as a research laboratory in the village of Culipán, not far from Oaxaca
City. As we walk through the convent, we pass room after room
of young researchers studying pottery shards unearthed over
many years of excavations at the Monte Albán ruins. "We are
trying to understand the function of the pottery now," Winter
says. "And to do that we are going into Zapotec villages and
documenting what the people do with vessels and cooking tools
today." Winter leads me to a room that contains hundreds of re-
constructed bowls and vessels in the distinctive Oaxacan gray
pottery style of Monte Albán I.

A huge proliferation of bowls in all shapes and sizes from the
early urban period (500 to 200 B.C.) at Monte Albán seems to
indicate that there was a sudden change in the way people ate,
Winter says. Examining the collection of gray pottery, I can't
help but think of all the little bowls of salsas, pickled peppers,
guacamole, and chopped condiments that are still common on
Mexican tables today. Some of the larger vessels look just like
the modern clay cooking pots called *cazuelas* that Zapotec
women set on hot coals to prepare beans, moles, stews, and
soups like *sopa de guias*.

"What do you think they used this for?" Winter asks me,
holding out a Frisbee-sized platter with a little elevated cup
about the size of a shot glass in the center. "It looks like a can-
dleholder, but I think they put some kind of condiment in this
little bowl in the middle."

"Maybe chile powder?" I volunteer.

Down the hall from the bowl room, Dr. Winter searches
through some cardboard boxes and comes up with something

else he wants me to see. He hands me fragments from two vessels that first gave shape to Mexican cooking some 2,000 years ago. One is a piece of a curved pottery tortilla griddle, or *comal*. During the early urban stage of Monte Albán, the *comal* became common in households all over the valley of Oaxaca.

In order to make *masa*, or tortilla dough, corn must be treated with lime. I ask Winter if he knows when this chemical processing of corn first came into use in Mesoamerica. No one can say for sure, he tells me, but it is a curious coincidence that *comales* became widespread at around the same time monumental architecture was developing. "Lime was used as plaster in Monte Albán," Winter observes. "It wouldn't surprise me at all if the whole process of soaking corn in lime to make *masa* started right here."

The clay *comal* is flat in the middle, with a curved edge that rises away from the center. It is identical in size and shape to the metal *comales* that are set over open fires to make Oaxacan tortillas today. By observing the use of the modern-day *comal*, archaeologists have deduced the reason for its shape. Then as now, the tortilla is formed and placed in the hot center of the *comal* to cook, then it is moved to the higher edge to turn the cooked tortilla into another familiar food—the tostada.

While modern-day Americans may value the tostada for its unique ability to stand up to a thick dip, in ancient Mesoamerica, its most important attribute was its long shelf life. While a regular tortilla would become moldy after a few days, a tostada would last unspoiled for weeks. "The tostada was one of the first nonperishable foods," Dr. Winter says. "What that meant was that people from Monte Albán could pack food to last them for several days. Mobility was a key factor in development at that time, and the tostada was the key to mobility." Portable nonperishable food made it possible to trade with distant lands, to tend fields in other places, or to attend a festival that lasted several days, Winter says as I picture the bean-covered *tclayudas* I ate a few days before.

The other vessel that Winter shows me (from the early urban period at Monte Albán) had an equally impressive effect on Mexican cooking. The Suchilquitongo bowl, named after a Oaxacan village where several complete examples were discovered, is a round vessel with thick walls. Winter points to a fragment from the inside of the bowl that shows heavy wear. While the metate was used for heavier grinding, the Suchilquitongo bowl was used to mash relatively soft foods. Like a modern food processor, the grinding bowl made it possible to mash things together to form a sauce. "We know they had avocados, because we have found fossilized avocado pits," Winter tells me. "And we assume they had *miltomates* [husked tomatoes] and chiles." Residue studies on the pottery fragments will someday yield a more exact ingredient list for Mesoamerican salsas.

"The innovations that took place at Monte Albán during the early urban stage were extraordinary," Winter says. Monumental architecture, astronomy, carved glyphs, and new methods of food preparation all appear to have originated by the second century B.C. and to have spread from Monte Albán, which is the oldest known city in Mesoamerica, to other civilizations. "Monte Albán was the ancient Greece to Teotihuacán's Rome," Winter says.

Driving away from Culipán, I am awestruck by the time line of Mexican food history. The Aztecs get most of the attention in any discussion of pre-Columbian cooking, but they didn't even arrive in the Valley of Mexico until the thirteenth century, just a few hundred years ahead of the Spanish. The food innovations of the Zapotecs, by contrast, date back to before the time of Christ. But what's even more astounding is that in the isolated villages of Oaxaca, you can still find purely Mesoamerican flavors five hundred years after the Conquest.

❧ Very Old-Fashioned Guacamole

Here's an idea of what guacamole might have tasted like 2,000 years ago. Tomatillos, also called *miltomates*, have a distinct tartness that makes up for the lack of lemon juice in this recipe. Serranos are green, bullet-shaped hot peppers that look like miniature jalapeños.

In an attempt to stick to their low-fat diets, many Americans have recently switched from fried tortilla chips to baked varieties. These "new" baked tortilla chips are the same sort of tostadas that originated at Monte Albán.

  3 large tomatillos, husked and washed
  2 large avocados
  1/2 serrano chile, minced (or substitute jalapeño)
  A basket of baked tortilla chips

Boil 4 cups of water in a saucepan. Add the tomatillos and turn off the heat. Allow the tomatillos to sit in the hot water for 5 minutes or until well softened. Remove the tomatillos from the water and puree in a blender. Chill in the refrigerator.

Cut the avocados in half and remove the flesh with a spoon. Combine the avocado and minced serrano in a bowl. Add the chilled tomatillo puree and mash until well combined.

Serve with baked tortilla chips.

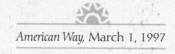

Wild and Wilder

The nose of the canoe parts the tall, slender stalks of grass as we paddle across a marsh called Mallard Lake in central Minnesota. Behind us the greenery slowly converges again, and our wake disappears. When I stand in the canoe to see over the vegetation, the lake appears to be a meadow. Don Wedll, the commissioner of natural resources for the Mille Lacs Ojibwe Reservation, is giving me a tour and describing the life cycle of the aquatic grass we call wild rice.

Wild rice kernels that fell to the lake bed after previous harvests begin to germinate and send up leaves in April, Wedll explains. Mallard Lake is three to five feet deep on average, and the leaves take about a month to reach the surface of the water. By June the leaves will resemble long green ribbons, and they will spread across the surface of the lake in what's called the floating stage. In early July aerial leaves and stalks begin to break the surface of the water, and blossoms are formed. Now, in late July, the lake looks like solid grass.

During the month of August, purplish red seed heads will form, and the plant will rise as high as eight feet above the water. In September, when the seeds are ripe, they will "shatter out," or fall away from the stalk. August is known as Manoominike-

Giizis, or "ricing moon," to the Ojibwe (also known as the Chippewa or the Anishinabe). It is the time when the tribe traditionally moved to lakeside camps to spend its days harvesting and processing wild rice.

The Ojibwe still harvest the wild rice that grows in places like Mallard Lake the way their ancestors did. Two people work together in a canoe. At the rear, one person stands up to see over the grass and guides the canoe. In the front, the other uses two sticks called knockers to bend the rice plants over the side of the canoe and knock the ripe grains onto the canoe's floor. "The Ojibwe harvesting method is inefficient," says Wedll. "It allows a lot of wild rice kernels to fall to the lake bed and provide future crops." The Ojibwe, who originally came from the woodlands to the east, took over the wild rice lakes from other Algonquian tribes in the mid-1700s.

In a good year, the lakes and rivers of Minnesota produce about a million pounds of wild rice. But the amount of this naturally occurring wild rice cannot be increased. In fact, the wild marshlands where wild rice grows are shrinking. "In the last century, we have probably lost something like half of the wild rice marshes," Wedll estimates. Dams, changing water levels, real estate development, and the introduction of excess nutrients into the water have all contributed to the loss of naturally occurring wild rice. But once upon a time, these lakes were the scene of incredible bounty.

"How did they cook it?" I ask Wedll as we paddle across the lake.

"How didn't they cook it?" he laughs. Wild rice was boiled; it was popped in a hot skillet to make a sort of popcorn snack; it was even made into a mush with maple syrup and wild berries, a sort of wild rice pudding. But probably the best-known wild rice dish was made by simmering game meat and wild rice together into a thick soup. The dish is still found on menus all over Minnesota. It's called wild rice soup, although most wild rice isn't really wild anymore.

"That black stuff you buy in the grocery store isn't really wild rice," Wedll maintains. "There's a world of difference between the wild rice harvested from lakes like this and cultivated wild rice."

Cultivated wild rice began to hit the market in the late 1960s, when Minnesota farmers first succeeded in growing wild rice in conventional rice paddies, where it could be harvested with combines. Rice farmers in California soon followed suit, and within ten years farmers were producing ten times more wild rice than was harvested in the wild. Today, nearly all the wild rice found in grocery stores is cultivated commercially.

"Unless you buy it from an Indian reservation, it's almost impossible to find anymore outside of Minnesota," Wedll says. "But we still eat it."

When it was first introduced, the cultivated wild rice sold for the same price as the hand-harvested product. The profit level made wild rice a very popular agricultural product, and wild rice farms proliferated. In 1985, California grew 8.3 million pounds and Minnesota 5 million pounds. When that glut of wild rice hit the market in 1986, the price plummeted.

The cultivation of wild rice has taken a toll on the Ojibwe, both economically and, some argue, spiritually. In a 1988 book called *Wild Rice and Ojibwe People*, Thomas Vennum Jr. describes the role that wild rice played in Ojibwe culture, myth, and religious ceremonies. "It was endowed with spiritual attributes, and its discovery was recounted in legends. It was used ceremonially as well as for food. . . . Consequently, many Ojibwe view the commercial exploitation of this resource by non-Indians as an ultimate desecration."

"Cultivated wild rice put us out of business for a while," says Mert Lego, the former wild rice manager of the Leech Lake

Reservation's Ojibwe tribe. "But now we're coming back." Lego has instigated several legal challenges that are attempting to change the way cultivated wild rice is marketed. New, Ojibwe-sponsored legislation in Minnesota requires that all wild rice sold in the state be identified as either "hand-harvested wild rice" or "cultivated wild rice" on the package, but even this fell short of what the Ojibwe really wanted. "We've tried and tried to stop them from using the word *wild*," says Lego. "But there's nothing we can do about it. Cultivated rice is not really wild, but you know, it's not really rice, either. It's a grass."

Dr. Ervin Oelke, an agronomist at the University of Minnesota, has been working with wild rice cultivators since 1968, and he is very familiar with the debate over the name. Oelke sympathizes with the Ojibwe point of view and doesn't disagree that marketing the cultivated product under the name *wild rice* is probably deceptive. But a Swedish botanist who examined samples of the plant in 1753 really had the last word on the subject. "Linnaeus called it wild rice, so what can you do?" says Oelke with a shrug.

"The original Ojibwe name was 'good berry,' *manoomin*," explains Oelke. "The first European settlers called it wild oats, blackbird oats, water grass—they had lots of different names for it. But it was the French name, *wild rice*, that stuck. By the 1700s, wild rice had already become an established trade item under that name."

"There is some discomfort in the scientific community about the name *wild rice*, too," Oelke admits. "We as researchers have discussed putting a hyphen in [between the two words]. Scientists are mainly concerned with the problem of confusion. If we call this wild rice, then what do we call the wild strains of *Oryza* [true rice]?"

Linnaeus chose the name *Zizania aquatica* for the wild rice specimen sent to him from the New World. Other wild rice species of North America include the endangered species Z. *texana* of Central Texas and *Zizaniopsis miliacea*, once common in the American South. Today, plant taxonomists distinguish between two strains in the wild rice–producing regions of Minnesota and Wisconsin. The South's Z. *aquatica* is taller and wider-leafed than the North's Z. *aquatica angustifolia*, which produces shorter, thicker kernels.

Wild rice is the only cereal native to North America, and unlike cultivated grains, which are hand planted from selected seeds, the naturally occurring varieties have remained genetically unchanged since they were first encountered by European settlers in the 1700s. In seeking to differentiate between the naturally occurring wild rice and the cultivated product, Ojibwe spokesmen point out that scientists like Oelke have genetically altered the plant.

"We are talking about a very minor difference," Oelke responds. "Two genes, to be exact." The genetic changes affect the seed-shattering characteristic of the plant, producing what agronomists refer to as a "nonshattering" wild rice, a variety that holds on to the plant longer and facilitates harvesting by combines.

"There are genetic differences from lake to lake in naturally occurring wild rice, too," Oelke says. "The elders will tell you that some lakes produce better rice, some produce easier-to-harvest rice. We have proposed to study the genetic differences from lake to lake, but the Indians don't want it done. They say, 'You'll just use the information to improve your cultivated rice.'"

"This is the ethical dilemma that has to be faced anytime you take a plant out of its native habitat and begin to exploit it," Oelke says. "As a scientist, I'd love to see how adaptable this food plant really is. Could this be a grain that could feed more people in climates that are too cold for other grains? It's a beautiful grain for cold-weather marshlands; it grows way up into the north of Canada. From the standpoint of science, it's a resource we should be working with—that's the philosophical approach. On the other side, there is the concern for the economic success of the people you're trying to help: the Minnesota farmers, the Ojibwe people. What would spreading this grain around the world do to them?" But in the end, you can't control a seed, Oelke says, and wild rice is already being grown as far away as Hungary and Australia.

The cultivated Hungarian product is especially vexing to the Ojibwe because it is packaged as "Indian rice" and promoted with brochures depicting American Indians in canoes. "We filed a lawsuit over there two years ago, but we never heard anything more about it," says Mert Lego.

But is there really any qualitative difference between cultivated wild rice and hand-harvested wild rice? I ask Don Wedll. To answer my question, he takes me to the Northern Grill Restaurant on the Mille Lacs reservation gambling casino, where they serve hand-harvested rice. There I order wild rice soup and walleye with wild rice on the side. The wild rice soup is very good, although I don't see any big difference in flavor. But the simple wild rice pilaf that comes with my fish is a revelation. The rice has the wonderful nutty flavor that I've come to expect, but it is lighter and fluffier than any wild rice I've ever eaten. Each grain has split and each side has curled until the individual grain resembles a tiny butterfly. There isn't a single unopened grain on the whole plate. This rice has the tender texture of al dente pasta. It is without a doubt the best I've ever eaten.

"But the real difference between paddy rice and lake rice is the way they're processed. Most commercial rice is parched until it's black. The Indians always said that only lazy people eat black rice. Black rice is tougher; it takes longer to cook, and it never gets tender."

In the traditional Ojibwe processing method, the rice was taken to shore and dried in the sun. Later, it was parched in a kettle over a slow fire until the outer husks split open. Then the rice was placed in a buckskin-lined hole where someone in clean moccasins tread on it until the husks broke away, a method called "dancing the rice." Finally, the rice was threshed by being tossed in the air so the wind could blow away the husks. There are still a few members of the Ojibwe tribe who process wild rice in the old way. They call their product "home-style rice," and it is much sought after by fellow tribe members.

I called Beth Nelson, executive director of the Minnesota Cultivated Wild Rice Council, and asked her why cultivated rice is black. "Because our market demands black rice," she said. The major market for cultivated wild rice comes from the companies that make wild rice blends, and they specify black rice.

This explanation makes a perverse sort of sense. I know I have stood in the aisle of the supermarket shaking the package of wild rice blend to see how many black specks are in it, and I guess everybody else does, too. If you used light wild rice in a blend, it probably wouldn't sell as well, even though it would taste better, because customers wouldn't be able to tell at a glance that they were getting their money's worth.

But is color really the only difference between lake rice and paddy rice? Don't the soil and climate and use of farm chemicals have some effect?

A Minnesota chef put it to me this way: "It's like the difference between regular commercial chicken and free-range chicken. The chicken in Grandma's backyard is always going to taste better than the one from the store. Commercial wild rice is dependable. But if you want something special, if you want to taste what our grandfathers tasted, you have to try lake rice."

I smiled as the chef continued with his lyrical rhapsody. To be completely honest, I can say that I prefer the flavor and texture of light wild rice to that of black wild rice. And since the only paddy rice I've eaten is black, I can say I like the lake rice better. This conclusion makes me very happy: it allows me to cling to the appearance of objectivity while I come down firmly in favor of the poetry.

Basic Wild Rice

Add 1 cup hand-harvested wild rice and 1/2 teaspoon salt to 3 cups boiling water and cook for 25 minutes or until tender. Cultivated rice must be cooked for 45 minutes or more.

Cream of Wild Rice Soup

The Leech Lake Wild Rice Company includes this basic recipe for wild rice soup in every package.

    2 cups cooked wild rice
    1/4 cup butter
    1/2 cup chopped green onion
    1/4 cup flour
    3 cups chicken broth
    1/2 cup sherry (optional)
    1 cup half-and-half
    1 tablespoon fresh chopped parsley

Melt the butter in a heavy 3-quart saucepan. Add the green onions and stir in the flour. Cook the mixture for 2 minutes, but do not brown. Stir in chicken stock and sherry, if desired; bring to a boil. Add the cooked wild rice. Reduce heat and simmer for 10 minutes, stirring occasionally. Add the half-and-half and parsley. Serve immediately.

Part TWO

I'll Have What He's Having

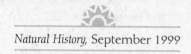

Stinkfruit

My Thai hosts are smiling and offering encouragement. "Eat some more; go ahead, it grows on you," they're saying. Before me on a plate are several soft, yellow sacs of durian, the sweetest, creamiest fruit I've ever tasted. I have already eaten one of the soft, custardy segments, but the smell of rotten eggs is so overwhelming, I suppress a gag reaction as I take another bite of the second.

I feel a little foolish sitting here in the formal living room of Prabhadpong Vejjajiva, Thailand's former deputy minister of finance. His palatial house, which is located in the middle of a durian plantation in the fruit-growing region of Chanthaburi, is named Barn Kradum Tong, or Golden Button Home. Golden Button is the name of an early-maturing variety of durian that has proven especially profitable for the former government minister. The news that an American is having his first encounter with durian has caused a small crowd to gather. I am the only one in the room with a plate of durian in front of him, and someone is snapping photos while I make my feeble attempt to eat the stuff.

Known as *stinkvrucht* in Dutch, durian is one of those foods that is at first repulsive and yet becomes highly desirable to some people. Watching Westerners experience their first bite of durian is a great source of amusement for Asians. And in this case, my hubris made the scene even funnier. As a veteran food writer who likes overripe cheeses and brutally hot chile peppers and has eaten bugs, barnacles, and goat brains in the line of duty, I expected to delight the crowd by eating a whole durian at my first sitting. But to my chagrin, I couldn't eat even two small sections.

Durio zibethinus doesn't look (or smell) like any European fruit I can think of. The husk is about the size of a man's head. With its covering of stout brown thorns, it looks something like a hedgehog. The glossy, malodorous flesh comes in colors ranging from pink to orange. The seeds are contained within the flesh, which fills five interior compartments of the husk. The durian flesh I'm eating is segmented, but not all durians share this feature. Plant explorer Otis W. Barrett described the aroma of durian as containing elements of decayed onion, turpentine, garlic, Limburger cheese, and some spicy sort of resin.

Thought to have originated in Borneo or Sumatra, the durian became an important trade item in Burma around four hundred years ago, where it was a favorite of the royal palace. There are hundreds of cultivars of the fruit, but the three major commercial varieties are the early-maturing Golden Button, the mid-season Golden Pillow, and the late-maturing Matong, the last being the favorite of connoisseurs.

Today Thailand and South Vietnam grow most of the world's durian. But to the chagrin of Thai fruit farmers such as Prabhadpong Vejjajiva, buyers throughout Asia are beginning to ask for "Singapore durian." This is the result of a brilliant marketing strategy, he says. The tiny island nation of Singapore is famously adept at filling orders promptly, meeting shipping deadlines, and promoting its products to the rest of the world. Which is why their campaign to sell "Singapore durian" to customers in Japan and elsewhere has met with such success. "But they don't grow any durian in Singapore!" the Thai fruit farmer loudly protests.

To say that durian is very popular in Southeast Asia is an understatement. In Thailand, it is called "the king of fruits." Every year, tourists from Japan and other parts of Asia come to Thailand's fruit-growing regions during the harvest season to participate in durian tours and durian festivals. I imagine it was overzealous durian tourists who caused several airlines in the region to institute their famous "no durian" policies. I have also heard of signs forbidding durian in hotel rooms and on public transportation.

We haven't had much problem with public durian eating in the United States—yet. But be on the lookout; *stinkvrucht* may turn up in your neighborhood any day now. According to the Thai Department of Export Production, the United States is currently the world's largest purchaser of frozen durian. And the market is growing. In 1996 Americans spent about $6.9 million on frozen durian. By 1999 that figure had risen to around $8.8 million. Frozen durian is sold primarily in Asian markets in major American cities but is considered a poor substitute for the fresh fruit.

So far, efforts to bring fresh durian to the United States have failed. The fruit does not survive the required quarantine process. But Asian Americans who long for fresh durian shouldn't give up hope. Durian may someday be cultivated in the United States.

A researcher named Surmusk Salakpetch, who is earning a Ph.D. from the University of Hawaii, reports that she has seen durian trees in Hawaii that seemed to be thriving. Salakpetch works at the Chanthaburi Horticultural Research Center, not far from the Golden Button Home plantation. She is the coauthor of a Thai publication titled *Technology of Durian Production*. Salakpetch says she has heard that some former sugar cane plantations in Hawaii were being considered as sites for American durian orchards.

If durian farming does come to Hawaii, I wonder whether they will plant the extremely pungent variety that true durian fanciers prefer, or a less aromatic cultivar that Americans might find more palatable. Odorless cultivars of the fruit have already been produced but have never gained acceptance. Asians simply like the odoriferous ones better. In fact, Singaporeans and Malaysians are very fond of a preserved form of durian that is even smellier than the fresh variety.

The durian's odor is produced by enzymes that break down two common sulphur–containing amino acids, methionine and cystine, into sulfides and bisulfides that have a very intense smell. To find out more about the chemistry, I call Dr. Ron Buttery, a research chemist at the U.S. Department of Agriculture's Western Research Center in Albany, California. Dr. Buttery points out that there are sulphur compounds in the aroma of many common fruits. In the smell of grapefruit, for instance, there is a tiny amount of a very intense sulphur compound called thio alpha-tepineol, the most potent odorant known. After rummaging around in his files, Dr. Buttery finds a paper on the aroma of durian. According to scientists R. Näf and A. Velluz, there are forty-three sulphur compounds in durian. The major ones are ethyl propyl disulfide, which is also found in onions; dialkyl disulfides, which are found in garlic; and also diethyl disulfide. Similar sulfur compounds are employed by skunks, Buttery notes.

My own reaction to durian surprises me. My disgust is completely involuntary, and there is no getting over it. A Thai friend who lives in the United States puts the phenomenon into perspective for me by comparing my reaction to durian to his reaction to cheese. As a child in Thailand, he had never had dairy foods, he says. To him, the smell of cheese is horrible, and as much as he wants to eat foods that contain cheese, he can never get them past his nose.

How does it happen? How do people from particular cultures come to love one smelly food and find another disgusting? I ask Dr. Paul Rozin, a professor of psychology at the University of Pennsylvania who specializes in the psychology of biocultural food habits and appreciation.

"Durian and blue cheese both have a rotten smell, which is offensive to most humans," Dr. Rozin says. "But this aversion is not innate. I believe that the disgust reaction comes from a universally acquired aversion that is probably taught in the toilet training process." Infants play with their feces, and animals show no particular aversion to it, Rozin observes. In the socialization process, we learn to feel disgusted by things that smell rotten—especially those, like blue cheese and durian flesh, that are mushy.

But the curious thing is that in many cultures, a small subset of rotten-smelling substances become highly favored foods, Rozin says. The category includes cheese for Europeans, fermented fish sauce and durian for Asians, and rotted whale meat for the Inuit—all things that taste much better than they smell. The food itself doesn't have the spoiled quality that the aroma indicates. And we get some pleasure from that—from a situation in which our body tells us no but our mind tells us it's okay. Rozin calls them "mind over body experiences."

"So it's a form of thrill seeking?" I ask.

"Sure, it's related to thrill seeking," he says. "But thrill seeking describes only the process, not the reason why."

"So what's the reason why?" I want to know.

Over and over again, humans develop strong likings for things that are initially aversive, Rozin tells me. Like riding on roller coasters, going to sad movies, and eating blue cheese and durian.

"We're crazy," Rozin chuckles. "What else can I say?"

That You May Know Heaven

Ode to a Caldillo de Congrio

Pablo Neruda

In the storm-tossed
Chilean
sea
lives the rosy conger,
giant eel
of snowy flesh.
And in Chilean
stewpots,
along the coast,
was born the chowder,
thick and succulent,

a boon to man.
You bring the conger, skinned,
to the kitchen
(its mottled skin slips off
like a glove,
leaving the grape of the sea
exposed to the world),
naked,
the tender eel
glistens,
prepared
to serve our appetites.
Now
you take
garlic,
first, caress
that precious
ivory,
smell
its irate fragrance,
then blend the minced garlic
with onion
and tomato
until the onion
is the color of gold.
Meanwhile steam
our regal ocean prawns,
and when
they are
tender,
when the savor is
set in a sauce
combining the liquors
of the ocean

and the clear water
released from the light of the onion,
then you add the eel
that it may be immersed in glory
that it may steep in the oils
of the pot,
shrink and be saturated.
Now all that remains is to
drop a dollop of cream
into the concoction,
a heavy rose,
then slowly
deliver
the treasure to the flame,
until in the chowder
are warmed
the essences of Chile,
and to the table
come, newly wed,
the savors
of land and sea,
that in this dish
you may know heaven.

From a distance, the fleet of seventy-odd wooden fishing boats bobbing together by the dock looks like a picture colored by a child with only three crayons. Each boat in the flotilla has a yellow hull, a cornflower-blue deck, and green trim. These are the colors that identify boats from the town of Ancud on the north coast of Isla Chiloé.

As I cross the dock, an Irish setter greets me, yawning and stretching on his front paws. The water is calm, and the morning mist the same gray as the sea. As I stand around waiting, a procession of divers appears, each carrying a regulator and a plastic sack full of bread rolls and lemons.

Someone signals for me to come aboard. Stepping across the blue decks of three other boats to get to the one called *Sebastiana*, I dodge big white puffs of wood smoke. The first mate invites me to join him in the little cabin below the *Sebastiana*'s foredeck, where he stokes the fire in a potbellied stove and coaxes along a huge kettle of water. Before starting the engine or checking the compressor, the first order of business must be attended to: making coffee.

The two Chilean divers on board regard me with amusement and curiosity. Why I would travel to this remote island in southern Chile to go out on a shellfish diving boat is a mystery to them. The first mate hands me a cup of coffee, and as the fishing fleet gets under way, I try to tell the crew what I am doing here in Ancud. My Spanish isn't that great, and in fact, I'm not really sure I could explain it much better in English.

I'm here because of a fish story, really. It all started a few years ago when a South American friend started waxing poetic about the seafood in Chile. "It is the best in the world," he swore, "an incredible array of fish, shellfish, crustaceans, and mollusks, many that you've never seen or even heard of before." Fantastic creatures from *20,000 Leagues under the Sea* swam through my imagination as he spoke, and all of them looked delicious.

A new acquaintance just back from Tierra del Fuego showed me his slides of Chilean fishermen and told me about a tiny village in Chilean Patagonia where the people made their livelihood gathering an exquisitely delicious shellfish called *picorocco* that exists nowhere else on earth. "It's sort of like a cross between a crab and a barnacle," he offered when I begged for a description. "But it tastes more like lobster."

Before long I was browsing Chilean guidebooks and drooling over their accounts of endless oyster beds and the fabulous clambake called *curanto*, with its piles of seafood steamed beneath leaves in a giant hole in the ground.

And then I read Pablo Neruda's recipe-poem "Ode to a *Caldillo de Congrio*." The poem about a simple peasant chowder ends with the promise that "in this dish / you may know heaven." It was all too much to bear. If there was a seafood heaven on earth, then by God, I had to get there.

When I arrived in Santiago, the beauty of the city nearly diverted me from my seafood quest. The old Spanish buildings and graceful parks reminded me of Barcelona, until I looked up at the sheer, snow-capped peaks of the Andes surrounding them. Gorgeous, well-dressed women sat at sidewalk cafés, flirting with the handsome young men cruising by in Acuras and BMWs.

My previous impression of Latin American capitals had been one of squalor and opulence existing side by side, of crime and corruption and broken-down public services. These preconceptions left me completely unprepared to meet a Latin American city of such affluence and grace: Santiago is bustling but clean, ambitious yet nearly crime free.

A growling in my stomach soon distracted me from the city's sights and reminded me of a dinner engagement, one of the strategy sessions I had scheduled with a few of Santiago's top food experts. That night, I found myself at a popular restaurant called Aquí Está Coco, chatting with elegant Laura Tapia, Chile's foremost restaurant critic. She gave me some suggestions about where to go and what to order when I got there.

Here, I plunged ahead without further guidance—straight for the *picorocco* appetizer. The plate came out covered with a pile of shredded seafood in butter sauce, topped by two strange claw-shaped projectiles. I sampled a forkful of the tender lobster-flavored white threads while considering these curved appendages. I couldn't conjure up the foggiest notion of what this creature might look like alive and in one piece, but was more than ready to attest that the butter-soaked mop of rich white flesh attached to the red pincers was one of my new favorite seafoods.

"Is this a claw?" I asked my hostess.

"No, that's the beak," she explained.

"What do *picorocco* look like?" I wanted to know.

"Well, they live in little apartment houses," she explained. There was obviously some kind of translation problem. As I sat and considered the sharp, curved beaks and the notion of little apartment houses, I puzzled over the anatomy of the *picorocco*.

Laura passed me an oyster from her own appetizer plate.

She said that if there was a seafood heaven on earth, it wasn't there in Santiago, but farther south on Isla Chiloé, where her oysters came from. "Notice the small size and the black lips," she said. "These oysters are among the best in the world." The oyster was excellent, though it was a little difficult to judge the subtle flavor with a mouth full of buttery *picorocco*.

Following Laura's suggestions, I made my way through the top restaurants of Santiago. I sampled simple preparations of *loco*, the South Pacific abalone; *centolla*, the king crab we know from Alaska; and *langosta*, the Chilean lobster—all good, but all only slightly different from their Northern Hemisphere cousins.

One of the only new aquatic acquaintances I made was *macha*, a pink-tongued mussel with a bold flavor. The unfortunate custom is to broil the mussels with a cheese topping, which masks the bivalves' pungency with Parmesan. But in one restaurant I found a *macha* soup that sent the flavor roaring across my taste buds at full throttle.

The soup was a standout, but I was still itching for something more exotic.

"Do you like the ceviche?" inquired Swiss-born Rene Aklin, one of Santiago's top chefs and a pioneer of Chilean salmon farming. Chile's fish-farming industry, only a dozen years old, is now the world's second largest, exporting more than 165 million pounds of salmon a year.

Rene, a portly, jolly man who loves to tell jokes in English, told me to meet him for lunch at a little eatery in a private home called Restaurant Ana María. He ordered a bottle of Chilean sauvignon blanc along with the ceviche.

"It's very good," I told him with my mouth full. If I didn't sound totally ecstatic it was because I eat ceviche all the time back home in Texas. I couldn't stop myself from wondering aloud if there wasn't something unusual on the menu, something I'd never seen before.

Rene got a gleam in his eye, called the waitress over, and ordered something called *erizo*. What came to the table looked like a plate of ostrich tongues. Wet, red, pointy, and slippery, they slid around on themselves as I tried to spear one with a fork. I finally wrestled one into my mouth and began to chew. The flavor was mineral and bitterly metallic with a melt-in-your-mouth texture like Italian ice. Rene was watching my face with great amusement. With a you-asked-for-it grin he said, "It's sea urchin. Do you like it?"

"No," I had to admit. But at that moment the waitress walked by with a steaming tray that left a heavenly vapor in its wake. The perfume reached Rene's nose at the same time, and we both swiveled our heads, following the waitress as if she were the girl from Ipanema.

The scent was of garlic and olive oil, with an intriguing fishiness to it. Rene craned his neck to get a look and burst into a smile. "Ah, now there's something you've never eaten before," he said with a finger in the air. When the waitress stopped by, he ordered a bowl of *puyes*.

They came to the table in a little crockery bowl full of hot olive oil, looking like worms. "Baby eels," chuckled Rene, scooping up a forkful. This time I followed his lead more tentatively, nibbling only a tiny bite.

They were outstanding—like smelts, crunchy and garlicky and delicately flavored. I was soon moving large bites into my mouth, trying not to examine their transparent little anatomies too closely on the voyage from the bowl.

Rene was impressed by my sudden addiction to baby eels. "Why don't you visit the fish stalls at Santiago's main market?" he suggested. "You'll see all kinds of unusual stuff there. You also ought to go down to Puerto Montt and Isla Chiloé to see where our seafood actually comes from."

The Saturday-morning sunlight slanted through the palatial cast-iron ceiling beams, gently illuminating the grand hall of Santiago's Mercado Central. I watched the fishmongers unload their trucks and set up their stalls, displaying a staggering variety of native Chilean seafoods.

I felt like I was observing the marine life of another planet. In the endless lines of fish stalls, there were king crabs, purple crabs and lobsters, all kinds of clams, and three colors of conger eel. There were mountains of sea urchins, shellfish that resembled huge clods of dirt, and dozens of different kinds of fish. Rene had supplied me with translations that helped me make sense of some of the fish names, but many had no English equivalent.

Finally, I ran across a stall full of *picoroccos*. Suddenly the apartment house translation made sense: *picoroccos* were barnacles. They were bigger than any barnacles I'd ever seen before, but they were definitely barnacles. Peeking out of a hole in a column of shell that must have measured three inches across was the now-familiar beak. The two curved points that I had mistaken for pincers now looked more like a pair of buck teeth. A long feathery appendage flitted out between them.

"They're strange, eh?" the fishmonger said in Spanish and affectionately tweaked one's beak. The *picorocco* immediately withdrew its snout into the safety of the shell. The white meat, I realized, was sealed behind the beak deep inside this tube of dirty, irregular, calcified crust. Dragging the depths of my memory for something to compare a *picorocco* with, the only image I came up with was the mouth of the monster that Sigourney Weaver battles in the *Alien* movies.

For half an hour I stood mesmerized in front of the *picorocco* stall watching a hundred little beaks protruding and contracting and sticking their weird hairy tongues out at me.

At last, I was distracted by the sight of a dapper elderly gentleman with a cap and a cane eating his breakfast standing at the *erizo* stall. As I watched, the proprietor of the stall cracked the hard shells of several sea urchins and handed them over to the enthusiastic old man. He fished the sections out with his fingers and ate them on the spot. Smiling, he offered me a section, and though I already knew I was no lover of sea urchin, I ate some anyway. Maybe I could get used to it eventually, but it still tasted like iodine sherbet.

Searching for a place to get the bitter aftertaste out of my mouth, I wandered into a section of the market set with tables and chairs and ordered an espresso. The restaurant I settled in was called Donde Augusto. Although it was still early in the morning, there were several tables full of people in evening clothes eating chowder and raw shellfish and drinking beer.

"Is that a common breakfast?" I asked my waiter.

"No, it's a hangover cure." He smiled. "They've been out all night."

After a few more hours of wandering around the market, I made my way back to Donde Augusto to try a few of their specialties for lunch. One of them was Neruda's *caldillo de congrio*.

The piping hot chowder with onions, tomatoes, hot peppers, and big pieces of lightly poached *congrio* was one of the most delightful things I'd eaten in Chile. Maybe it was Neruda's gushy poem that made it taste so heavenly, but I was completely won over to his point of view.

As I scribbled in my notebook, a large white-haired man came by to join me. Augusto Vasquez Salinas, better known as Don Augusto, was the owner of the restaurant and, by dint of experience, one of the most knowledgeable men in Santiago on the subject of seafood. He has worked in Santiago's Mercado Central for forty years, and his restaurant has been open for eleven of them.

"The flavor of Chilean seafood has no equal," he rhapsodized. "And with 3,000 miles of coastline, we have more varieties of seafood than anywhere else in the world.

"In Santiago you can see the greatest variety of seafood, because Santiago pays the best prices. But Santiago is an inland city. To truly experience Chilean seafood, you must eat it while it is still dripping with saltwater. Tomorrow, you will fly south and go to sea with the fleet."

Speechless, I pictured myself eating sea bass sushi on the deck of a Chilean fishing trawler. Meanwhile, Don Augusto sent the waiter for his cellular phone.

"It's all set," he said as he hung up. "Fly down to Puerto Montt in the morning, and my friend Jaime will pick you up and show you around Isla Chiloé."

Isla Chiloé is the wellspring of Chilean culture. It remained a stronghold of Amerindian civilization long after the Spaniards had vanquished most of South America's native peoples. Like the Amerindians they are descended from, many inhabitants of Chiloé still make their living by gathering shellfish. Centuries ago, Chilotes simply waited for the tide to go out to gather all they could carry. But the clam beds on the beaches and mudflats were depleted long ago, and now shellfish are gathered by divers.

Yesterday, I visited Quellón, on the south coast of Chiloé, a windblown town whose main street looks like Dodge City in an old Western. Horses blew steam into the cold air as they stood hobbled in front of the weathered-wood storefronts. The main street has buildings on only one side. Across the street a seawall overlooks a huge marina, home base for a diving fleet that works the desolate 1,000-island archipelago that stretches hundreds of miles to the south.

On the way home from Quellón, I stopped to meet the new breed of Chilote fishermen. Pesquera Mar de Chiloé is a salmon farm in a long saltwater inlet. The "fishermen" pulled up one of their pens to show me the swarm of silvery salmon. Each deep-water pen contains 6,000 fish. Grown from the eggs of Norwegian Atlantic salmon, these transplants to the Southern Hemisphere will average around nine pounds apiece by the time they are two years old.

Environmentalists have shown little enthusiasm for fish farms. But salmon farmers point out that fish farming is the logical alternative to massive overfishing of the world's oceans. Fish farms may be the wave of the future, but they are a strange contrast to the shellfish- and clam-gathering culture of the Amerindians that is still going strong here on Isla Chiloé.

After our island tour, my guide, Jaime, takes me home for a traditional Chilote dinner. His wife and mother-in-law cooked the legendary *curanto*: clams, mussels, pork, sausage, chicken, potatoes, and dumplings are all steamed together until the flavors meld into a sort of sauceless stew. Like a New England clambake, it is a method of cooking that European settlers learned from the native peoples. With the *curanto*, each diner takes a bowl of a thin *pebre* sauce made of lemon juice, water, onions, cilantro, chives, and hot peppers; the sauce is eaten with spoons like a soup.

Jaime is a very gracious guide, even if he finds my fascination with seafood a little bizarre. When he drops me off at the dock early the next day, he takes the crew aside to tell them about me. His explanation draws a few raised eyebrows and some barely suppressed laughter. To people whose everyday reality is shellfish gathering, explaining the purpose of my transcontinental journey is hopeless.

So we settle into the rhythms of the waves and sit waiting for the divers twenty feet below us to finish their work. The first mate is down below watching a Chilean game show on TV, and I bask in the sun on the foredeck. My mouth waters as I remember the *curanto* with the clams that tasted like sausages and the sausages that tasted like clams. Slowly it dawns on me that I skipped breakfast and I'm starving.

I can follow the divers' progress as the huge green bubbles of their breath streak to the surface above them. They wear no scuba tanks or buoyancy vests. As with old-fashioned helmet divers, their air hoses are connected to a compressor on the boat.

The *Sebastiana*'s hold is already loaded with several hundred pounds of clams. Now the divers are gathering some other kind of seafood that I've never heard of. The sky is turning blue as the sun breaks up the morning mist, and some of Ancud's fleet is already passing us on their way in to the docks.

Finally, the divers break the surface and start to throw their catch up on the deck. They have been collecting the strange dirt clod-like shellfish I saw in the Santiago market. The clumps are called *piure*; the first mate has to spell the unfamiliar name for me in my notebook. They feel like hardened sponges, yielding slightly to the touch.

As the boat gets under way and joins the fleet on the way back to the docks, the crew members gather round with their lemons and their rolls. They are opening clams and dousing each with lemon juice. Still cold and alive, fresh from the seafloor, the clams taste like brine and lemon; the succulent meat has a nutty crunch. Someone slices the *piure* in half. Inside the brown casing are several smaller chambers, each containing a bright red glob of meat, which the divers enthusiastically pop into their mouths. Now they offer me some.

The flavor is very strong, less bitter than sea urchin, but with an odd fishy tang. "¡Levanta muertos, eh!" somebody laughs to me. I agree—a flavor to raise the dead. I chase the *piure* with a couple more clams, but soon I'm back for more. Do I like it? they want to know. Well, hunger makes everything taste great, I smile.

I came here in search of exotic seafoods, but sampling oddities hardly seems like the point anymore. To experience a day in the life with these modern-day shellfish gatherers is more exotic and thrilling than any strange sea creature they might pluck from the deep.

Side by side with the rest of the coloring-book fishing fleet, we eat our clams and *piure* and throw the empty shells back into the water. The waves of cirrus clouds are distant whitecaps in the intense blue Patagonian sky above us. The velvet green cliffs of Isla Chiloé are a few hundred meters to starboard, glistening with foam as the waves crash in.

Cruising across the calm gray sea, bringing our shellfish home, I feel the ancient culture powering this simple daily ritual as surely as the diesel engine below my feet. I think of Pablo Neruda's ode to the chowder as one of the divers, still in his wetsuit, sucks another icy clam out of its shell. How fitting that my "taste of heaven" should turn out to be a profound appreciation of somebody else's everyday lunch.

Prickly Paradox

When I woke up, *El Regiomontaño*, an express train en route from Monterrey to Mexico City, was chugging up a hill outside San Luis Potosí. Opening the window shade of my Pullman berth, I squinted at the blindingly sunny morning. In the sudden brightness, the scene outside my window burned itself into my memory like a snapshot. A farmer dressed in white stared at the train. Behind him a terraced plantation of tree-high prickly pear cacti climbed the hillside in neat rows, the bright green pads and fat purple fruits glowing in the slanting rays of the early sunshine.

The snapshot image came back to me as I wandered around Mexico City's sprawling Mercado Merced looking at the produce a few days later. Standing beside a perfectly stacked column of cactus pads that must have weighed several hundred pounds, a woman in rubber gloves stood patiently scraping the pads one by one with a potato peeler.

Cactus pads, known on both sides of the border by the Spanish name *nopalitos*, are eaten as a vegetable sautéed with onions, garlic, or cheese. But before they can be sliced and cooked, they must be scraped clean of the tiny spines that grow in clusters and are barbed on the end.

At a market stall nearby, I bought a purple cactus pear that was slit open for easy eating and trimmed of spines. The fruits, called *tunas* in Mexico, taste sort of like honeydew melon. As I ate the *tuna*, I discovered that the fruit has a lot of seeds. My efforts to discreetly spit them into a piece of paper caused howls of laughter among the prickly pear sellers. An amused *tuna* salesman finally demonstrated in a gulping pantomime that you aren't supposed to spit the seeds out; you're supposed to swallow them. The seeds aren't small and I didn't have much luck chewing them, so I ended up swallowing them whole like a mouthful of pills.

On my way home to Austin, the image of the farmer in his cactus field came to me again as I drove across the vast expanse of South Texas, a region where prickly pear grows in abundance. I had eaten *nopalito* tacos in Tex-Mex restaurants, and I'd seen prickly pear fruit in some supermarkets, but I had never seen a cactus plantation in the United States. Was there such a thing? Or did we actually import all our prickly pear products from Mexico, despite the prickly pear all around us?

I made a few phone calls when I got home to see if I could find anybody who knew about the cactus business. Friends in the produce industry gave me the name of Jay McCarthy, a chef in San Antonio. McCarthy was doing some interesting new things with *tunas* and *nopalitos*, I was told, and he was working on a cactus cookbook. People in the food business were starting to call him the Cactus King. So late in the summer, I went down to San Antonio to visit Jay McCarthy and find about his cactus obsession.

The lanky, curly-haired chef told me the story with some amusement. The whole thing started with some five-gallon glass jars he bought to decorate a restaurant on San Antonio's River Walk, he told me. McCarthy grew up in Jamaica, where bars and restaurants often displayed big glass jars full of rum and fruit, which they used to make punch. McCarthy figured he'd do the same thing in this Southwestern restaurant by substituting tequila for the rum. And what better fruit to soak in tequila than that of the prickly pear fruit?

So McCarthy ordered a couple of cases of *tunas*. Within a few days of filling the jars, the purple cactus pears had stained the tequila to a deep scarlet tint that looked great in the sunny bar. And when the time came to make cocktails, McCarthy was delighted by the blood-red color and tart flavor he got when he blended the *tuna*-flavored tequila with the puréed, strained fruit pulp. McCarthy called the frozen prickly pear fruit margaritas "Cactus Ritas" and put them on the menu.

The drink quickly became the talk of the town, and before long, the restaurant was selling as many as 1,500 "Cactus Ritas" a week. But that meant McCarthy needed to find fifty 15-pound cases of prickly pear fruit every week. During the July-through-September Mexican harvest season, this was easy enough to do—a case goes for $12 to $15 at that time of year. But out of season, a case of *tunas* runs as high as $60—if you can find one.

McCarthy was desperate for cactus fruit, so he looked for an alternate source, and learned about Dr. Peter Felker at Texas A&M University at Kingsville. Felker was working on a project to turn prickly pear cactus into a Texas cash crop. Felker was already assisting Texas farmers who were experimenting with a new, nearly spineless variety of prickly pear developed by Texas A&M for the *nopalito* market.

Felker hosts a yearly symposium for people interested in cactus agriculture, McCarthy informed me. The next seminar was just a few weeks away, and the chef suggested that if I wanted to find out more about cactus cultivation, I ought to attend. So on the appointed date, I drove down to Kingsville and sat in on the proceedings. There I met cactus experts from Israel, Mexico, and South America.

I learned that although prickly pear is a food source in semi-arid countries all over the world, much of the scientific research in the United States has focused on finding efficient methods to eradicate it. Felker's cactus seminar is a new attempt to bring farmers and ranchers, scientists, and food professionals together to consider the prickly pear as an agricultural product instead of a nuisance.

"I just planted ten acres of *nopalito* cactus," laughed Robert Mick, a farmer from Sinton, just outside Corpus Christi. "Eighty years ago, my grandfather spent his days clearing our land of prickly pear. Now I'm planting the stuff." But prime farmland is not a requirement of this crop. Much of its appeal for farmers is that it will grow in marginal areas where other crops have failed. Even in poor, rocky soil, it can produce as much as 18,000 pounds of fruit to the acre.

"I see it as an enormous opportunity," Felker told me. "After all, prickly pear grows naturally on 70 million acres in Texas. We are already studying dozens of fruit-producing varieties, trying to find the ones best suited to withstand our winters."

During the symposium, Dr. Felker and Dr. Eulogio Pimienta, an expert on cactus genetics and the dean of the Faculty of Biology at the University of Guadalajara, Mexico, examined specimens in the Texas A&M test plots while I tagged along. They were carving up cactus pads looking for the causes of various diseases.

"How long have cactus been cultivated in Mexico?" I asked Dr. Pimienta.

"Roughly sixty centuries, according to the anthropologists' estimates," Felker translated. As they worked, I noticed that they were getting lots of spines stuck in their fingers.

"How many of those do you get stuck with every year?" I asked the prickly pear pros.

"Too many to count," said Felker. "And if there's one thing to educate the public about it's how to get them out. Use a pair of tweezers! Your first inclination when you can't get hold of them with your fingers is to try and pull them out with your teeth. If you do that, odds are you will end up with one stuck in your tongue. And that's a mistake you won't make twice."

Felker is still searching for a fruit-bearing prickly pear that can withstand temperatures as low as ten degrees Fahrenheit. The search could take awhile, if only because there are so many varieties of prickly pear fruit in Mexico to experiment with. White, yellow, purple, pink, and green *tunas* are all popular. So far, Dr. Felker has considered 130 different clones.

To provide a break from the serious business of agriculture, the town of Kingsville sponsored a cactus cook-off after the symposium. As a food writer, I was pressed into service to help with the judging. While there were a few awful combinations (*nopalitos* with Durkee canned fried onions and Campbell's mushroom soup), most of the dishes were very good. A cold *nopalito* salad with oranges and jicama was the best of the show. Other unlikely standouts included a *nopalito* pie, which tasted like a tart apple pie, and a hot shrimp-*nopalito* casserole served in tomato sauce. The *nopalitos* looked and tasted a little like green beans, but with a pleasantly tart aftertaste. I had hoped someone would submit a *tuna* casserole, but no one did.

As we sat around the picnic tables in the public park eating our cactus dishes, I finally got my questions about cactus plantations in the United States answered. As it turns out, the spineless and fruitless variety of prickly pear grown for *nopalitos* is not the only cactus farmed in this country. Prickly pear fruit orchards like the one I had seen out of my train window in Mexico also exist in the United States, I learned. And while I was surprised by this news, I was even more amazed by the story of how they got here.

"Most people in the Southwest think that everybody who eats prickly pear fruit is Hispanic," said Jim Manassero, the executive vice president of D'Arrigo Bros. Produce Company of

California. "Not so. The Italians have been growing prickly pear since the sixteenth century. Sailors brought the plant back from the New World. In Italy the fruits are known as *fichi d' india*, or Indian figs, and they are extremely popular in Sicily."

D'Arrigo Bros. Produce Company was founded in the early 1900s in Boston by two brothers who sold fruits and vegetables from a pushcart in Italian neighborhoods. The business thrived, and in the 1950s one of the brothers went to California to buy farmland where the company could grow foods such as broccoli and prickly pear fruit that were in high demand among their Italian customers but were not grown by American farmers of the era.

With a 270-day growing season, the California fields now turn out around 3 million pounds of cactus fruit a year, which is sold primarily in the Italian neighborhoods of New York, Boston, and Toronto. Demand for the fruit is high these days, and even more prickly pear orchards are being planted.

What's more, in the wake of the Southwestern cuisine movement, prickly pear fruit has begun to break out of its ethnic niche. Now that innovative chefs have shown us how to make cactus-fruit margaritas, salsas, jellies, and sorbets, people want to try these recipes at home. Knudsen, the juice company, has already introduced prickly pear fruit to the mainstream market in the form of their "lime cactus quencher," which is made with a yellow *tuna* and, according to a company spokesperson, tastes like a margarita.

In fact, Karen Caplan, a distributor of specialty produce in Los Angeles, thinks that prickly pear could follow kiwifruit as the nation's next fruit fad. But first, she suggests a name change. Kiwifruit never did very well by its original name, Chinese gooseberry, she observes. And she doesn't think names like prickly pear fruit, Indian fig, or *tuna* are going to catch on in the United States either.

To make the fruit sound more appealing to U.S. consumers, Caplan suggests that from now on growers should call their fruits "cactus pears." Unfortunately, the marketing expert had no advice on what to do with the seeds.

Jay McCarthy's "Cactus Ritas"

> 10 large purple prickly pear fruits
> 1 bottle (750 ml) white tequila
> Crushed ice
> Limes
> Triple sec or Cointreau

Peel each prickly pear fruit and discard the skin. Put the peeled fruit in a large glass jar and then pour in the tequila so that the fruits are completely submerged. Seal tightly and allow to sit for 3 to 4 days.

For each margarita, remove one *tuna*. Mash the fruit through a large mesh strainer into a bowl to remove the seeds. Discard the seeds.

Put the strained fruit in a blender. For each drink, add 1/2 cup crushed ice, 2 jiggers of the *tuna*-flavored tequila, 1 jigger of triple sec or Cointreau, and the juice of 1 lime. Blend and serve.

Natural History, May 1999

A Rose by Any Other Name Would Taste as Sweet

Ever so gently, the young woman gasped as I set the platter down on the table. It was a few days before Valentine's Day, and for dinner I had made quail in rose petal sauce. Laura Esquivel's novel *Like Water for Chocolate* made the dish famous. Tita, the Mexican cook whose dishes literally express her emotions, makes the sauce from roses given to her by Pedro, her forbidden lover. Putting this recipe together, I felt a little like I was preparing a witch's potion. And the most magical of the ingredients were the red roses.

Flowers aren't really unusual in cooking. In fact they are often essential. Bouillabaisse wouldn't be bouillabaisse without the intoxicating aroma of saffron threads, which are the orange-yellow stigmas of the purple crocus. Hot-and-sour soup wouldn't taste right without dried day lilies, known in China as "golden needles." And in New Orleans, no self-respecting bartender would dare serve a Ramos gin fizz without a splash of orange-flower water. But in none of these flower-flavored concoctions can you actually recognize any blossoms. As the book title

Please Don't Eat the Daisies suggests, actually putting whole blossoms in your mouth seems a little strange.

Roses in particular, with all their romantic connotations,
look odd on an ingredient list. After all, when a man sends a
woman a dozen roses, he doesn't expect that she's going to be
making salad out of them. But in fact, roses have been eaten
since ancient times. At some flower-strewn Roman feasts, rose
petals were sprinkled on the food, the table, and all over the
banquet hall. Rose petals—fresh, dried, and crystallized—as
well as rose water and rose syrup, are still widely used in the
cuisines of the Middle East. Greek baklava, for instance, is au-
thentically served with a drizzle of rose syrup.

Though roses are one of the most common flowers in our florist
shops, we Americans hardly ever eat them. Which is a good thing,
because modern systemic pesticides have made them highly toxic.
And according to Cathy Wilkinson Barash, author of *Edible Flowers: From Garden to Palate*, even if you could eat modern hybrid
roses, you'd probably be disappointed. "Queen Elizabeth has very
little flavor," she reports. "Tropicana has none at all." Barash grows
flowers organically so that she can use them in cooking. And she
has eaten dozens of roses in her quest for good-tasting varieties.
"My favorite eating rose is the beach rose (*Rosa rugosa*), which
grows wild along much of the Atlantic coast," she says. "It has
great aroma, and it tastes as good as it smells."

If you're looking for a cooking rose to grow organically in
your garden, Barash recommends the David Austin varieties,
which are throwbacks to old garden roses. "Gertrude Jekyll is
my pick of his cultivars," she says. Among the modern hybrids,
Mr. Lincoln, a deep velvety-red rose, and Tiffany, a light pink
hybrid, are tastiest. Carrot slaw on a bed of pink Tiffany petals is
one of Barash's favorite salads.

Flowers are also popular these days with innovative and romantic young chefs like Danielle Custer, the executive chef of

Laurels Restaurant in Dallas. "I use a rose petal–infused oil for salads," she says. "I also serve my lobster bisque with rose petals sprinkled on top." We can thank the organic farming movement for the return of edible flowers to our cuisine. The pesticide-free cooking roses used by most American chefs come from organic gardeners in California who airfreight them to specialty food suppliers around the country. Chefs pay around $17 for fifty fresh thumbnail-sized blossoms.

So what does a good eating rose taste like? "I don't think roses really taste like much of anything on the palate," says Custer, "but there is an aroma and a texture and an association with their eye appeal that makes them very sensual, almost— what's the word?—aphrodisiacal."

In *Like Water for Chocolate*, Tita's quail in rose petal sauce certainly had that effect. After eating it, her sister Gertrudis "began to feel an intense heat pulsing through her limbs." Dripping with rose-scented sweat, Gertrudis went to the wooden shower stall in the backyard to wash. "Her body was giving off so much heat that the wooden walls began to split and burst into flame." Having set the shower stall on fire, Gertrudis stood in her backyard, burning hot and smelling of roses, until she was suddenly swooped up by one of Pancho Villa's men, who charged into the backyard on horseback. "Without slowing his gallop, so as not to waste a moment, he leaned over, put his arm around her waist, and lifted her onto the horse in front of him, face to face, and carried her away." The naked Gertrudis and the crazed soldier made love at a full gallop. The moral: cook and eat flowers at your own risk.

I followed Tita's recipe pretty closely, except I added more roses. Not only did I use rose petals and rose water, as called for in the recipe, but I also garnished the dish with an extra dozen tiny red buds. The young lady who ate the quail with me did not set my house on fire. (I kept a pitcher of water nearby just in case.) But the striking beauty and the deep perfume of all those roses certainly made her cheeks flush.

✿ Quail in Rose Petal Sauce

Adapted from *Like Water for Chocolate: A Novel in Monthly Installments, with Recipes, Romances, and Home Remedies*
My local Middle Eastern store had plenty of rose water on hand. I ordered the edible roses from Heart of Texas Produce, a specialty food company in Austin. Tita's recipe also calls for *pitaya*, a delicious cactus fruit. But *pitaya* was out of season, so I substituted a dark red prickly pear fruit puree. You can also use frozen raspberries.

  6 quail
  3 tablespoons butter
  Salt and pepper to taste
  1 cup dry sherry
  Petals of 6 fresh organic red roses
  6 peeled chestnuts (boiled, roasted, or canned)
  1 clove garlic
  1/2 cup *pitaya* or red prickly pear fruit puree
     (or substitute raspberries)
  1 tablespoon honey
  1/2 teaspoon ground anise seed
  1/4 teaspoon ground cinnamon
  14 teaspoons rose water

Rinse the quail and pat dry. In a large frying pan over medium-high heat, melt the butter and lightly brown the birds on all sides. Add sherry, and salt and pepper the quail. Lower the heat and cover and simmer 15 minutes. Turn the quail, cover, and cook another 10 minutes. Remove the quail, reserving the pan juices.

Rinse the rose petals in cold water. Place half the petals in the blender with remaining ingredients and the pan juices. Puree until smooth. Transfer to a saucepan and simmer 5 minutes. Adjust seasoning with more salt, pepper, and/or honey. Pour sauce over quail and sprinkle with the remaining rose petals.

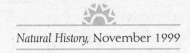

Morgan's Extra Special Tasty Dulse

Fishy asparagus? Spinach in mussel juice? Chef Dale Nichols and I are trying to find words to describe the flavor of the frilly black vegetable on the plate in front of us. Its cultivators market it as Sea Parsley, but it is actually a mutant strain of dulse that marine biologists found in the Bay of Fundy some twenty years ago.

According to the company's brochure, the seaweed spans a wide range of flavors, from parsley to shellfish, depending on how it's prepared. Nichols is the head chef at the CP Hotel Halifax in Halifax, Nova Scotia, and we are in his kitchen doing a little taste testing. We both agree that the company's claims are a trifle exaggerated, but we also agree that a filet of grilled halibut with "Sea Parsley hollandaise" on top makes for some fine eating. Fried and then chopped into the sauce, the salty, dark-green seaweed gives the hollandaise a flavor we decide to describe as a combination of bacon and fishy spinach.

"The term 'seaweed' itself does not have any taxonomic value," observes V. J. Chapman in his book *Seaweeds and Their Uses,* "but is rather a popular term used to describe the common large attached (benthic) marine algae found in the groups

Chlorophyceae, Rhodophycyae, and *Phaeophyceae* or green, red, and brown algae, respectively." Chapman's book catalogs commercial uses for seaweed throughout history.

Seaweed has always had a "something for nothing" charm that appeals to economic sensibilities. Farmers, foragers, and fishermen have gathered and attempted to sell various seaweeds for a variety of purposes over the years. Algaes have been touted as fertilizers, sources of potash, and foodstuffs. Lately, academics have gotten into the act, writing papers on the potential of massive seaweed farms to consume carbon and thus halt the greenhouse effect.

Supplements containing seaweeds such as spirulina are sold at health food stores with claims that they can boost the immune system. Mainstream nutritionists discount such claims but note that seaweeds are rich in minerals and can contain beta carotene and vitamin C. They also caution that seaweeds are high in salt and should be avoided by anyone on a low-sodium diet.

The earliest records of seaweed as a food come from Chinese poetry of around 800 B.C. Porphyra, the seaweed used to make nori, was the first cultivated in China. It also played an important role in the history of Iceland, where it was one of the few vegetables available. Known as laver in England, porphyra grows naturally on sticks and stones in the ocean, where it was once harvested by foragers.

In the 1940s, British phycologist Kathleen Drew discovered the life cycle of porphyra. Her observations made possible the cultivation of the seaweed. "She became a saint in Japan," chuckles John van der Meer, director of research at the Canadian Institute of Marine Biosciences. "I have heard that nori growers have built shrines to her. Nori is a billion-dollar-a-year business in Japan. I'm not sure if it's true anymore, but as of about five years ago, the nori industry in Japan was worth more than all of the fish aquaculture and shellfish aquaculture industries in the world combined."

"The North American seaweed business got started at the beginning of the Second World War," van der Meer says. "The Japanese produced all of our agar-agar, which was required for microbiology, so when the war started, people went looking for substitutes." That, in turn, spurred the American alginate and carageenan industries—and, he deadpans, inspired all the practical applications we see today, such as the carageenan thickening in McDonald's triple-thick shakes and the little red pimientos in your martini olives.

It is obvious from my silence that I have never heard of either, and I suspect van der Meer is slapping his knee on the other end of the phone. "My martini olives?" I finally inquire, dumbfounded.

"It was too difficult to coordinate the olive and pimiento seasons," van der Meer explains. So food technologists started turning the red peppers into a slurry, adding alginate to make a sheet of elastic-like pimiento, and then cutting it into strips as needed to stuff olives. Seaweed-based gums are also used to thicken and smooth ice cream, sausage, candy, and toothpaste.

Unbeknownst to most of us, we have been eating algae all our lives. But undisguised seaweeds are relatively new to the Western table. In Boston, when I noticed that the lobster at Legal Seafoods came garnished with seaweed instead of parsley, I asked consulting chef Jasper White about it. He said he thought it would be a nice touch, and besides, the *ogo* keeps indefinitely in the lobster tanks, while parsley takes up room in the refrigerator and quickly turns yellow if it isn't used.

The Sea Parsley that Chef Nichols and I experimented with is also used by chefs as a garnish. Cultivated in saltwater tanks in Nova Scotia greenhouses, it is descended from an unusual strain of dulse. *Palmaria palmata*, as dulse is known to scientists, seems to be one of the few edible seaweeds that comes exclusively from the Western culinary tradition. It has long been eaten in Ireland, particularly in the mashed potato dish called champ. In Nova Scotia and Maine, dried dulse is often served as a salty cocktail snack. Bar owners in the Maritime Provinces put it out free to induce thirst. According to the marketing brochure, Sea Parsley is a dwarf dulse discovered by Canada's National Research Council.

"About twenty years ago, Peter Shacklock and Keith Morgan, two employees of the National Research Council at the time, were sorting through samples from a commercial dulse harvester in the Bay of Fundy when they found some highly subdivided, frilly dulse," van der Meer remembers. "These are mutations or morphological variants of normal dulse plants, small frilly out-growths from the normally flat plant. We pinched it off and propagated it, and it has maintained that form for twenty years now."

"We snack on the stuff all the time while we work on it," van der Meer says; he actually likes it better fresh than dried. But Keith Morgan was especially fond of the dwarf dulse—although they didn't call it that. Van der Meer says, laughing, "We actually called it Morgan's Extra Special Tasty Dulse. It was a joke around here." The little frilly dulse plants were sweeter and milder than regular dulse, and not as thick, so they had a nicer texture. "Except for our occasional munching, the stuff just sat there for fifteen years in our culture collection."

But then entrepreneur Ed Cayer came along. He was taking a tour and asked if anybody was doing anything with the stuff. He registered the name *Sea Parsley* and started growing it in tanks. The National Research Council gets a royalty on the gross sales.

Van der Meer isn't terribly impressed with the product or its sales. "It's very early yet, but I don't think Sea Parsley will ever be more than a niche market," he says. The researcher cautions that the seaweed industry may look like a bright new idea, but in fact it is a very old business with a poor track record. Canada's carageenan industry failed in the 1980s because of competition from the Philippines. Kelp, which was once used for potash, has also declined in importance over the years.

Appealing to Western tastes with seaweed products may be a hard sell. But van der Meer has high hopes for one Canadian edible seaweed product. A company called Acadian Seaplants Limited is cultivating a selective clone of *Chondrus crispus*, better known as Irish moss, and the source of carageenan. Through a tenderizing, drying, and coloring process, this Irish moss variety is being turned into an imitation of a Japanese sea vegetable called *marista*, which has been drastically overfished. The end user reconstitutes the imitation dried, pink sea vegetable, and the product is selling very well in Asia. "We're talking about something there that's going to be worth tens of millions," says van der Meer proudly. Canada's National Research Council helped develop the cultivation and food processing technology that made the tasty product possible.

I ask van der Meer about promising future uses for seaweed. "I hear the Japanese are working on a microalgae for scrubbing CO_2 from waste gases," he says.

"And what about the giant seaweed farms that could slow global warming?" I ask.

"I think that one was a lot of hot air," he says. I suspect he's slapping his knee again.

Dulse Champ

I brought a bag of dulse home from Nova Scotia. It tasted like iodine chewing gum. I offered some to my kids, but they wouldn't eat it. They said it smelled like fish food. I checked the fish food label and, sure enough, it contained algae meal.

But when I cooked the dulse with butter and mixed it into our mashed potatoes, the way they do in Ireland, the kids loved it.

1-1/2 pounds potatoes
1/2 pint hot milk
1/4 cup butter
1/4 cup dry dulse, tightly packed
Salt and pepper to taste

Peel potatoes and cook in salted water until tender. Drain and return to the flame for a minute to dry the potatoes out. Mash with the hot milk. In a saucepan, melt the butter and add the dulse. Stir until it is reconstituted. Add the dulse and butter mixture to the potatoes and beat until smooth.

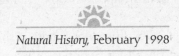

Ewe Bet

Hal Koller's old white clapboard farmhouse and big red barns sit on a bluff above the rolling green hills. If there were some black-and-white Holstein cows in the picture, it might be a picture postcard of a Wisconsin dairy farm. But unlike most of his neighbors around Star Prairie, Hal Koller doesn't milk cows.

"You should see the looks I get when I tell people I milk sheep," Koller says as he shows me around the farm. "Some people actually say, 'Don't you mean goats?' I want to slap myself in the forehead and say, 'Oh, so that's what they are!'"

Dairy goats have become fairly commonplace on small family farms in Wisconsin, thanks to the growing popularity of goat cheese. Dairy sheep are something new around here. But with premium sheep's milk selling for $75 a hundredweight, about five times the going rate for cow's milk, Koller is very happy to milk sheep, even if his neighbors do give him odd looks.

Sheep dairying sounds weird to many Americans, until you start talking cheese, he says. Most people don't realize that many of their favorite cheeses are made from sheep's milk. Among the sheep's milk cheeses the United States imports are such classics as Italian Pecorino Romano; Spanish *manchego*; Greek, Bulgarian, and other fetas; and French Roquefort. In

1990 the United States imported some 50 million pounds of sheep's milk cheeses.

After watching Koller's sheepdog round up the flock, he and I hop in the car and head for Spooner, Wisconsin, to find out about the progress of the American sheep dairy business. On the way, Koller explains his own reasons for getting into sheep. "In Wisconsin, you have to find something else to do on a small farm besides milk cows, or you're going to go under," he says. "Family farmers can't compete with the big agribusiness dairies anymore. Ten years ago, on the drive from my house to Amery, I passed eight family dairy farms. Today, there is only one left."

At the University of Wisconsin's Spooner Agricultural Research Station, a French-born researcher named Yves Berger takes us on a tour of the experimental sheep dairy operation. As Hal Koller eyes the state-of-the-art milking parlor with envy, I ask Berger how the sheep dairy industry got started in the Upper Midwest.

"In 1970, while I was a graduate student, I worked with Bill Boylan at the University of Minnesota," Berger says. "Bill was working with ten or twelve different sheep breeds, trying to increase lamb production. Some of the most prolific breeds, like the Finn, had trouble producing enough milk to feed their lambs. In 1985, after traveling in Europe, Bill got the idea of building a sheep-milking parlor so he could determine exactly how much milk various breeds produced. He was interested in developing a prolific ewe that had sufficient milk for its lambs; he had no intention of getting into the dairy business. But once he had all this sheep's milk, he didn't want to throw it away. That's when he discovered that local cheese makers were eager to buy the milk. It was an accident, really, but little by little, the project started moving toward sheep dairying."

"When I heard about Bill Boylan's milking parlor and the market for sheep's milk, I started milking my Dorsets," Hal

Koller interjects. "But I only got about a hundred pounds of milk in a 120-day season." In 1991 the University of Minnesota helped Hal Koller acquire British Columbian sheep that were half East Friesian, a northern European dairy sheep, and half Arcott Rideau, a Canadian sheep raised for meat. By crossing them with the Dorset, a breed long raised for meat in the Upper Midwest, Koller produced sheep that gave twice as much milk.

After Bill Boylan retired and the University of Minnesota got out of the sheep dairy business, the University of Wisconsin brought Yves Berger to the Spooner Agricultural Research Station to do further research with dairy sheep. Earlier in his career, Berger had worked at a sheep dairy research station in La Fage, France, about ten miles from Roquefort. In the future he hopes to compare crossbreeds of East Friesians with crossbreeds of Lacaune, the French dairy sheep of Roquefort.

"I think the sheep dairy industry is extremely promising for Wisconsin," says Berger. "There are many small farms and small cheese plants here that need to diversify. But it's not just Wisconsin that's working on this. They are making sheep's milk cheese in Vermont, New York, and British Columbia too."

"But are Americans ready to buy sheep cheeses?" I ask.

"I think so," says Berger. "Fifteen years ago, nobody in America ate goat cheese—now it's everywhere. American tastes are evolving. Gourmet cheeses like Roquefort are in demand, but there is a limited supply."

"Now that goat cheese has reached a plateau, I think this will be the next big wave in cheese," says Jim Path, cheese outreach specialist at the University of Wisconsin's Center for Dairy Research. Path is helping Wisconsin cheese makers move from commodity cheeses to the more profitable specialty cheeses. He cautions that sheep and goat dairying aren't for everyone. They will always be cottage industries as compared to the enormous cow's milk business. "But I see no reason why sheep's milk cheeses won't become even bigger than goat cheeses in this country. Cheese makers like Scott Erickson are turning out sheep's milk cheeses that are as good as any in the world."

I stopped by the Bass Lake Cheese Factory in Somerset, Wisconsin, to talk to Scott Erickson and ask why cheese makers are so crazy about sheep's milk. "Sheep's milk has about twice the fat and twice the solids of cow's milk," he told me. "So you get twice as much cheese." But the volume of solids is not the only difference between sheep's milk and cow's milk.

"If you look at them both under a microscope, you see that the fat globules in sheep's milk are about half the size of the fat globules in cow's milk," Erickson continues. "That gives sheep's milk a smoother texture and makes it easier to digest." It also makes it possible for Erickson to freeze the sheep's milk until he has enough for a 4,000-to-6,000-pound batch. "You can't freeze cow's milk, because the large fat globules will burst, but the small fat globules in sheep's milk freeze very nicely."

But Erickson really waxes poetic about the milk's flavor. "We call it a lipase flavor," he says. Lipase is an enzyme that breaks down the fat in milk, creating free fatty acids. "The lipolyzed free fatty acids in sheep's milk have a unique tangy taste and aroma that is very desirable to cheese makers. It's that slightly rancid aroma you associate with Italian Pecorino. In Italy, when they make cow's milk Parmesan, they add lipase extracts to it to imitate that flavor."

Erickson participates in the University of Wisconsin's Master Cheesemaker Program, which brings artisanal cheese makers from around the world to Wisconsin to demonstrate their techniques. Inspired by an Italian cheese maker, Erickson made a basket-formed sheep's milk cheese he called Canasta Pardo. The cheese won first place in its category at the American Cheese Society Conference.

"Once people try these cheeses, they're hooked," Erickson says as he cuts into a basket-formed sheep's milk cheese he calls

La Rosa. The cheese is about the size of a round loaf of sour-dough bread. It is rust-colored on the outside and it retains the ridges and indentations of the basket it was formed in. The inside is creamy white and dense with a crumbly texture. I eat a little piece expecting an explosion of flavors on my tongue, but compared to Roquefort or Pecorino, this cheese is mild. The characteristic lipase taste is identifiable but not overpowering, and the crumbly texture turns to velvet in my mouth. It is an exceptional cheese, and I start trying to negotiate to buy some.

"Sorry, this is the only one I have," Erickson laughs. "All our La Rosa and Canasta Pardo cheeses are still aging. We like to age them at least five months. When they're ready, they'll sell for around $13 a pound, plus shipping and handling." I stare longingly at the basket-formed cheese with visions of quesadillas dancing through my head.

"We also make a blended cheese we call Kassari," Erickson says. "It's 25 percent sheep's milk and 75 percent cow's milk. It still has the sheep's milk taste, but it's a lot cheaper. And I have some Kassari I can sell you right now." Cheese experts predict that because of their lower price and milder flavor, these blended-milk cheeses will be the first domestic sheep's milk cheeses to gain large-scale consumer acceptance in the United States.

I buy some Kassari, and I also beg and plead for a little piece of the La Rosa until, finally, Erickson relents. In the parking lot, I lovingly tuck the deliciously rancid-smelling sheep's milk cheese into the passenger's seat, where I can easily reach it. On the long drive home, I nibble at the cheese and imagine a picture postcard of Wisconsin, America's Dairyland, with sheep where the cows used to be.

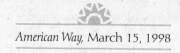

The Tropic of Spam

There was a long line at the convenience store in Kailua-Kona, and I was in a hurry. When it was my turn to pay, I rattled off my purchases: "Ten bucks' worth of gas, a large cup of coffee, and. . . ." My eyes darted around, looking for a quick breakfast. There was a large glass display case on the counter, the kind usually stocked with breakfast tacos or stuffed croissants, but this one was filled with a different morning treat.

"And one of those," I blurted.

"And one Spam *musubi*," said the clerk handing me the thick, warm square of rice topped with Spam and wrapped up with a strip of seaweed.

As I zoomed up the highway, trying to make my tee time, I sipped my coffee and considered the Spam-covered rice. In the pink light of a Hawaiian sunrise, it didn't look half bad. Besides, I was hungry. So I bit in. The spices and grease of the fried Spam had soaked into the sticky rice, giving it a sweet, oily tang. I washed the Spam sushi down with the rest of my coffee and made it to the golf course with time to spare.

The Hawaiian Islands consume 4.3 million cans of Spam a year, more than any other state in the Union. Hawaiians eat Spam *musubi* for breakfast, they pack their *bento* boxes with

Spam and rice for lunch, and they eat grilled Spam with Hawaiian pineapple for dinner. One of Hawaii's most famous chefs, Sam Choy, serves Spam dishes in his popular restaurants. And like most Hawaiians, he gets a little touchy if you needle him about it.

For the rest of the world, Spam is an icon of absurdist humor. The can, with its huge yellow letters on a dark-blue background and the photo of the pink pressed meat loaf decorated with cloves, looks like a Warhol-inspired parody of itself. Just the word *Spam* can provoke laughter. In a *Monty Python's Flying Circus* restaurant skit, waiters in Viking helmets sing "Spam, Spam, Spam, Spam" over and over as hapless customers try to order something else. At Spam-carving, Spam-eating, and Spam-cooking contests all over the country, tongue-in-cheek contestants ham it up with Spam slapstick.

People at Hormel, the makers of Spam, have a good sense of humor about it all. They have even authorized a mail-order catalog to sell Spam neckties, Spam boxer shorts, and a T-shirt featuring the music to the Viking waiters' song. And why not? In 1994 they sold their 5 billionth can of Spam. As long as Americans continue to consume Spam at the average rate of 3.6 cans per second, they can afford to keep laughing.

But as the world's second largest per capita consumers of Spam (after Guam), Hawaiians don't get the joke. They have Spam cooking contests in Hawaii, too, but with a difference: the contestants take the cooking seriously.

"I'm proud to serve Spam in my restaurants, and I don't care what mainlanders think about it," said Sam Choy when I stopped to see him at his restaurant on the Big Island. "In fact, I hope to do a Spam cookbook someday."

"Isn't there already a Spam cookbook?" I asked.

"Yeah, but I want to take it to the gourmet level," Choy said without a trace of irony. Spam became a part of Choy's menu through his involvement in the Hawaiian regional cuisine movement. The chefs who started the trend were trying to include indigenous Hawaiian foods such as the delicious local fishes and exotic fruits in their cooking. But Choy, the only native Hawaiian among the upscale chefs, argued that Spam was a Hawaiian food tradition, too. Like most Hawaiians, he'd grown up with Spam and wasn't willing to abandon it just because mainlanders laughed at it.

Choy's reverence was shared by most of the Hawaiians I talked to. As incongruous as it may seem, the canned luncheon meat from Austin, Minnesota, is deeply imbedded in Hawaiian culture.

There are many explanations for the popularity of Spam in the Hawaiian Islands. Most trace the beginnings of the phenomenon to World War II. The American military popularized Spam, serving it frequently to soldiers, sailors, and base personnel. Others note that Spam kept well in the tropical climate at a time when refrigerators were scarce. And then there's the livestock issue. Since sugar and pineapple production always dominated Hawaiian agriculture, there was never a large supply of local meat.

All of these explanations make a certain amount of sense. But the war has been over for more than fifty years now, Hawaiians have plenty of refrigerators, and frozen meat is pretty inexpensive. So why does Spam persist as a Hawaiian favorite?

I got an insight when I returned to Choy's restaurant to taste a few of his Spam specialties. Sam was off in Oahu, but his sister, Claire Wai-Sun Choy, who manages the place, was ready for me. She served me Spam in creamed corn, Spam with homemade papaya marmalade, and Spam *musubi*, and she sat down at the table with me to talk Spam for a while. I was embarrassed to admit that none of the Spam dishes was really winning me over.

Claire got up and walked over to the cooler. She came back with a little dish of lavender goop and set it down in front of me.

"Have you ever eaten poi?" Claire asked.

"No," I had to admit. I knew that poi, a starch made from ground taro root, had been Hawaii's most important food throughout history, but I had also been warned that it tasted like wallpaper paste.

"Poi is like yogurt," Claire said philosophically. "It tastes bad all by itself." I sampled a little of the ice-cold sour goo and agreed with a grimace. "But when you combine poi with other flavors, something happens." She handed me a plate of slow-cooked *laulau* pork, and I followed her instructions. The pork was excellent, but when I ate it with the poi, the poi tasted good, too. What had once seemed sour now seemed sweet. In fact, the combination of pork and poi was much more interesting than the pork alone. At Claire's direction, I also sampled poi with fried *poki* fish.

"Now eat some of this," said Claire, shoving the Spam and papaya toward me. I cut off a big hunk of Spam and started to chew. As usual, it tasted too salty, too greasy, and too sweet.

"Now eat some poi," Claire directed. I shoved a huge spoonful of poi into my mouth with the Spam and continued to chew. The salty, sweet greasiness of the hot Spam was perfectly offset by the thick, starchy sourness of the ice-cold poi. It was better than poi with pork or poi with fish. When I got over my disbelief, I took another mouthful of the culinary odd couple. Then I started to smile as I realized what Hawaiians had figured out long ago.

Claire summed it up with a shrug. "Nothing tastes better with poi than hot, crispy Spam."

Keep On Shuckin'

They put a couple of ice cubes on top of each raw oyster at Gilhooley's to keep it cold. I push the ice aside and squeeze a few drops of lemon juice onto my next victim. The naked shellfish wiggles helplessly on the little fork as I lower it wickedly into my mouth. There is no flavor quite so delicate—a little briny with a fleshy sweetness—and no texture quite so slippery and sensual on the tongue. Raw oysters are one of the most exquisite culinary experiences on the planet. I will continue slurping them until shortly before I die. (And you're probably thinking that might not be long from now.)

A lawsuit stemming from the death of Mike Matthews, a Houston barber who ate an oyster contaminated by the bacteria *Vibrio vulnificus*, has prompted a lot of discussion on the subject of oysters around here lately. In a recent letter to the editor, Jim Yarbray says he has a one-word reaction whenever he sees somebody eating raw oysters: dumbass. Millions of Americans have come to the same conclusion. People in the United States don't eat oysters like they used to, raw *or* fried. Total oyster sales in the last few years have been running half of what they were in 1989. Yarbray sums up the cautious attitude: "Eating a delicacy is not worth a life," he says, "no matter how small the risk."

I don't agree, so count me as one of the aforementioned dumb-asses. About twenty of the approximately 20 million raw oyster eaters in this country die each year for their culinary pleasure, so the odds of expiring from eating an oyster are a million to one. Eating raw oysters is well worth the gamble, in my book. It's like the lottery in reverse: you win every time you play—unless you hit the jackpot and die. I also will gladly roll the dice with juicy, rare hamburgers—like the one I just ordered at Gilhooley's.

A reader named Ken Ryback recommended this funky bar after I complained about the difficulty of finding a rare hamburger these days. "If you go to Gilhooley's on FM 517 in San Leon and ask for a rare hamburger, they ask you, 'Cold rare or warm rare?'" he wrote. "Order it warm; the cold rare is easily healed with a Band-Aid."

I started falling in love with Gilhooley's as I pulled into the unpaved oyster-shell parking lot. The outdoor bar, with its ramshackle patio furniture, is overgrown with vegetation. The interior is all worn woodwork and old furniture, the rafters seemingly held together by the license plates that cover them. Children are forbidden here, no doubt in part because of the risqué artwork and "Show us your tits!" photos that grace the walls. But it's the menu that made my blood race. Gilhooley's Raw Bar may be the last place in the country where you can get a dozen raw oysters *and* a rare hamburger for lunch. Maybe they ought to call this the Double Dumbass Combo.

In the pursuit of pleasure, you probably take bigger risks than eating these potentially lethal foodstuffs all the time. Ever go skiing, bicycling, horseback riding, or boating? You dumbass! Don't you know you could die from those activities? According to the National Safety Council, the chances of dying in a boating accident (1 in 5,092) are much higher than the one-in-a-million odds of dying from eating oysters. Do you consider the risk of drowning every time you go swimming? Why not? It's a hundred times more likely that you will die from drowning (1 in 7,972) than I will die from eating oysters.

It's a dangerous life we lead, when you think about it. But I laugh in the face of danger—especially in months with an *r* when I am not taking antacids.

Vibrio vulnificus, the bacteria that killed Mike Matthews, is very common in the Gulf of Mexico. You could get infected by stepping on a sharp shell while walking on the beach. The bacteria is present to some extent in every oyster in the Gulf. In the winter, the level is fairly low; in the summer, it gets much higher. Hence, the folk wisdom about not eating oysters in a month without an *r*. Researchers are trying to determine at what level the bacteria should be considered dangerous, but this is complicated by the fact that the vast majority of people have no reaction to it at any level. The at-risk group includes people who have liver trouble, immune system disorders, and it is now suspected, those taking antacids.

The antacid connection was noticed by researchers at the Food and Drug Administration's Gulf Coast Seafood Laboratory. Under normal circumstances, your stomach acids kill *Vibrio vulnificus*, but when you neutralize those acids, it seems, you give the bacteria a much better chance of surviving the voyage into your intestines. This finding makes me wonder if antacids aren't a factor in other cases of bacteria-related food poisoning. And it leaves us with a chicken-or-the-egg question to ponder: if you get food poisoning, is it the bacteria or the antacids that are to blame?

My rare cheeseburger is delivered by a sexy, tough-talking waitress wearing a tube top that leaves her midriff exposed—the better to show off her belly-button piercing. The burger has been cooked over a wood fire, and the bottom bun is soaked through with meat juices. I load it up with the tomato, onion, lettuce, and pickles provided, then cut it in half. It's bright red inside. There's no mayo on the bread, and no mustard, ketchup, or any other sauce. I want to ask the waitress for something to spread on the bun, but she's nowhere in sight. I take a bite while I wait to get her attention and suddenly forget all about the mayo. Gilhooley's rare cheeseburger is so juicy, all it needs is a little salt and pepper.

I've tried to look up the odds of dying from eating rare hamburgers, but I can't find that statistic. The Centers for Disease Control *do* report that every year in the United States foodborne pathogens cause 76 million people to get sick, 325,000 people to go to the hospital, and 5,200 people to die. Food that makes people sick is particularly abhorrent to Americans. The public outcry following the tainted-hamburger deaths of a few years ago caused changes in cooking, inspection, and hygiene practices in restaurants across the country. Some think these changes were for the better, but I think the quest for sterility has gone too far. Corporate restaurant management types are insisting that employees wear plastic gloves while throwing pizza dough (which doesn't work), and health department restrictions have made hand-formed hamburger patties almost nonexistent. Paradoxically, it was one of those perennial winners of the health department inspection game, a fast food franchise, that set off the tainted-hamburger scare in the first place.

"What Americans really want are artisanal foods that have been untouched by human hands," remarks New Orleans food writer Pableaux Johnson. And oddly, few of the people I've shared that remark with see any contradiction in it. As a culture, we no longer seem to make any connection between handmade, artisanal foods and the hands that make them. And now we're attempting to force the rest of the world to adopt our ideas about food safety. The American effort to raise international sanitary standards and require pasteurization of all milk products has long been seen as a threat to French cheese makers and

European culinary culture in general. At the heart of the debate are completely different attitudes about food.

"Americans shouldn't eat *fromages au lait cru*," an Alsatian wine maker once chided me when I bemoaned the fact that we can't get these lively raw milk cheeses in the States. He wasn't kidding: raw milk cheese that tests high for the dangerous *Listeria monocytogenes* bacteria is detected quite often in Europe, he explained. And people sometimes die from eating such cheese. In a notorious outbreak in Switzerland, Vacherin Mont d'Or cheese, made with unpasteurized milk, caused thirty-four deaths between 1983 and 1987. While efforts should be made to keep the food supply reasonably safe in Europe, some degree of uncertainty is considered a fact of life there, the Alsatian maintained. But if an American ever died from eating French cheese, the repercussions would be horrific. Americans should stick with antiseptic cheeses that come in plastic wrappers, he thought.

Listeria monocytogenes is actually more common in meats than in cheese, European cheese makers contend, and indeed the naturally occurring bacteria has been identified in hot dogs, coleslaw, and pasteurized milk. "This is really a war of norms and contrasting tastes, not about scientifically proven health and sanitary issues," Antoine Boissel, director of a French cheese company, told *Time* magazine. "The French hear American health arguments in favor of pasteurization, and then ask why it is the U.S. remains the world champion in reported listeriosis cases." (Maybe it's the antacids?)

My dining companion has his own observations about European and American food culture. He thinks, for instance, that Gilhooley's is the perfect place to bring visiting French intellectuals. "They always find some little detail to complain about at Cafe Annie," he says. "But they love it when they think you're feeding them the local peasant food."

He isn't impressed, however, with Gilhooley's shrimp gumbo, which he refers to as "Protestant gumbo" because of its exceedingly mild flavor. The shrimp and sausage étouffée, too, is long on sausage but short on other flavors. The daily lunch special, spaghetti and meatballs, doesn't look very tempting, either. And I'm afraid there isn't much else on the short menu at Gilhooley's to recommend.

But if you're one of the few, the proud, the dumbasses (or a visiting French intellectual), you'll go to Gilhooley's for the rare find of raw oysters and red burgers. Just be sure to have your doctor check your liver and immune system first, don't take any antacids, and don't blame me if you get sick.

Part THREE

Chicken-Fried Soul

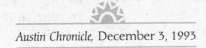

Dinner at Darrington: The Dying Art of Black Southern Cooking

Benny Wade Clewis is fixing me dinner. Watching him assemble the ingredients, I'm not very hopeful. A pair of frozen hamburger patties, two potatoes, flour, a stalk of broccoli—that's about it. For spices there's salt and pepper. "We gotta make do with what we got," smiles Benny, holding three huge pots with long handles. "We never had any skillets at home either, just ol' stewbo'lers like these, so this is gonna be real authentic soul food."

Benny Wade Clewis is a convict at the Darrington Unit, a Texas penitentiary. He is also something of a legend in the food world. He writes long letters to editors of food magazines, and his recipes have turned up in several cookbooks. He learned to cook from his grandmother in Palestine, Texas. He has been cooking in the Texas prison system for forty years. Benny remembers the days when black prisoners supplemented their meat ration by bringing the cook a rabbit or a possum they had caught in the cotton fields. In short, Benny is a culinary time capsule.

I'm getting a tour of the prison kitchen as I follow Benny, who's looking for cooking oil. A Texas Department of Corrections

(TDC) officer goes wherever we go to protect my safety. As an avid student of Southern cooking, I've eaten in strange circumstances before. During my career as a cab driver, I used to stop late at night to buy barbecue sausage in a vacant lot where the rest of the crowd played a loud game of craps. I've eaten at shade-tree barbecue stands and catfish camps where you could watch the proprietor wade into the pond to catch your fish. But this was the first time I'd ever gone to prison for dinner. Unfortunately, it's the only way to taste Benny Clewis's remarkable cooking.

Black Southern cooking is a dying art; integration ruined many restaurants where it once flourished. Outstanding black eateries like the Southern Dinette on East 11th Street in Austin were once popular with blacks and whites. They were the meeting ground of the races in the days of segregation. But these bustling black restaurants lost their steady clientele when segregation ended and the black middle class moved to the suburbs. Today, the last of the inner-city black Southern restaurants are fading away despite a resurgence of interest in regional cooking.

Benny throws a bunch of flour into a bowl, adds some oil, a pint of milk that mysteriously appeared when a friend of his walked by, and some baking powder. He makes no measurements and he mixes the dough with his hands. It's obvious that Benny could make biscuits in his sleep. Isolated from modern trends in commercial kitchens, his cooking is unique; he has never heard of many conveniences and shortcuts. He uses few mixes, and he has no microwave. In fact, today, he can't even find a skillet. He isn't cutting down on fat or red meat—the people he cooks for do backbreaking work in the fields all day and don't have much trouble keeping their cholesterol low. He carries on the traditions of his grandmother, who taught him how to clean a possum, smoke a hog, and find sassafras in the East Texas woods. Benny is a down-home purist. He cooks like he lives on a Southern cotton plantation—which he does. Darrington sits in the middle of 8,000 acres of cotton fields, and the inmates still pick cotton by hand.

Benny is busy at the stove now, stirring a roux, heating oil, blanching the broccoli, preheating the oven, and patting out his "cat heads" all at the same time. The enormous kitchen is bustling and noisy. Black men in clean, white clothes sing while they carry potatoes and use paddles the size of boat oars to stir broccoli in sixty-gallon pots. There are bars and cages on the windows, barbed wire out the back door, and every scrap of food is padlocked. But Benny doesn't mind. He is the king of the prison kitchen. The other men who work there stop by to observe his technique as he chicken-fries my hamburger. He sometimes teaches classes in commercial cooking for other inmates.

Benny tried applying for a cooking job at the Hilton Hotel in Fort Worth once when he got out. When asked about his experience, he would only say, "I cooked here and yonder." He didn't think he'd get hired if they knew he'd been in prison most of his life—but without references, the Hilton wouldn't hire him anyway. So he tried a few chain restaurants, but the instant mixes and modern commercial kitchen apparatus intimidated him. He felt he couldn't compete. "I just know how to cook from scratch," Benny says, showing me his brown roux.

He calls my attention to the change of water he gives the broccoli. "Gotta 'bleach' your broccoli in berling water first to raise the bugs—lookit here," he says, fishing a green winged insect out of the first pot. "Tha's a 'stinky Jim.' If you crush it, it go'n' stink like a skunk." This broccoli is obviously fresh from the field. Like most of the ingredients in the Darrington kitchen, it was grown on a Texas prison farm. "Back in the old days, we only ate what we grew on the farm. We'd grow peanuts and send them to 'Bama, and they'd send back peanut butter. We'd grow sugarcane and send it to Imperial Sugar, and they'd send us back our sugar." Benny recites the names of the ten Texas prison farms clustered in the fertile flatlands south of Houston and tells me which crop each produces.

Pounding out his dough, he begins cutting his "cat heads" with a plastic glass. I asked him what cat heads were, and he told me that cat heads were what got him started cooking at the Gatesville School for Boys in 1952. "When I got to Gatesville, I seen all these little black dudes running around in the kitchen. They had they little blue-jean pants on, and they little blue shirts, and they was clean, they was real clean.

"I said to one of the dudes, 'What is that right there?' He said, 'That's a cat head.' I had them cat heads on my mind all night. They called them that because they looked like a cat head. They was tight and round across the top just like this." He shows me the biscuits as he slides them into the oven.

In the reform school, fifteen-year-old Benny did everything he could to get transferred to kitchen duty, where everyone wore clean clothes and biscuits were free for the taking. Eventually he got his chance, working under a retired cook from Fort Hood named Tucker. "He was one hell of a cook," says Benny. "He taught us how to cook soul food—ham hocks, pinto beans, oatmeal, grits, greens, corn, rice, and cat heads."

Benny batters some french fries in egg, flour, salt, pepper, and an ingredient he makes a show of concealing. "Us chefs always got to have our secret ingredients," he winks as he throws the fries in the hot oil. Benny's first adult prison was Central Unit no. 2 in Sugar Land, one of the oldest penitentiary complexes in the Texas prison system. It's the "Sugar Land" made famous by Leadbelly's song "The Midnight Special."

One day, Captain Montgomery, a warden there, observed Benny standing for hours in the kitchen, diligently fanning the flies away from a pot of beans he was cooking. Montgomery was so impressed, he arranged to have Benny transferred to his house for duty as his family cook. Over the years, Benny has worked for a long line of wardens' families, learning "fancy cooking," as he calls it, along the way.

Benny has borrowed some yellow food coloring from the bakery, and now he is making a "cheese" sauce for my broccoli out of flour and butter and yellow dye, which he adds to my finished plate with a flourish. He serves me my dinner in the warden's dining room. He has battered the hamburger patties and chicken-fried them. They are served smothered in brown gravy with battered french fries and broccoli in "cheese" sauce with biscuits on the side.

The cat heads are among the best biscuits I've ever had. The hamburger, fried while the patties were still ice cold, is crunchy on the outside, moist and pink in the middle. Since Darrington raises its own beef, the meat is very fresh, flavorful, and more coarsely ground than commercial ground meat. The battered french fries are excellent; I guess the secret ingredient is cayenne. The "cheese" sauce can only be appreciated by someone who hasn't eaten real cheese in a long time, and the gravy could use some herbs. But considering the limited ingredients, the cooking is sensational.

The genius of black Southern cooking has always been to turn the most common ingredients into bold, flavorful dishes. Benny remembers a time when catfish were too expensive for his family, and they had to learn to cook carp. He remembers making a stew to feed twenty out of one rabbit.

"Soul food is called soul food because the cook had to make do with what they had," says Benny. "They made up for the missing ingredients by adding some of their soul."

While I eat, Benny talks about how different it was learning to cook for the warden's families. "One time Mrs. Montgomery told me she was having some people coming over for the weekend, and she wanted me to cook a good meal. She told me to write down what I would need from the store. I didn't know but a few things to cook, so I told her to get some rice, neck bone, sweet potatoes, mustard greens. When she saw this list she said, 'This is nigger food! I don't feed neck bones to the dog.'

"She gave me the cookbook put out by the Chicago Institute of Cooking. This was my first cookbook. I carried it everywhere I went. It was like a Bible to me. Most of the inmates would sit around the tank and talk about girls, getting drunk, stealing cars. I would sit around the tank and talk to Smokey and the rest of the cooks and steal cooking knowledge from them."

Benny worked for a long succession of wardens in his ten trips to prison. His cooking made him a coveted houseboy. "I know how to do the shuffle," says Benny. "I know how 'please white folks. Cooking is about pleasing folks." Mopping up gravy with a cat head, I am inclined to agree. Benny Clewis is a charmer.

But Benny has also been convicted of a murder he committed while in prison. "Yeah," he says, "we was mixin' it up, and I cut a guy up pretty bad." With ten convictions and three life sentences, he is considered a career criminal.

I told Benny that I wished I could eat his cooking in a restaurant, and I asked if looking back over his life, he didn't wish all of this could have been different. I asked if society or the prison system couldn't have gotten him back into the mainstream somehow.

"I've been asked this question often, and I've analyzed it." says Benny Wade Clewis. "I never woulda knew how to turn a spoon if I wasn't forced to cook in prison—I wasn't really forced, I had a choice. I coulda tried to been a good cook, or went out into the fields with a cotton sack on my back from sun up to sun down, rippin' and a-runnin' up and down those turn rows. I seen blacks drug, I seen 'em beaten, I seen 'em stomped, I seen 'em die out in those cotton fields. I chose cooking."

Benny's eyes fill with tears as he tells me about the kindness of the wardens' families and the other black prisoners who taught him to cook—kindness that he never found in the free world. "I think this was my life," says Benny softly. "I think this was the best thing."

Summer and Smoke

The sport of barbecue was still new to me. So I didn't know quite what to expect when I was asked to be a judge at the Taylor International Barbecue Cook-off. What I encountered, as I wandered around Murphy Park in Taylor, Texas, were a lot of middle-aged men proudly parked beside their custom-built barbecue trailers. Some of the trailers featured walk-in kitchens and wet bars; all of them were equipped with huge smokers and a good supply of perfectly cut and aged hardwood.

The competitors were organized into teams with names like "Harley's Hogs" or "The Fat Boys." Many of them had been cooking since late last night. The main team activity in the heat of the summer afternoon was relaxing around the smoker, drinking beer, and debating the relative merits of hickory, apple, peach, post oak, pecan, and mesquite wood, and the perfect combination of time and temperature for smoking beef brisket.

For the smoke-seasoned souls who tow their barbecue trailers across the South each summer, barbecue is more than a cooking style; it is a way of life. There is no shortage of venues for competitive pitmasters. In Texas alone, over one hundred barbecue cook-offs are held each year. The grand champion of the Taylor cook-off will win a trophy and be invited to compete in two of

the national championships of barbecue, the Kansas City Barbecue Society American Royal Invitational in Kansas City, Kansas,
and the Jack Daniel's Invitational in Lynchburg, Tennessee.

Sitting around drinking beer and watching meat smoke may
seem like an odd activity to judge competitively. Of course it
was a blind tasting of the smoked meat that determined the
winner. The judging criteria included aroma, taste, texture,
moistness, and the quality of the smoke ring. The smoke ring
identifies authentic slow-smoked barbecue. When the meat is
sliced, this band of color can be observed about a half inch in
from the edge. The color ranges from pink to a dark red depending on the kind of wood and the intensity of the smoke.

At the Taylor Cook-off, there are separate categories for
pork, beef, poultry, goat, lamb, wild game, and seafood. I was a
judge in the wild game division, in which I tasted venison,
javelina, wild boar, quail, and rabbit. The wild boar tasted very
much like regular pork, and the venison was excellent, but I
gave my top marks to the quail that was basted with a spicy
honey barbecue sauce.

Unfortunately, cook-offs don't offer prizes for best beer drinking or tale telling, but there is no doubt in anybody's mind that
lounging around the smoker is really the most enjoyable part of
the barbecue experience. It occurred to me, as I opened a beer
and sat down with a perfect sparerib, that this uniquely American leisure activity is tied up with the very origins of the barbecue tradition.

Many imaginative etymologies for the word *barbecue* have
been advanced over the years. I have often heard the French
phrase *barbe à queue*, meaning "beard to tail," cited as the source
of the English word. The phrase supposedly refers to the fact
that barbecuers roast the whole animal. But the Oxford English
Dictionary considers that theory "absurd conjecture," as do
most barbecue scholars.

It was the Carib Indians of the West Indies who gave us the word along with a few of their smoking methods. The Spanish word *barbacoa* is a variation of the Arawak-Carib word *babracot* and the root of the English word *barbecue*. A *babracot* was a grill of green sticks that the Caribs would place a good distance above a slow fire. They would then arrange their meats on the grill and cover them with leaves to retain the smoke.

Of course, the Caribs didn't invent barbecue. Smoke has been used to preserve meat since prehistoric times. Some speculate that the preservative qualities of smoke were first discovered in the Neolithic Age, when smudge fires were built under racks of meat and fish that were drying in the sun. According to this theory the smoke was originally intended to keep the flies away. But when it was found that the meats cured with smoke kept longer than regular air-dried meats, the practice became standard. The Roman epicure Apicius gave a recipe for curing ham that included seventeen days of salting, two days of open-air drying, and two days of smoking.

Scientists don't fully understand the chemical reactions that give smoke its preservative properties. Of course, the smoke's heat plays a major role in the cooking and drying, and the open-air draft aids in retaining moisture in the meat. But wood smoke contains upwards of two hundred other components, including alcohols, aldehydes, acids, phenolic compounds, and various toxic substances. The phenolic compounds retard fat oxidation. The organic acids and aldehydes inhibit the growth of bacteria and fungi. But what else happens when we apply this ancient chemical treatment to our meat remains something of a mystery.

It is also something of a mystery why the early European settlers had to learn this ancient technique from the natives. Perhaps indoor kitchens caused European cultures to give up smoking because the technique was better suited to the outdoors. Whatever the reason, the early Spanish settlers on the island of

Hispaniola regarded the Caribs' barbecue as unique enough to borrow the name.

The Caribs smoked small game animals and fish on their grills, but their taboos prohibited the Spanish cows and pigs, as well as salt. It could be argued that when these Europeans began to apply the Caribs' techniques to beef and pork and added a little salt, American barbecue was born. But if you hang around with barbecue crazies, this theory will lead only to very long debate about just what barbecue is.

Some argue that the definition of barbecue is meat with a spicy sauce, but some of the best barbecue in Texas is smoked meat with no sauce at all. Some say barbecue means smoked meat, but in Memphis some of the most famous barbecue pork ribs are simply grilled with sauce and no smoke. In the Carolinas, barbecue most often means a sandwich of slow-cooked pulled pork in a spicy sauce. And for a huge number of Americans, "barbecuing" just means cooking hamburgers and hot dogs on a grill in the backyard.

The word *babracot* is probably the reason for this ambiguity. The word was a noun for the grill itself. Since the Caribs' grill was used for smoking, and they had a preference for highly seasoned foods, and we didn't have a special word in English for the meat itself, the word *barbecue* seems to have come to mean all sorts of things. The same word now describes the grill, the meat that is cooked on it, the process of doing it, and the party surrounding it. No wonder we can never agree on what barbecue really is.

Other languages have a variety of words that shed a little light on barbecue history. The Spanish word *charqui* means "dried meat" and is the root of the words *jerk* and *jerky*. The word *jerk* ties the barbecue traditions to its Caribbean roots. Of all the barbecue techniques I've seen, the one that comes the closest to the historical descriptions of the Caribs' methodology is Jamaican jerk barbecue.

In 1994 a Jamaican friend and I visited Jamaica's most famous jerk shacks in the little town of Boston Beach. The wood of the allspice tree is used to smoke the meat in Boston Beach; you can smell the smoldering logs all over the village. The meat is spread across a grill and suspended above an open pit of smoldering coals, just as in the descriptions of the Carib method. Metal grills have replaced the grate of green sticks, and a galvanized sheet of metal has replaced the leaves. But my Jamaican friend told me that as little as twenty years ago, banana leaves were still used in Boston Beach. The jerk pork I ate would have done well here at the Taylor barbecue competition. It was spicy and so tender that it fell apart in my fingers.

Women often do the cooking in Jamaican restaurants, but none were in evidence at Boston Beach. There were, however, a lot of guys sitting around the fire drinking Red Stripe beer. The male camaraderie I witnessed around those smoky pits and at the Taylor Barbecue Cook-off brings to mind another word for barbecue.

The French word *boucan* came from Tupi, a Brazilian Amerindian language, and was used by the French as a synonym for the Carib word *babracot*. A derivative of the word entered the English language in the form of *buccaneer*. The buccaneers (or *boucaniers*) were a crew of mostly French and English outlaws who lived on the island of Tortuga, off the northern coast of Hispaniola, in the mid-1600s. Although they would later be known for their seafaring exploits, their original fame was in the barbecue business—hence their name.

The buccaneers hunted the wild cows and pigs that were the survivors of failed Spanish settlements on the island of Hispaniola. Then they smoke-cured the meat and sold it to passing ships. Hunted themselves by the Spanish, the buccaneers banded together for protection. Eventually they gave up on the meat business and went to sea. Soon they discovered that capturing Spanish vessels by surprise attack was a lot more lucrative than chasing wild pigs.

But the part of barbecue history that fascinates me most is the association between barbecue and leisure time. We can thank the Caribs for several inventions that helped create this tradition. Not only did they contribute the word *barbecue* to the English language, they also taught us the word *hammock*. They might as well have invented summer weekends.

The relationship between the *babracot* and the hammock in Carib society is critical to understanding our own barbecue culture. By Carib custom, a hunter or fisherman retired to his hammock after he had been out hunting or fishing in order to recover his strength. There in the hammock, he would wait for his meat or fish to slowly smoke to perfection.

An incredulous French observer of the seventeenth century once reported that the Caribs, on returning to their homes after fishing expeditions, "had the patience to wait the roasting of a fish on a wooden grate fixed two feet above the ground, over a fire so small that it sometimes required the whole day to cook it."

That a hungry man could relax in a hammock all day waiting for his dinner to be properly smoked obviously dumbfounded the Europeans. But walking around the Taylor International Barbecue Cook-off, watching the smoke rise and smelling the meat cooking while The Fat Boys and Harley's Hogs stretch out in their lawn chairs, I feel connected to a noble, indigenous American tradition. If a seventeenth-century Carib were to fall to earth here in Murphy Park this afternoon, I am sure he would feel right at home.

Boston Beach Wet Jerk Rub

Rub the meat thoroughly with this paste. For larger cuts, such as pork roasts, slash the meat at two-inch intervals and force the jerk rub into the cavities. Allow the meat to marinate overnight before smoking over a slow fire until well done.

1/2 cup fresh thyme leaves
2 bunches (about 15) green onions
4 tablespoons finely diced fresh ginger
3 Scotch bonnet or habanero peppers, stemmed
1/4 cup peanut oil
5 garlic cloves, chopped
3 bay leaves
2 teaspoons freshly ground allspice
1 teaspoon freshly ground nutmeg
1 tablespoon freshly ground pepper
1 tablespoon freshly ground coriander
1 teaspoon freshly ground cinnamon
2 teaspoons salt
Juice of 1 lime

Combine all the ingredients in a food processor. Blend to a thick, chunky paste. You can store the rub in a tightly sealed container in the refrigerator for several months.

Yields 2-1/2 cups

Chicken-Fried Honor

A steaming chicken-fried steak slides down the stainless-steel bar top at Ouisie's Table and comes to rest below my nose. The golden-brown Southern-fried crust is so perfect that the cream gravy is served on the side. I nibble on the mashed potatoes, the mustard greens, and the custardy corn pudding. The undulating curves of battered steak are endlessly alluring, but the free-form fried meat is still too hot to eat. I finger the gravy boat. I want to pour the gravy at just the right instant: wait too long and the meat is not hot enough anymore, but pour too early and you either burn your mouth or sit in frustration while that awesome crust goes soggy.

As I wait for that moment to arrive, I fume about something I read in the paper. "Only a dupe believes in such a thing as the best chicken-fried steak in Texas," read the subhead of an article by my fellow *Houston Press* food writer, George Alexander. He'd insulted everything I hold sacred.

"The phrase 'chicken-fried steak' is, itself, striking and memorable in a *Hee Haw* kind of way," George opined. But "there is no such thing as a great chicken-fried steak." The tough round steak should be braised, not fried like the tender veal used in Wiener schnitzel, and no good cook would ever use béchamel on beef, he wrote. "Finally, to make this dish truly hilarious, the contemporary Texan food humorist serves it with a side of mashed potatoes so that there is little contrast in color, flavor, and texture between the sauce and side dish, and a minimal contrast with the battered, fried beef." He also questions the historical pretensions of the dish, since the earliest mention of it in print dates back only to 1952.

George, I understand how you could have made this mistake. There are a lot of bad chicken-fried steaks out there, just as there are lots of bad Wiener schnitzels, bad béchamels, and bad caviars. But ignorance is no excuse. You shot yourself in the foot on this one. And your foot was in your mouth at the time.

I will address each of your contentions in a minute. But first, I need to pour some gravy. I like to start modestly with a couple of tablespoons over a quarter of the battered steak and then quickly cut off a big chunk. That way the batter is still crunchy and each bit is instantly swaddled in the salty warmth of cream gravy and savory meat juice. I close my eyes and savor the moment. Ouisie's Table serves a world-class chicken-fried steak—without a doubt, one of the best in Texas.

Not that I am an authority. I have been eating chicken-fried steak (or CFS, as it is known in the trade) for only thirty years and writing about it for ten. I hope someday to become a full-fledged expert, like Bud Kennedy of the *Fort Worth Star-Telegram*, who can describe the nuances of every CFS in every small-town café within a hundred-mile radius of the Fort Worth stockyards. Kennedy learned from a master, the late Jerry Flemmons, also a columnist at the *Star-Telegram*.

"As splendid and noble as barbecue and Tex-Mex are, both pale before that Great God Beef dish, chicken-fried steak," wrote Flemmons. "No single food better defines the Texas character; it has, in fact, become a kind of nutritive metaphor for the romanticized, prairie-hardened personality of Texans."

Flemmons and his buddy Dan Jenkins hung out at an old Fort Worth roadhouse called Massey's, which is famous for its CFS and ice-cold beer served in frozen cannonball-sized schooners. Jenkins wrote a comic riff about chicken-fried steak in his novel, *Baja Oklahoma*. Only after years of studying these masters of CFS literature did I dare to try writing about the "Great God Beef dish" myself.

There is a chicken-fried steak recipe in *A Cowboy in the Kitchen*, the cookbook I coauthored with Fort Worth chef Grady Spears. (Check out the sexy close-up of a CFS dripping with cream gravy on the cover.) Which, of course, brings up the subject of my conflict of interest. I will admit that the CFS is buttering my bread, and it would not be in my financial interest to bad-mouth it.

So don't take my word for it, George. Take your basic premise, that there is no such thing as a great chicken-fried steak, over to Ouisie's Table. (Call first—they serve CFS only on Tuesdays or as a daily special.) Here's how to eat it: first you cut off a nice big chunk of steaming meat with plenty of batter, then put some potatoes on top with your knife, and then some mustard greens (properly doused with pepper sauce). Now lower the whole forkful directly into the gravy bowl for a drenching.

Not enough contrast? What I get is a montage of texture and flavor, the vinegary pepper sauce on the bitter mustard-flavored greens burning through the mashed potato and creamy gravy and mixing boldly with the meat juices. This perfect bite is properly washed down with a swallow of cold beer. (Go ahead and get the Pilsner Urquel if Shiner Bock isn't good enough for you.) If you still can't tell the meat from the potatoes after a bite like this, then maybe it's time to take your palate in for a checkup.

The meat is a little tough, you complain. Duh, George. What did you expect? Tough beef has been the main indigenous ingredient in Texas regional cooking for quite some time now.

Which is why we also invented the hamburger, chili con carne, and barbecued brisket here. That's also why we tenderize the steaks before we batter and fry them.

But just for the sake of argument, let's consider your contention. "Frying, especially batter-frying in a pan, is for tender meats. Think Wiener schnitzel," you say. In James Beard's *American Cookery*, the recipe for Wiener schnitzel calls for a veal cutlet. "In our terminology, the cutlet is cut from the leg and has the round bone still in," says Beard. This one-half-to-one-inch-thick round steak is then pounded with a meat mallet to the thickness of a quarter inch or even thinner and then breaded and fried in deep fat. Sound familiar?

After you beat it with a hammer for a while, what's the difference between veal and beef round? Surely tenderness is not the issue. Veal tastes milder because it comes from milk-fed calves. But there wasn't any milk-fed veal available in Texas years ago. So they made the same dish with a similar cut of beef. Chicken-fried steak is essentially a Texas variation on the breaded veal cutlet, an American dish that James Beard tells us was patterned after Austrian Wiener schnitzel and Italian veal Milanese and has been popular in the United States for 150 years.

Which brings us to the topic of history. "Most Texans probably first heard about the dish when they went to see the 1971 movie . . . *The Last Picture Show*," says George. Wait a minute, let me get this straight: he thinks Bubba started eating chicken-fried steak because of an arty black-and-white film by Peter Bogdanovich?

According to the *Lone Star Book of Records*, the CFS was invented in 1911 by Jimmy Don Perkins, a cook in a small café in Lamesa, Texas, who misunderstood a customer's order and battered a thin steak and deep-fried it in hot oil. Unfortunately this oft-reported food fact is a complete fable. Nobody is really sure when the CFS was invented, but it was long before 1952. In the

Best Read Guide to San Antonio, Carol B. Sowa reports that the Pig Stand Drive-in locations in San Antonio started serving chicken-fried steak sandwiches when they opened in the 1940s. *Gourmet* columnists Jane and Michael Stern speculate in *Eat Your Way across the U.S.A.* that the chicken-fried steak was a Depression-era invention of Hill Country German Texans. My own guess is that the dish existed as beefsteak Wiener schnitzel long before the catchy Southern name was coined.

Finally we come to the cream gravy problem. "It is also known to all professional cooks that you would never, ever use béchamel sauce on beef," says George. In speaking for all professional cooks, George truly puts his foot in his mouth. Elouise Cooper and Robert Del Grande, two of Houston's best chefs, serve chicken-fried steaks with cream gravy. So what is George trying to tell us? That Cooper and Del Grande aren't professional cooks?

At Del Grande's Rio Ranch, the chicken-fried is a sirloin dipped in buttermilk batter and served with cream gravy. Rio Ranch helped invent the upscale cowboy cuisine that has taken the common chicken-fried to new heights in Texas. Over the last ten years, chicken-fried venison steaks, chicken-fried rib eyes, and chicken-fried tuna steaks (all in cream gravy) have been featured in high-class restaurants across the state. No doubt George will discover these innovations someday soon and report back to us breathlessly about them.

We can forgive George his miscues; he has just moved back to Texas after a long absence. But the real problem here isn't the lack of local knowledge; it's the haughty attitude. Telling Houstonians that there is no such thing as a great chicken-fried steak is like telling Philadelphians that there is no such thing as a great cheese steak, or New Yorkers that there is no such thing as a great pizza. It's not just a snobby opinion. It's a civic slur.

Creole Country

The turtle soup at Brennan's of Houston takes you on a magic carpet ride. From the moment the bowl of black stew hits the white linen, it commands your attention. Musky alligator snapper meat, dark roux, and intricately spiced veal stock shimmer behind a veil of steam. And just as you lift your spoon, the waiter steps in. Your silverware hovers in the air as he uncorks the sherry bottle and lets the Creole genie out. A sudden whiff of sherry, bay, garlic, and spices rises up, lifting you gently from your chair. Then you take a bite and go flying—through a version of history as exotic and opulent as anything in *1001 Arabian Nights*.

Consider this ancient urban legend: it's 1762. King Louis XV of France is playing cards with his cousin King Charles III of Spain. Louis is losing but thinks his hand is a sure thing, so he goes all out and bets the French territory of Louisiana. Charlie smiles. His cards are even better. In a fit of giggles and a flash of powdered wigs, Louisiana goes from French to Spanish rule.

Cut to a darkly lit interior on the other side of the globe: in the slave quarters of a Louisiana mansion, an elegantly dressed French aristocrat slips quietly into the bedroom of his lover and the mother of his children. The beautiful black slave girl is named Marie Therese. Whispering in French, her lover, Claude Pierre, promises her an impossible future. He will set her free and buy her a cotton plantation

But I'm getting ahead of myself. Let me start from the beginning: Brennan's dining room is dark and cozy, with a rose-colored granite floor and dark wood columns wrapped with Christmas garlands. It looks inviting, but I'm not allowed in.

"I'm sorry, sir," says the manager. "Gentlemen are required to wear jackets at Brennan's. But we will gladly lend you one." I sheepishly select a large from the rack of identical blue blazers. I have never understood this strange custom of eating dinner in somebody else's jacket. But it's too late to retreat, so I sit down with my date and look over the menu.

Brennan's is the most famous Creole restaurant in Houston, and I am here to see what this style of cooking is all about. But what I read on the oversize menu makes me dizzy. Truffled *maque choux!* Foie gras on braised frisée with praline liqueur and pecans! Sweetbreads and foie gras on rutabaga cakes!

At Brennan's, you have to decide if you want classic Creole, nouvelle Creole, or Texas Creole. We shuffle the deck. For appetizers, we order the nouvelle truffled shrimp *maque choux* and the classic turtle soup. For our entrées, we select old-time seafood stew Pontchartrain and Texas pecan-crusted trout. The *maque choux* is a disappointment; I can barely smell any truffles in the corn-and-pepper stew, and the shrimp on top have no connection to the dish. You know about the turtle soup. The pecan-crusted trout is pleasant enough, but very delicate. Seafood stew Pontchartrain is a crustacean orgy, an obscene amount of lump crabmeat covered with shrimp on a bed of roasted trout with oysters swimming in butter and cream sauce. It is "as delicious as the less criminal forms of sin," as Mark Twain once described Louisiana seafood.

Near the reservations desk, I find a copy of a new Creole cookbook, *Commander's Kitchen*, by Ti Adelaide Martin and

Jamie Shannon, the owner and chef of Commander's Palace in New Orleans. (The Brennan family has owned ten restaurants during the last fifty years, including Brennan's in Houston and the flagship, Commander's Palace in New Orleans.) In the book, the authors explain the lineage of the historic Creole cooking style, which has been lovingly preserved and handed down by famous old New Orleans restaurants.

In 1780 the Spanish government gave special rights to persons of European heritage, whom they called *criollos* or "Creoles." These refined souls embodied the affluent spirit of old New Orleans, and they loved to mimic the French and Spanish courts with elaborate banquets. The food was created by their African servants from classical French recipes and New World ingredients. To the existing French-African–Native American cooking style of Louisiana, the Spanish introduced the ingredients that completed the New Orleans pantry—tomatoes, chiles, and exotic spices from their far-flung empire. (The French still thought tomatoes were poisonous.) And thus the foundations of Creole cuisine were created.

As the truffled *maque choux* and foie gras creations on the menu will attest, Creole cooking is neither static nor immune to innovation. Former head chefs at Commander's Palace include Paul Prudhomme and Emeril Lagasse, each of whom has launched stylistic variations of his own. But the menus of the Brennan family restaurants also preserve such classics as turtle soup and shrimp *rémoulade*, both of which trace their heritage all the way back to the bons vivants of the late 1700s.

George Thomas is blowing a soulful rendition of the line "Chestnuts roasting on an open fire . . ." on the flügelhorn. His four-piece jazz band is set up in front of the fireplace at the Creole Shack. The crowd is mostly black, and everybody is in a good mood. Several families have brought their kids, who bounce their feet in time to the music and stare at the huge flocked Christmas tree covered with blinking colored lights. On Friday and Saturday nights, the Creole Shack is a "fat café." "A fat café is what they call a restaurant that has music back in western Louisiana," the bartender tells me.

I get a catfish poor boy, a cup of gumbo, and a cold beer. The gumbo comes first; it's loaded to the brim with chicken, crab, oysters, and a sausage. A woman at the next table leans over and says, "That's fine gumbo, ain't it?" I agree.

"We're Cajun, and we come here every night," her companion says.

"What's the difference between Cajun and Creole gumbo?" I ask.

"No difference," he says.

The sandwich arrives with a piping hot fried catfish fillet on top of a large roll sliced in half and slathered with *rémoulade*, then dressed with cold lettuce and sliced tomato. It's too hot to eat, so I suck on my beer while it cools and get rewarded with the ultimate poor boy combination: hot-as-your-mouth-can-stand-it seafood on a bed of cold lettuce and tomato. A couple of shakes of Cajun Chef hot sauce adds a little edge to the spices. So what's the difference between Creole and Cajun? I wonder.

I know the Cajuns, or Acadians, were French-Canadians exiled from present-day Nova Scotia and environs by the British. Their diaspora spread them around the world—a great many ending up in French-speaking Louisiana, particularly in the swamps and bayous of western Louisiana. The Cajun cooking style they developed was heartier and spicier than the Creole cooking in New Orleans but seems similar to what they call Creole in western Louisiana. Confused? So was I. So I e-mailed Pableaux Johnson, the author of *World Food: New Orleans*, a foodies' guide to Louisiana from Lonely Planet Publications.

I tell him that I've just eaten at two Creole restaurants in Houston—Brennan's, where I had transcendental turtle soup and seafood stew Pontchartrain, and the Creole Shack, an inexpensive black hangout where I had a catfish poor boy, gumbo, and cold beer.

"Are they both the same kind of Creole?" I ask him.

"No," he replies. "The two restaurants you are talking about are using two different definitions of Creole. Brennan's, being an outpost of the Crescent City restaurant dynasty, is using 'Creole' to define a style of cooking invented by the old European settlers of New Orleans. It's sophisticated, old-fashioned city food—essentially classical French cooking adapted to New World and Spanish ingredients by African cooks. Heavy on the seafood, lots of butter and cream sauces, gumbos with tomato, rich, elegant quasi-European stuff.

"The Creole Shack, on the other hand, is a classic 'south Louisiana Creole' joint," he continues. "Here 'Creole' is being used as an ethnic distinction. In the eighteenth century, French-speaking Afro-Caribbean free people of color (*les gens de couleur libres*), including Haitians and freed slaves of French owners, settled in French Louisiana. Pockets of these French-speaking black folks flourished in both New Orleans and out in the bayous. The foods of the south Louisiana Creoles are simpler and more rustic (similar to Cajun food), with a different set of influences than the 'European Creole' of old New Orleans."

No wonder I was confused.

"'Creole' is a dangerous word to throw around, but everybody does it," Johnson says. "The seemingly simple term means a lot of different things. Linguists have a technical definition, 'a mixed-language dialect used as a group's mother tongue.' Louisiana historians have another one, 'direct descendants of New Orleans's early colonial French and Spanish settlers.' 'Creole' means something altogether different in the French West Indies and in other parts of the Caribbean. And then there are several culinary definitions. Just remember, anytime somebody tries to tell you exactly what Creole means, take it with a grain of salt."

Does that include you?

"Especially me!"

Thanks to Pableaux Johnson's explanation, I now understand that when Roland Curry, the owner of the Creole Shack, says "Creole," he's referring to Louisiana's French-speaking blacks. In fact, Curry is related to one of the most famous French-speaking free people of color in Louisiana history, Marie Therese Coin Coin, a Creole woman who owned an antebellum plantation outside of Natchitoches. Curry goes on to tell her story:

"It was the time of the Spanish rule," he says. "Marie Therese Coin Coin was a slave from western Africa. A white French aristocrat named Claude Pierre Metoyer fell in love with Marie and fathered fourteen children with her." The man's family was scandalized, Curry continues, so they tried to keep him from seeing her anymore. As a compromise, he made a deal with them that if they would grant her freedom, he would stop seeing her. They agreed, just to get rid of her, but they insisted on keeping the children as slaves. Well, Metoyer was in good with the Spanish king, and he got Marie a land grant on which she built a plantation called Melrose. And every year, with the money she made, she bought back one of her children. They say that just a few months before she died, she finally raised enough money to buy back her baby. "A lot of the Creoles in Natchitoches are descended from Marie's fourteen children—including me," Roland Curry says.

Cajun, New Orleans Creole, and African-French Creole are three distinct cuisines from three of the world's most fabled cultures.

On my second visit to the Creole Shack, I taste the difference. Roland Curry's style of Creole is part African, part Choctaw Indian, part French, and part Spanish, he tells me. "It's a little different from Cajun food, with more tomato sauces and different spices," Curry says.

The Creole Shack's shrimp étouffée drowns juicy shrimp in a spicy sauce, which is made with a little roux and a lot of tomatoes, green peppers, and onions. It's different from Cajun shrimp étouffées, which are brown sauces thickened with dark roux. It's closer to a New Orleans shrimp Creole, only spicier.

My buddy gets okra Creole, which is perhaps the most unique illustration of black country Creole on the menu. It's a spicy hash of okra (African); corn and peppers (Native American); onion, celery, and andouille sausage (French); and shrimp in a thick tomato sauce (Spanish), served on a plate with French bread. It's like nothing I've ever seen in a Cajun restaurant—or in a New Orleans Creole restaurant, either.

The Creole Shack and Brennan's occupy opposite ends of the spectrum. Brennan's is one of Houston's most elegant restaurants, a place to experience historic New Orleans cuisine and some innovations unique to the Bayou City. The Creole Shack is a fun and inexpensive joint whose spicy stews and well-dressed poor boys offer an interesting, if subtle, alternative to Cajun food. Go to Brennan's for a stellar fine-dining experience. Go to the Creole Shack for a poor boy, a cup of gumbo, and a jazz show on Friday or Saturday night. Either way, you will be experiencing authentic Creole culture.

Houston Press, April 5, 2001

The Inkblot Test

There are eight customers in the Triple A Restaurant at 10:30 in the morning. All of them are men, and four sport comb-overs. The wood-grain Formica on the tables and the orange vinyl on the chairs are a little worn. There is a picture of a 1935 high school football team hanging on one wall. My waitress is named Betty; she grew up in the Heights and has been working at Triple A for eighteen years.

I am interested in a menu item that occupies almost half the page: "Two Farm Fresh Eggs (Any Style) with. . . . " The "with" options include a pork chop, a breakfast steak, chicken-fried steak with cream gravy, and bacon or ham or choice of sausage. The sausage choices constitute another sublist. All of the above includes grits or country-style potatoes and toast or biscuits. Betty describes the three kinds of sausage available: the home-made pan style is a free-form patty that's been spiced up hot; the country sausage is a big link like kielbasa; and the little links are the regular kind. I order two eggs with chicken-fried steak and hash browns and biscuits. And I get a side order of that home-made sausage, just out of curiosity.

"How do you want your eggs?" Betty asks.

"Over easy and greasy," I smile.

"It's going to take a while," she says. "We batter the chicken-fried steak from scratch. It's not the frozen kind."

Neither are the crunchy potatoes; they are big pieces of fresh spuds fried crisp. The eggs are just right. The chicken-fried steak is piping hot with a wrinkly brown crust and a peppery tan cream gravy on the side. The biscuits are average. The biggest problem with Triple A's breakfast is the vehicle on which it is served: the oval platters are too small for the portions. I end up eating from three plates. I split my biscuits on the right-hand plate and pour a little cream gravy on them, while I eat the eggs, potatoes, and chicken-fried steak from the middle plate. From the left, I sample the homemade sausage, which is extremely spicy and fried extra brown.

Betty is gabbing with the other waitresses, and it takes a lot of gesturing to get my coffee refilled. But it's a sunny day outside, and from the window by my booth I can see the farmer's market next door. I also see an old black shoeshine man working on Triple A's front porch. His customer is sitting against the wall, so I can't see his face, just his brown brogues. The shoeshine man is spreading the polish with his fingers. I linger over my coffee until 11:20 and leave just as the lunch crowd arrives.

If the scene above were an inkblot test, how would you characterize it? Inviting? Depressing? Boring? Charming?

Before you answer, consider the following inkblot:

At 11 in the morning, almost all the tables are occupied at Century Diner on the corner of Main Street and Texas Avenue. There are some young, hip guys lingering over books and magazines, and a lot of downtown business folks in nice clothes eating lunch.

The vinyl booths by the window are two-tone, pastel green and off-white. The tables are covered with brand-new Formica in a bright pattern of circles and shapes, a design that was called "modern" forty years ago. The waiters wear black-and-white bowling shirts with slogans such as "Something Superior for Your Interior" on the back. The menu is sprinkled with little nuggets about old diner lingo, such as the fact that "Adam and Eve on a raft" once meant ham and eggs on toast.

But ham and eggs on toast is not on the menu. Instead, the place offers a contemporary take on diner food, including "The Total New Yorker," a bagel with Nova Scotia salmon and cream cheese, and "The Health Kick," an egg-white omelet. Although two eggs with ham, bacon, or sausage aren't offered, the menu does feature "Eggs N' Hash," two eggs with hash browns and New York–style corned-beef hash.

My waiter is a young guy with dyed black hair. He's too busy to chat, so I don't get his name. I order two eggs. They don't have hash browns at lunch, so I settle for french fries. The waiter doesn't know what the breakfast meats are, but he checks. I order the sausage and a side of biscuits and gravy.

"How do you want your eggs?" he asks.

"Over easy and greasy," I smile.

Coffee comes in a little stainless-steel Thermos, which is a nice touch. It reminds me of the little glass "hottle" you used to get at coffee shops in the 1960s. The eggs are just right. The french fries are excellent. The link sausage is precisely what you'd expect. The biscuits are huge, and the gravy has lots of bacon pieces in it. Unfortunately, it has been spooned over the top of unsplit biscuits. I try to break them up to soak up some of the gravy.

At a table just across the divide from mine, two men and a woman in conservative business suits are gossiping about somebody's chances in some election. The conversation is spirited, and the woman's eyes sparkle as she laughs at one of the men's observations. I can't hear what he said, but it must have been pretty funny. I pour myself some more coffee and copy down this quote from the big shiny menu: "'The character of a diner builds up the way grime does'—Douglas Yorke."

My own reactions to these diner-shaped inkblots are not hard to predict. Breakfast at Triple A puts me in a warm and wonderful mood. And the retro-chic at Century Diner feels phony. But I'm pretty much alone in this opinion.

One friend calls the breakfast at Triple A "a heart attack on a plate." Another finds the dark wood paneling, worn-out furniture, and fat old guys with comb-overs "depressing." And she thinks the Century's decor and waiters' costumes are "precious."

What does the inkblot test tell you?

The same restaurant can feel entirely different to you and me. I can walk into a truck stop alone and feel right at home. But a beautiful young woman walking in by herself might feel differently. My mother is obsessive about cleanliness; she'd rather eat at McDonald's than at a place with character if there's the threat of grime. And then there are deeper prejudices.

When I moved to Austin from Connecticut to start school at UT (the University of Texas), I was seventeen years old, 2,000 miles away from my parents, and high on my newfound freedom. I drove my motorcycle all over town discovering funky places to eat. I loved little luncheonettes run by crazy old ladies, drugstore soda fountains, and old urban institutions like the Southern Dinette on East 11th Street in the heart of the black east side.

Why did I love these places? It wasn't always about the food. I was also seeking a level of comfort. As a newcomer, I was fascinated by the characters in these old places and by the vestiges of a disappearing Texas. As a long-haired geek from the East, I was scared of the rednecks and fraternity boys who prowled the trendy campus hangouts. Maybe I ate in eccentric dives and places on the wrong side of the tracks because I felt like an outcast myself.

Sometimes friends who grew up in Texas, people who are concerned with healthy diets and whose families struggled with poverty in their childhood, don't find these funky joints nearly as endearing as I do. In another's eyes, these places are outdated, high-cholesterol slop houses, full not of colorful characters but of boring old farts. I understand these biases, and I want to be honest about my own.

It's still not always about the food with me. Sometimes I think a restaurant review needs to stick closely to the subject at hand. But in other cases, I'm more interested in food as a reflection of culture, and so it is with this case. There are some differences in the food at Triple A and Century Diner. But having breakfast at an old diner one morning and a new retro diner the next brings up intriguing questions.

Like, do you prefer sanitized imitations of old institutions to grimy old institutions themselves? And why does a retro-chic diner in the oldest part of Houston get its history lessons (and breakfast dishes) from New York? Does the architectural preservation downtown make any sense absent some cultural preservation?

Several letters to the editor lately have complained about my ramblings—that my restaurant reviews are too personal and not focused enough on food. To this charge I proudly plead guilty.

When I began reviewing at the *Austin Chronicle* in 1991, I was influenced by the very personal narratives of food writer John Thorne. Thorne's own inspiration was Mark Zanger, who under the pseudonym Robert Nadeau reviewed restaurants for the *Boston Phoenix* in the late 1970s. "He was teaching himself eating and drinking and simultaneously wondering out loud what he should be making of it, gnawing away at all pat assumptions," wrote Thorne. "He taught me that honesty means nothing if there's no real risk to it, no genuine self-examination."

Lofty aspirations for a restaurant reviewer, no doubt, but at least it's a worthy goal. In that spirit, I offer you this nonreview. And I invite you to visit Triple A and Century Diner for some genuine self-examination of your own. Which one do *you* like better?

Folk Art on Bread

The skinny flute of bread is split in half and toasted, always a good sign. "Do you want your oysters well done?" asks the woman behind the counter at Original New Orleans Po' Boy.

"No, I want them juicy," I say. They come from the fryer in the back, six to a pie plate. The sandwich maker coats the toasted bread with a spatula-full of tartar sauce and prepares a bed of lettuce on one side. Then she lays the golden oysters down one after the other. They fit perfectly. A couple of slices of tomato and the other half of the bread are put in place, and I take my poor boy down the cafeteria line to the cashier.

Steve Wertheimer of the Continental Club told me about this place; he's partial to the cheeseburger poor boy here. Two taxicabs are parked out front, so I assume the drivers are eating here, too. As a former driver for hire, I always take notice when cops and cabbies frequent a restaurant.

The sandwich costs $5.14, tax included. The oysters are hot and juicy. I douse them well with Louisiana hot sauce, push the top layer of the twelve-inch roll down hard, and attack. The oysters gush into the lettuce, tomatoes, and tartar sauce, creating that perfectly moist and creamy texture. It is one of those rare foods in which every bite tastes better than the last. Along with soft-shell crab poor boys (which are rare), oyster poor boys are my favorite sandwiches. I am not alone in my high opinion of them.

"The grinder of New England is a cousin to the hoagie of Philadelphia, and both are kissin' kin to the ubiquitous submarine," opined William Rice, food and wine columnist for the *Chicago Tribune*. "But in the sandwich equivalent of the Social Register, none ranks higher than the poor boy (or po' boy) of New Orleans, and the pride of that family is the oyster poor boy."

I have tried oyster poor boys all over Houston. Nowhere else did anyone ask me how I wanted my oysters done. They just went ahead and overcooked them. Nowhere else did they use authentic skinny bread, so that the ratio of bread to oyster remained low enough for you to actually taste the juicy mollusks. And nowhere else were the sandwiches so moist. This is clearly the best oyster poor boy in town. And yet, when I try to tell people about Original New Orleans Po' Boy, they look at me like I've lost my mind.

"You mean that grimy little green-and-yellow place on Main Street?" one woman asked in astonishment. "Yuck," she quickly added.

"You're not talking about that greasy spoon with the painted windows?" my editor asked in disbelief when I said I wanted to write about it.

"Yes," I assured them both. "That's the place." Neither seemed to think that a dive like Original New Orleans Po' Boy was a good candidate for a review.

The best oyster poor boy I've ever eaten came from St. Roch's on St. Claude Street in New Orleans. St. Roch's is an eyesore. The dilapidated wooden structure sits in the down-and-out Marais district, across the tracks from the French Quarter. There are only a couple of communal tables, and the crowd always seems to include at least one homeless person smoking cigarettes and panhandling. The place smells like a fish store, which in fact it is.

Original New Orleans Po' Boy is positively antiseptic by comparison. Granted, the restaurant has seen better days. A new coat of red paint was recently applied to the front of the building, accented with some sloppy white lettering. As for the green and yellow paint on the windows, one assumes the original builder had no idea how hot it would get inside the structure—or how high the electric bills would be—when the summer sun poured through the glass. So somebody painted over the windows.

The tall sign in the potholed parking lot is probably the restaurant's most distinguishing feature. On the top is a silhouette of a guy with a cane and a strangely wide top hat. But the sign has been painted over in fire-engine red, so you can't see the guy anymore, except in your imagination. I envision him as an R. Crumb caricature of Southern elegance.

The inside of the restaurant features orange plastic chairs, worn Formica tables, and an old terrazzo floor that still bears the scars of previously built-in furniture. The walls are dominated by a collection of Coca-Cola artifacts. There are hundreds of eight-ounce Coke bottles commemorating everything from Enron Field's opening last year to the Kentucky Wildcats' national basketball championship in 1978. There are also Coke bottles in Arabic, Korean, and other scripts that I can't identify, along with Coca-Cola jigsaw puzzles, clocks, mirrors, trays, pins, and refrigerator magnets. It's a funny-looking place, all right. But what do you expect from a poor boy joint?

I find the answer to that question hanging on the wall. In a framed review that appeared in this paper, Brad Tyer tells us that Antone's defines the "state-of-the-art" in Houston poor boys, while Original New Orleans Po' Boy is a "low-brow variant."

I am puzzled and vaguely insulted—*a lowbrow variant?* Of a poor boy? The sandwich got its name during a streetcar strike in

New Orleans in 1929, according to Louisiana food historians. The city sympathized with the strikers, and the Martin Brothers restaurant offered to feed those "po' boys" for cheap. Any striker who showed up at the eatery's back door at closing time could get a meal for a nickel—essentially a sandwich of leftover French bread filled with "debris" (meat trimmings) or potatoes, then topped with gravy. Thus the "po' boy" sandwich was born. It was an instant hit, and the Depression years that followed made it an icon. The Martin Brothers restaurant would ultimately commission a bakery to make the skinny flutes that are now the traditional poor boy bread.

Eventually, in Catholic-dominated New Orleans, meatless poor boys had to be invented for Friday meals and Lent. So cheap varieties of seafood, especially fried oysters, became a popular stuffing.

Given its history, the idea of a highbrow poor boy is a little ludicrous. The other day, I asked Tyer what he was thinking when he wrote the review. I particularly wondered why he didn't mention the oyster poor boy. He said he didn't sample the sandwich because he doesn't like oysters. He also said he was just filling in as a restaurant writer and felt the need to apologize for his plebeian tastes. Like many people, he assumed that food critics generally focus on fancy restaurants. I explained my own philosophy to him.

A couple of weeks ago I went to hear the Houston Symphony perform a fascinating program of Beethoven works, including the *Mass in C-major*. A couple of weeks before that, I went to Miss Ann's Playpen in the Third Ward for its Monday-night blues jam. I had a great time at both places, and I don't see anything inconsistent about that.

In music, as in food, there is high art and there is folk art. Like many people, I enjoy both. But the fact is, in Texas, we are better known for the latter. We are far more famous for the blues than for classical music. Likewise, we are better known for barbecue than fine dining. You don't read much about the symphony or the opera in the *Houston Press* music section. So why should the café section be all about haute cuisine?

When food writers and chefs from New York, California, and Europe visit Houston, they want me to take them to smoky meat markets for brisket or Tex-Mex temples for enchiladas or soul-food joints for Southern breakfasts. It's not that we're bereft of brilliant chefs and great restaurants. We have plenty, but so does every other city. Chefs come and go, but classic peasant dishes are forever.

And likewise, on my first visit to France, I was much more interested in sampling cassoulet, pot-au-feu, bouillabaisse, and *choucroute* than I was in eating at trendy restaurants. The French understand this point of view, and they set an excellent example by respecting both ends of the food spectrum.

You can't compare a gritty poor boy shop to the fanciest restaurant in town. But you can judge both on how well they accomplish what they set out to do. And with its rendition of the folk art form known as the oyster poor boy, the humble dive called Original New Orleans Po' Boy approaches greatness.

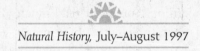
Pods of the Gods

By mid-July, there isn't much left in my garden. The brutal heat of Texas summer burns up the tomato plants and shrivels the cucumber vines. The only survivors of the annual inferno are the chile peppers and the okra. The okra, in particular, seems to like the heat. The scraggly plants grow so tall that I sometimes need to climb on a chair to harvest all the fuzzy pods before they get too big to eat.

In a 1974 survey by the United States Department of Agriculture, Americans named okra as one of the three vegetables they like least. I was never much of an okra fan myself. Raising a forkful of the little green circles to my mouth and watching the slime drip away from the fork was usually enough to convince me that I didn't really want to put them in my mouth.

Then I started eating at Dot's Place, a little Austin restaurant where aficionados of Southern cooking meet for lunch. The owner, Dot Hewitt, is one of the foremost practitioners of black Southern cooking in Texas, and okra is one of the best dishes in her lunchroom.

A few years ago, a California food writer asked me to help her find some great African American cooks to contribute to a cookbook she was writing. I introduced her to Dot, and she asked for Dot's okra recipe. Dot's cooking method is deceptively simple; you stew whole okra pods in tomato sauce. By keeping the pods whole, you all but eliminate the slime. When the book came out, I was distressed to find that the author had called for sliced okra in the dish, effectively ruining Dot's recipe. Whole okra stewed in tomato sauce is a wonderful vegetable dish. Sliced okra produces so much mucilage that it's good for thickening gumbo.

Though everyone complains about okra slime, the mucilage is actually very useful. It soothes the digestive tract; in fact, a preparation made from the mucilage is sometimes administered to ulcer patients. A gummy extract made from okra pods is also used to extend blood plasma.

The okra plant, *Hibiscus esculentus*, is a member of the mallow family (Malvaceae), which includes cotton. Although found in Asia, it is most closely identified with Africa, where the plant has long been a vegetable staple. The tapered, finger-shaped pods will grow as large as nine inches if left on the plant, but at that length they become fibrous and tough. Immature pods of five to six inches are the most tender and tasty. Picking the immature pods also stimulates the plant to bear more abundantly.

According to every cookbook I've ever read on the subject, African slaves brought okra to the New World. Its popularity in the American South, the Caribbean, and the state of Bahia in Brazil, all areas where large populations of African slaves once lived, seems to support this conclusion.

The word *okra* comes from the Twi word *nkruman* or *nkrumun*. In Umbundu okra is called *ngombo*, from which the English word *gumbo* is derived. The connection between *ngombo* and the Louisiana stew called gumbo has long obsessed food writers. Some speculate that a gumbo without okra isn't really gumbo. In truth, there are many gumbo recipes that don't include okra, and they may actually be more true to the dish's historical origins.

According to food authority Waverly Root, the Louisiana dish we now call gumbo was first invented by Native Americans, who thickened a catchall stew with powdered sassafras leaves, also known as filé powder (as in, "jambalaya, crawfish pie, filé gumbo"). Powdered sassafras also has a slimy consistency when it is mixed with liquids. African Americans used *ngombo* instead of filé powder as a thickener in their version of the stew and renamed the dish. Though the stew is now known throughout the country as gumbo, Root observes that many traditionalists in Louisiana (who probably don't know they are being traditionalists) still prefer to thicken their gumbo with filé. On the subject of how *ngombo* got to Louisiana in the first place, Root writes, "Okra was introduced into the Western Hemisphere by black slaves from Africa. . . . "

As I strolled barefoot through the okra patch that used to be my garden one sticky summer morning, picking a few pods, I started wondering about these accounts of okra's arrival in the New World. I split an okra pod open with my thumbnail and squirted a few seeds into my palm. According to the cookbooks, the captive Africans secreted okra seeds in their hair or inside their ears during the long journey to America. The okra seeds in my palm were about the size of BBs. The idea of a few rattling around in my ear made me wince.

Although it was before eight o'clock in the morning, it was already ninety degrees and the cicadas had begun their shrill, daylong choir practice. As I walked back to the kitchen with my okra pods, I tried to imagine myself a captive West African being led away in irons by white men with whips and guns. How would I react? Seething with anger, weeping with sorrow, and screaming in rebellion all came to mind. Sticking some okra seeds in my ear did not.

"I've never met a scholar who believed that the slaves really brought seeds with them to the New World," Dr. Robert Voeks, associate professor of geography at California State University at Fullerton, told me on the phone. "The notoriously brutal conditions imposed during capture, transportation, and sale must largely rule this out. These legends about slaves bringing okra seeds and other plants to the New World come from *candomblé* folklore."

Candomblé is the African-Brazilian religion of the Yoruba ethnic group, who originated in the present–day West African nations of Gambia and Benin. *Candomblé* is an African religion that has remained nearly intact on this side of the Atlantic. It is the most widely practiced religion in Bahia, where it coexists with Catholicism. It's also closely related to the Santería religion of the Caribbean.

During his fieldwork in Brazil, Dr. Voeks was initiated into a *terreiro*, or holy house, of *candomblé* in order to learn more about the religion's fascinating ethnobotany. In his book *Sacred Leaves of the Candomblé*, he describes the practices of *candomblé* herbalists, priests, and priestesses who employ some two hundred different kinds of plants in their rituals, celebrations, and healing ceremonies. Foods like okra, black-eyed peas, and yams are among the plants that have religious significance.

The nature spirits of the *candomblé* religion are called *orishas*, and each has a unique personality and favorite food. Shango, the *orisha* of thunder, is a womanizer, and predictably enough, he is fond of goat. Yansan, the wind spirit, likes the black-eyed pea fritters called *acarajé*. Oshun, the *orisha* of freshwater, likes *xin-xin de galinha*, chicken cooked in palm oil with peanuts and dried shrimp. On each *orisha*'s feast day, *candomblé* adherents prepare the god's favorite food.

Carurú, an okra stew, is the food of the Ibeji, the twin gods of procreation and reproduction. The festival of the twin spirits is also called *carurú*, and on this event, the consecrated dish must be prepared according to an elaborate ritualized recipe. Deviation from the precise order of preparation is considered a sacrilege. *Carurú* may be the food of the *candomblé* gods, but Dr. Voeks doesn't recommend it. "It tastes like slime with seeds in it," he said. "It isn't my favorite dish, but most people in Bahia love it."

But if the slaves didn't bring the *candomblé* gods' favored foods to the New World, then who did? Dr. Voeks has done a lot of detective work on the mystery of how West African medicinal herbs and native plants important to *candomblé* came to be transplanted to the New World. He has shown that in some cases, freed slaves actually returned to Africa and shipped the missing magical ingredients back to Brazil. But in the case of okra, yams, and black-eyed peas, he thinks there is a much simpler explanation. "There is no documentation," he says, "but the logical conclusion is that the Portuguese brought them over."

The African slaves were given garden plots to grow their own food, and slave owners made an effort to bring in foods that slaves already knew how to grow. We know that the Portuguese imported the African oil palm to Brazil so the slaves could have their familiar cooking oil, the red palm oil known as *dendê*. "The Portuguese were smart," Dr. Voeks says. "It made good business sense to keep the slaves healthy. Okra is nutritious, it's a West African staple, and it grows like a weed."

Okra is a fair to good source of calcium, potassium, vitamin A, and vitamin C. It also supplies about seven grams of protein per one hundred calories. It is high in fiber and very filling and is especially popular in the tropics, where it thrives during the heat of the summer, when other green vegetables wither.

Having dismissed the legends of slaves bringing okra seeds to the New World in their ears, I am left to ponder how such a dubious explanation became so universally accepted. I suspect that like many religious myths, the stories caught on because they hint at a larger truth.

Okra was a sacred food for the Yoruba people of tropical West Africa, and thanks to Yoruba slaves and their descendants, okra is now a sacred food in Brazil and an important part of Caribbean and African American cuisine. Even if the African slaves didn't physically carry okra seeds with them, there is no doubt that they deserve the credit for spreading the pods of the *candomblé* gods all over the New World.

Dot Hewitt's Stewed Okra

Don't cut the okra. Don't boil the okra. Just rinse off the pods and stew them in tomato sauce. If you give it a chance, it will change your mind about okra.

2 tablespoons vegetable oil or bacon drippings
1 yellow onion, halved and sliced
1/2 pound okra, rinsed
1 large can (14 ounces) crushed, stewed tomatoes
    with their juice
1 teaspoon salt
1 teaspoon pepper

In a heavy saucepan over medium heat, warm the oil. Add the onion and sauté until soft, about 5 minutes. Add the okra, stir and sauté for 2 minutes or until the pods sizzle a little. Add the tomatoes and juice. Bring to a boil and reduce the heat. Cover and simmer for 25 to 30 minutes, or until the pods are tender but intact.

Houston Press, September 6, 2001

Blue Crab Standard Time

The sun is getting ready to plunge into East Galveston Bay. The slanting light casts a pink glow on the platter of barbecued crabs in front of me. I suck a tangy claw and admire the still life with shellfish. It's Saturday evening at Stingaree Restaurant on the Bolivar Peninsula, and the place is hopping. About ten minutes ago, a bunch of people filed outside to take seats on the open deck, where they are now drinking beer and facing west. I am sitting in the air-conditioned dining room behind them, looking over their shoulders at the sunset, and methodically disassembling the blue crabs native to the Gulf. I have eaten four so far, and it looks like there's about six left.

Under the heading "Crabs, Crabs, Crabs," Stingaree's menu offers "Bosco's barbecued crabs," "Vieno's fried crabs," and "seasoned boiled crabs." No mixing is allowed with regular or large orders, but you can try them all if you get the all-you-can-eat special, which of course I did. The crustaceans are all native Gulf Coast blue crabs, and they range in size from small to enormous. Barbecued crabs are a tradition around here, and I've always wanted to try them.

My roommate at the University of Texas, the late Phil Born, grew up in Port Arthur, and he used to talk fondly about eating barbecued crabs. He was a very slow eater, a trait that he claimed was essential to great crab connoisseurs. "My grandfather and his friends would sit and eat crabs for two hours straight," Phil used to tell me. When Phil and his family went to the beach, they went to Bolivar, like most Port Arthur and Beaumont residents. It was here in the crab shacks along the East Texas Gulf Coast that barbecued crabs became famous.

Stingaree Restaurant is on the second story of the Stingaree Marina in the little town of Crystal Beach. There is a white shack at the end of the marina under a sign that reads, "Bait Camp." The Intracoastal Waterway runs so close beside the restaurant that you could lob your crab shells into it from the deck. Giant barges glide by every fifteen minutes or so, reminding you that this part of the Gulf Coast is, first and foremost, industrial.

This is the first time I've been to Bolivar, and I am utterly charmed by the funky grace of it all. Verdant vacant lots sprinkled artfully with rusted autos and propane tanks line the main route, Highway 87, between the settlements. And each hamlet is a guileless variation on the Gulf Coast resort format—a restaurant, a liquor store, a bar, some whitewashed cottages, a couple of mobile homes, and a bait camp. The cynicism of high-dollar resort projects has yet to overtake the native patterns of development.

"This is what Galveston Island used to be like," my companion sighs as we drive up the peninsula. She spent a lot of her childhood on Galveston; in fact, she uses the screen name "islandgirl" on-line. Before West Beach was dominated by condo complexes with let's-pretend-we're-somewhere-else names like Inverness by the Sea and Bahia Mar, it looked a lot like this, she says. Maybe we should have Bolivar set aside as a cultural reserve, the last redoubt of that rare bird, Gulf Coast innocence.

From the front deck of the ferryboat *Robert C. Lanier*, we watch in awe as an oil tanker passes. The ferry has yielded the

right-of-way to the enormous vessel, which towers over us like a
ten-story building passing by. A lone dolphin leaps dramatically
in front of the ship, cavorting in its bow's wake to the delight of
the ferry passengers.

To get to Bolivar from Houston, you drive down to Galveston and catch the ferry from the east end of the island. It's a
short ride, and it crosses some of the most active shipping lanes
in the Gulf. There's nothing like looking at an oil tanker from
the waterline to help you appreciate the massive scope of this
region's maritime industry. There's also a nice breeze on the water, even on the hottest days. Bring along a bag of potato chips if
you want to feed the seagulls off the rear deck.

We left Houston at around 5, which put us in Galveston by 6
and Bolivar by 6:30. I hadn't thought about catching the sunset
at Stingaree, but the timing worked out perfectly.

My second and third plates of crabs are inexplicably delivered at
the same time. There are four boiled crabs on one and four
deep-fried crabs on the other. But I am only halfway through my
first plate of barbecued crabs.

I am not very fond of the boiled ones, which taste watery and
bland after the barbecued variety. I am up in the air about the
fried ones. Barbecued crabs were made famous by a place in
Sabine Pass called Granger's; later, Sartin's took over the tradition. The recipe called for blue crabs to be cleaned and broken
in half, dipped into a spicy seasoning mix, and then deep-fried.
Crabs prepared this way can be spectacular, or if the grease is
not at the right temperature or a little too old, they can be
pretty foul. Stingaree barbecued crabs are first boiled, then
dipped into seasoning and broiled. They are far superior to
boiled or deep-fried crabs, in my estimation.

Dinner at Stingaree begins with a bowl of creamy coleslaw,
which is served as a starter course. They go through quite a bit

of the stuff, so it's always nice and crunchy. We also had an order of delicious but incendiary New Orleans–style barbecued shrimp. The peel-and-eat shrimp are tender, but you have to resist the impulse to lick your fingers in order to avoid overdosing on the spicy coating.

Islandgirl orders the charbroiled red snapper fillet, a stunningly simple piece of fresh fish that arrives a little black on the edges and extremely moist in the middle. She finishes her snapper while I'm still on my third crab. She starts to get bored watching me eat, so she excuses herself somewhere around crab no. 7 and goes outside to watch the sunset with the crew on the deck. This is fine with me. While she sat there eyeballing me, I felt pressured to hurry up and eat.

The slow pace is why Gulf Coast crab shacks and restaurants that specialize in barbecued crabs are becoming rare, Stingaree's owner, George Vratis, tells me on the phone a week later. "Crab shacks are going the way of the drive-in theater," he says, "because neither one is a very good way to utilize the space." Modern corporations look at restaurant tables as real estate. You make money by renting them out, and the shorter the stay, the more money you can make. An all-you-can-eat crab customer is going to squat at a table for an average of ninety minutes, Vratis explains. A fifty-minute turnover is the average in a dinner house. Which is why the chain version of the concept, Joe's Crab Shack, gives you only four crabs for $10.95, he says. Stingaree customers hang around a long time.

"But I don't care," says Vratis. "As long as you enjoy my crabs, you can stay all night." Some of his favorite customers are old-time crab lovers who will sit at a table for hours and eat twenty or thirty crabs.

I wish Phil could have been here to cheer me on. I know I could have made the big leagues. But islandgirl needs to get back to Houston, and I am getting a little bored smashing crabs

by myself. Besides, my thumb is bleeding from where I acciden-
tally stabbed it with one of the needle-sharp little points under
a claw. (This maintains a personal record: I have never eaten
crabs without bleeding.) So I reluctantly call it quits after con-
suming fourteen in an hour and twenty minutes.

Not very impressive, really. Next time, I promise to do better.

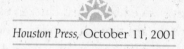

Houston Press, October 11, 2001

Third Ward Fried

Sitting at a long, shiny stainless-steel table outside Frenchy's Chicken, my daughter Julia and I juggle three pieces of too-hot-to-eat fried chicken. There aren't any plates, so we have to keep the chicken in the air while we tear up the bag for use as a place mat. It's a sunny and cool fall morning on this part of Scott Street in the shadow of the University of Houston's Robertson Stadium. Black families in dressy clothes walk by, heading for the Baptist church next door.

While the Third Ward goes about its business, we marvel at the mystery of Frenchy's chicken. There isn't any grease dripping from it; there's no greasy shine to it, either. As far as I can tell, the dry, spicy coating is a mixture of flour, salt, pepper, and cayenne, and they aren't shy with the cayenne. The amazing spicy crust doesn't slip off the chicken with your first bite. It sticks to the skin and the skin sticks to the chicken in a way that allows you to appreciate all three together. Is there a miracle adhesive involved?

"Fried chicken doesn't get any better than this," my daughter sums up as she cleans every morsel of crust off one of Frenchy's thighs. I suspect she's right, but we are about to put it to the test with a Sunday-afternoon drive-by sampling of Third Ward fried-chicken stands.

This isn't the first time I've eaten fried chicken in the Third Ward. In fact, it was an ethereal fried-chicken experience I had just a couple of weeks ago that got me started on this taste-test idea. It was "Blues and Barbecue" night at Miss Ann's Playpen at the corner of Dowling and Alabama. Richard Earle was performing some cuts from his new CD, *Greyhound Blues,* and owner Bobby Lewis was cooking ribs. Bobby's ribs were excellent, but after many beers and even more blues, I was hungry again on the way home.

"Try the new chicken shack over on Ennis," longshoreman Rory Miggins told me as I left the club. "It's called Henderson's. The chicken is awesome, and it's open late." Miggins has given me some great tips before, so I took his advice.

They don't start frying your chicken until you order it at Henderson's Chicken Shack. It takes about twenty minutes. I ordered a thigh and a breast in a two-piece basket with fries and sat down to wait. There's a jukebox in the little lobby, so I punched in the numbers for "Dock of the Bay" by Otis Redding, a great song for wasting ti-i-i-i-ime.

I ate most of the great red-peppery fries in the car on the way home. The chicken had a wonderful thick spicy crust, and it came on two slices of white bread to soak up any juice. There were also some pickles and a jalapeño pepper in the basket. It was a great late-night snack, but I couldn't help noticing that the breast was a tiny bit dry in the center.

A few evenings later, I stopped at the legendary Frenchy's and ordered the exact same thing. The Frenchy fries were limp and greasy, but the chicken was stupendous. The crust was thinner and a tad spicier, while the white meat was juicy throughout. The chicken had gotten cold on my drive home, though, so I decided it wasn't a fair comparison. I vowed to start eating chicken all over again.

Fried chicken is more than a food in the South. It's a cultural icon. That's why Jason Alexander, the actor who played George on *Seinfeld,* seems like such a strange choice as the new spokesperson for Kentucky Fried Chicken. The bald New Yorker is definitely a departure from the hirsute Southern colonel. In the commercial, Alexander claims that chicken isn't fast food but rather some order of slow cooking.

Bob Garfield of *Advertising Age* magazine had this to say about the campaign: "Deep-frying is slow cooking like rape is seduction. The stuff is tasty, all right, but to suggest that it is somehow morally superior to other fast-food fare more than strains credulity. . . . Let's get real here: The paper napkins after a KFC meal look like the gauze dressings at a liposuction."

Evidently the New Yorker is supposed to help KFC make some inroads into regions of the country where whiny and rude is fashionable and fried chicken is not. The "Chicken—it's not fast food and it's not just for Southerners anymore" strategy was devised by KFC's new ad agency, BBDO Worldwide in (who would have guessed?) New York. Divorcing a regional food from the ethos that spawned it and finding a celebrity to "make it more mainstream" is the sort of cultural demolition project that Madison Avenue does best.

But fried chicken has a Southern soul that the marketing geniuses can't deny. Don't take my word for it. Run a search for "fried chicken" on Google. Among the first ten hits you'll find a personal Web site in Dallas called "God made fried chicken" and a Southern literary journal in North Carolina called *Lonzie's Fried Chicken*.

Lonzie was the black maid at the childhood home of editor E. H. Goree. "Queen of all Thursday's fragrances was fried chicken, waiting in one of Mother's serving bowls on the yellow linoleum countertop by the stove," Goree says. "It was close to impossible to resist the urge to pick off a piece of crust. In early 1998, when I needed the most descriptive name for a literary magazine of accessible Southern fiction and poetry . . . there was no debate. What other thing in my life was as pleasing, there for the taking, and precious for the moments you savor it?"

I bet Lonzie's fried chicken didn't stain the napkins. Contrary to popular belief, great fried chicken is not greasy. John Martin Taylor, author of *Fearless Frying*, writes that if the oil is hot enough, a batter-coated food submerged in it should instantly seal itself and not absorb any oil. That's the idea behind deep-frying.

"There are no secrets to fried chicken," Taylor writes. You cut up the chicken, sprinkle it with salt and pepper, dredge it with flour, and fry it in very hot deep fat. What about KFC's "eleven secret herbs and spices"? That claim was debunked in a 1983 book called *Big Secrets* by William Poundstone, Taylor says. Poundstone hired a laboratory, which detected only flour, salt, pepper, and MSG in the Colonel's chicken.

It's 11:40 A.M. when we finish our Frenchy's taste test. Henderson's Chicken Shack won't be open until noon. So to kill some time, we go eat chicken at Popeye's. I figure Popeye's will serve as a sort of control group in our fried-chicken experiment. I suspect that Frenchy's and Henderson's will both get stellar ratings, and I want to put them in perspective with some ordinary fast-food chicken.

I order two thighs and some red beans and rice at the drive-through window of the Popeye's franchise at the corner of Scott and Holcombe. We pull into the vacant lot behind the restaurant and attempt to eat the chicken. The thighs are very small, dark brown, and shiny with grease. Julia's piece is wet with the stuff. After a few bites we throw the chicken away in disgust, but our greasy fingers set off a slapstick routine. I drop my pencil, Julia drops her soft drink, and I drop my pencil again. The paper I'm writing on is spattered with oil, and we have trouble opening the red beans and rice, which is mostly rice and very bland.

I usually like Popeye's chicken. Maybe the fryers weren't up to full steam so early in the day. The franchise chain, which was founded in New Orleans, has spread the Creole version of fried chicken across the country. The difference between Louisiana's Creole fried chicken and the traditional Southern variety is pretty simple. Creole chicken is spicy—usually adding a touch of cayenne is all there is to it. But Popeye's also has introduced traditional Creole accompaniments like biscuits, red beans and rice, and jalapeño peppers to the rest of the chicken-eating world.

We order two thighs, a breast, and some red beans and rice at Henderson's Chicken Shack just after it opens. The little building is still festooned with colored pennants from its grand opening. You order at a window that looks into the spotlessly clean kitchen.

We're thrown off by Henderson's chicken. There are three pieces, but they look like three breasts. I finally figure out that the thighs are actually bigger than the breast. "Yeah, that's what he said too," the woman in the window says, pointing to the fry cook.

Is it the maturity of the chicken that makes these thighs so huge and the meat so white? Or is it a special breed of bird? I don't know, but we both agree these thighs are better than the ones they use at Frenchy's or Popeye's. The breast is juicy all the way through too. The coating is not as dry and perfect as Frenchy's, but it isn't very greasy, either. These three pieces of chicken make a huge portion. The red beans and rice are okay, but I don't taste any pork or sausage in them.

Henderson's Chicken Shack isn't a franchise or a chain. It's owned by a Creole woman named Ann Henderson, who was born in New Iberia, Louisiana. Henderson's Chicken Shack does a lot of things right. Cooking the chicken to order seems like a nuisance when you're waiting, but it's worth it once you bite into the hot, crunchy chicken. And if you're getting your order to go, as most people do, the chicken will cool off in the car, so it's the perfect temperature when you get home. Is it as good as Frenchy's? Well, yes and no.

Percy Creuzot, another Louisiana Creole cook, opened Frenchy's in 1969. By now, it has become the most famous chicken stand in a city that is crazy about fried chicken. The chicken here isn't made to order, but it doesn't have to be. The fact that there are always people standing in line at Frenchy's guarantees that every piece of chicken you get has just come out of the fryer. This creates a sort of self-perpetuating cycle: the reason Frenchy's chicken is so popular is that Frenchy's chicken is so popular. The red beans and rice, studded with big chunks of sausage, doesn't hurt their reputation any, either.

I highly recommend that you take the Third Ward Creole fried chicken–shack taste test for yourself. As for our results, I'd have to say that for the quality and size of the chicken pieces, the new Third Ward contender, Henderson's Chicken Shack, gets the nod this Sunday. But for the spicy crust, the lack of grease, the overall flavor, and the red beans and rice, Frenchy's is the winner and still champion. Popeye's finishes a distant and pathetic third.

And as for KFC—don't get me started again.

Part FOUR

Those Cranky Europeans

The War of the Cheeses

The flag of Gruyère flutters over the stone ramparts of an ancient walled castle on an Alpine cliff. The flag is white with a fierce-looking bird in the middle of it. Legend has it that the first ruler of Gruyère went out hunting one day with the intention of naming his county after the first thing he killed. He killed a crane (*grue* in French), and thus became the Count of Gruyère.

I thought I'd run across some cheese makers here in the walled village of Gruyères (the name of the village is spelled with an *s* on the end to distinguish it from the name of the district), but there aren't any. As it turns out, this fortified village wasn't built to produce the stuff; it was built to defend it. Defending cheese may sound like a strange idea, but by now I'm used to it. In fact, I've just traveled all the way from my home in Texas to the Swiss Alps because I'm feeling so defensive about cheese.

Who would have thought that a recipe for cheese enchiladas I wrote for *American Way* would end up turning me into a target for European nationalists, the enemy of a secret society, and ultimately a combatant in an ancient and bitter international rivalry?

All I said was that the Gruyère enchilada I ate at a Paris Tex-Mex joint was one of the best I'd ever had. I gave a recipe and said that it was no wonder the French made great cheese enchiladas since they have the world's best cheese. That little recipe article was enough to suck me into an improbable international food fight.

A reader named Frank Binzoni of Pleasanton, California, wrote to challenge my veracity on the subject of cheese and to suggest that I must be something of a yokel. "Gruyère is a cheese made only in Switzerland," Binzoni wrote to my editor. "Walsh should get out of Texas more often."

I was sure that Gruyère was made in France as well as Switzerland, since I'd eaten a lot of French Gruyère, so I looked into the matter. Then I naively called Binzoni at his home one day and read him a citation from *Larousse Gastronomique*, the French food encyclopedia. The article stated that Gruyère was made in both France and Switzerland. Binzoni was not impressed. The fact that the encyclopedia was written by Frenchmen seemed to make its accuracy doubtful to him. This was starting to reek of a larger controversy.

Maybe it's Gruyère's militaristic background that makes the subject so contentious. The Romans first encountered the hard cheese of the Jura Mountains when they invaded the area around 40 B.C., but it was in the Middle Ages that Gruyère cheese became a central part of Swiss life.

The Gruyère culture began when the farmers in the valleys of the Jura Alps all began to take their cows up into the mountains for the summer. The idea was to save the grass in the valleys for winter hay. With the timber they cleared to create mountainside pastures, they built the summer houses known as chalets. But the summer pasturing created another problem: what to do with all the milk? They couldn't carry it down the mountain, and they couldn't store it. So they started making it into cheese in the shape of the familiar wheels. The hardness of this style of cheese was made possible by abundant supplies of brine flowing from saltwater springs in the mountains.

Cheese had been around for a long time. But this kind of hard cheese was unique because, unlike the soft variety, it would keep for years. It was handy for feeding the family, but since a herd of only thirty cows would produce a seventy-pound wheel of the stuff every day, soon the Swiss farmers had a lot more cheese than they knew what to do with. So they started trading their cheese wheels for things they needed. Before long, their hard cheese had become a famous and valuable commodity.

It wasn't a gourmet who first realized how valuable hard cheese really was; it was a military man. One of the biggest problems of marching a large army around the snowy Alps was feeding it. The hard cheese of the Juras was one of the best nonperishable protein sources available. And therefore the storehouses full of cheese became like banks—huge reserves of accumulated wealth. Predictably enough, people started robbing the banks.

The walled village of Gruyères was founded to keep the local farmers' cheese and grain safe from thieves and freelance armies. And for the protection of their wealth, the farmers paid a tax to the counts of Gruyère—in the form of cheese.

Eventually the counts of Gruyère got into debt, borrowing money from Swiss bankers to finance their military expeditions. When the counts of Gruyère defaulted, the Swiss banking system took over the county and the cheese and became the dominant political force in the region. But the article in the food encyclopedia went on to explain that both the French and the Swiss claim to have invented Gruyère and that the argument has never really been settled.

As a food writer who has judged hot sauce contests, beer tastings, and bagel bake-offs, I figured I'd make the call. Per Binzoni's advice, I would get out of Texas, taste the cheeses in question on their respective home turfs, and vindicate the authenticity of French Gruyère.

But what looked to me like a cheesy little argument over bragging rights turned out to be a major cultural battle, one of the longest-running trade disputes in food history. It was not a subject to be joked about, at least not within the confines of this Swiss castle.

In the courtyard of the Chateau de Gruyères, a secret society assembles to repeat its ceremonial rites. Everyone is dressed in flowing white robes with bright red and yellow sashes; each wears a medal of a crane standing on a wheel of cheese. They stand before a table spread like an altar with the implements of cheese making. In the center, a huge wheel of Gruyère is elevated on a wooden yoke once worn by a farmer to carry wheels of cheese down from the mountains.

Placing one hand on the cheese, each member of the Twenty-Seventh Chapter of the Confrérie du Gruyère swears to uphold the honor of their beloved Gruyère. New members are taught the secrets of the society. "We teach them how to love Gruyère," says the group's governor. "It's a holy mission."

But the mission of the Confrérie du Gruyère isn't just to run around in flowing robes and pledge allegiance to the cheese. The society is also involved in a long-running crusade to convince the world that only the Swiss make true Gruyère—and to combat infidels like me who say otherwise.

In fact, the Swiss have been trying to secure the exclusive rights to the name *Gruyère* in international legal skirmishes since 1939. The treasured AOC *(appellation d'origine contrôlée)* designation, the same territorial guarantee that applies to Bordeaux, Champagne, and Roquefort, would greatly increase the value of the more than 7,000 tons of Gruyère cheese that Switzerland exports each year. And that would make the members of the Confrérie du Gruyère very happy.

The border between Switzerland and France cuts straight across the top of the Jura mountain range. On the French side is the province of Franche-Comté. They make cheese here too. For centuries, they called their cheese Gruyère.

The Swiss claim that the French usurped the name. Not so, say the French. In the Middle Ages, an officer of the French government called a *gruyer* presided over forest lands and collected taxes—in the form of cheese. It is this *gruyer* that their cheese is named after, claim the French, and they can show tax records dating back to the 1100s to prove it.

With the assistance of an army of scholars, historians, and lawyers, the French have successfully foiled every attempt the Swiss have ever made to lock up the name of Gruyère. The legal issue boils down to one simple question: was it the Swiss or the French who made Gruyère cheese first?

"It was neither," says Jean Arnaud, a seventh-generation French cheese man. "I have 150 books in my library about this cheese," he smiles. "Twenty-five of them are just about the subject of the competition between the Swiss and the French over the name *Gruyère*."

Arnaud's family business, Fromageries Arnaud Frères, is in Poligny, just across the mountains from Switzerland. In a meeting room above the cheese-ripening vaults, he gives me the benefit of his own considerable knowledge on the subject. On a blackboard he draws a big oval. "You see, this is the Jura mountain range," he says. "In Roman times, the Jura region was the homeland of an ethnic group called the Sequanes," he says, writing their name inside the oval. "Roman texts dated from 40 B.C. describe the cheese process used in Sequany—the wood, the milk, the salt. It is the same process."

He slashes a chalk line down the middle of the oval from north to south, dividing the ancient land of Sequany in two. "This is the modern border between France and Switzerland," he informs me. "The first Gruyère was neither Swiss nor French, because in 40 B.C. neither country existed."

In 1959, after decades of fighting over the name, cheese makers in the Franche-Comté region decided that protecting the name *Gruyère* was hopeless and applied for an appellation under the name *Comté*. "In France, everybody knows the name *Gruyère*, but *Comté* has a problem," explains Arnaud. In light of the confusion, Comté cheese producers market their cheese as "Comté, the king of Gruyères."

"Comté is still a Gruyère," Arnaud tells me as we descend the stairs to his underground cheese vaults. But nowadays, the term *Gruyère* has come to describe a family of cheeses, he says. Down in the vaults, I get a practical lesson in the Gruyère family history.

With a tool that resembles a hollowed-out ice pick, Arnaud cuts a core sample out of a huge wheel of Comté. After I break some off to taste, the little cylinder of cheese is neatly plugged back into the wheel. Then he takes a similar sample out of a Swiss Gruyère. There is a big difference in flavor. The Comté is mild and nutty; the Swiss Gruyère is stronger and creamier.

Swiss Gruyère is made with full milk. Comté is made from milk from which the cream has been skimmed, so Comté has 10 percent less fat, Arnaud explains. Both cheeses are outstanding, but I confess to Arnaud I am partial to the stronger flavor and creamier texture of the Swiss. In that case, Arnaud insists, I must taste Beaufort, another French Gruyère from the Savoy region.

Beaufort is made the old-fashioned way. While Comté and Swiss Gruyère are made in large cooperatives these days, there are still farmers who make cheese in the mountains as they did in the Middle Ages. This kind of cheese is called *fromage d'alpage*, and it is made from the full milk of one herd of cows that have been grazing in the sweet grass and wildflowers of a mountain pasture. The Beaufort sample is buttery and fruity—without a doubt the fullest-flavored Gruyère cheese I have ever tasted.

Of course, the Swiss have their own *fromage d'alpage* called L'Etivaz, which I also taste in Arnaud's cellar. It is even stronger than the Beaufort—a wonderful, rich cheese with a creamy texture and nutty aftertaste. I can't decide whether I like the Beaufort or the L'Etivaz better, but I imagine either one would make a pretty awesome enchilada.

After tasting my way through the family, it easy for me to understand why the Swiss are having so much trouble trying to insist that one kind of cheese is the true Gruyère. Arnaud points out that cheeses called Gruyère are also made in Wisconsin, Argentina, and Australia these days. Surprisingly, Arnaud confesses that he has recently been consulted by a delegation of Swiss cheese authorities who asked his advice on their latest effort to gain their own appellation.

"I told them it would be nearly impossible to get an appellation for Gruyère now," says Arnaud. "Swiss Gruyère is really good cheese, and I hope we find a way to recognize it, but it's just too hard at this point to tell everybody else in the world to stop. Maybe they can get an appellation if they call it Gruyère of Switzerland or Fribourg," he says with some sympathy.

And so the cheese feud continues. The Swiss maintain that theirs is the only true Gruyère, and the French refuse to concede.

And I thought my friends back in Texas were passionate about barbecue.

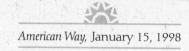

Sauerkraut Pilgrims

Like a mountain peak on a cloudy day, the spire of the Strasbourg cathedral soared out of vision into the scudding gray fog.
The light jacket I'd brought in anticipation of cool autumn
weather was no match for the bone-chilling wind blowing in
over the Rhine. Across the main square, I noticed the imposing
half-timbered, four-story building that housed Maison Kammerzell, a well-known local restaurant and the nearest place to
get in out of the cold. So my traveling companion and I took a
seat in the cozy old dining room. As I looked over the menu, my
eyes began to widen. There was an entire page devoted to elaborate sauerkraut dishes. *Choucroute,* as the dish is known, is a
specialty in the Alsace region of France.

The menu included sauerkraut with pork, sauerkraut with
duck, sauerkraut with skate and capers, and sauerkraut with fish
and bacon, which my friend ordered. We had never heard of fish
and sauerkraut before, but the combination proved delicious. I
opted for a menu item called Choucroute Formidable, which
turned out to be a mound of tender, steaming, Riesling-scented
sauerkraut piled high with three kinds of glistening sausage, a
rosy loin of pork, juicy pork ribs, crispy bacon, intense black
pudding, delicate liver quenelle, and meaty pig's knuckles. I dug

into my Formidable with glee. As a sauerkraut lover, I had hit the mother lode.

Most of my earliest childhood food memories involve sauerkraut. At my grandma's house we ate sauerkraut with everything. The combination of sauerkraut and mashed potatoes still makes me weepy with nostalgia. And who could forget Grandma's sauerkraut *paghachy*, an Eastern European *stromboli* made by folding a pizza crust over a filling of sauerkraut sautéed with bacon?

When I was a college student, my chums and I would sit around and reminisce about the comfort food back home. It was then that I realized I was a little out of sync with American culture. My friends would lovingly describe Mom's meatloaf, pot roast, fried chicken, or apple pie. But when I began to wax poetic about Grandma's sauerkraut, the gang would generally heave a collective yuck and look at me like I was crazy.

Sauerkraut is one of those foods that you either love or hate, and most Americans seem to fall into the latter camp. In the States, it is generally associated with hot dogs and with that pariah of world cuisines, German food. Over the years, I learned that cooking sauerkraut is a good way to alienate dinner guests and to cause the fellow tenants of your apartment complex to complain about the smell emanating from your domicile.

So as an adult, I learned to suppress my sauerkraut desires in order to fit in. Now and then, when no one was around, I made myself solitary sauerkraut feasts.

And then I took that first trip to Alsace. What a liberation. What a joy it was to discover a place where my fetish for fermented cabbage seemed completely normal, a land where they treated sauerkraut as lovingly as Grandma did. It was not only the land of sauerkraut but also a part of the Western world's most respected culinary tradition. Sauerkraut as French cuisine: what a concept.

On that first trip, my Alsatian wanderings centered on the string of vineyards and tasting rooms known as the Alsatian wine trail. In one of the little inns where I stuffed myself with sauerkraut every day, I came upon a brochure for another sort of tourist trail. It was called La Route de la Choucroute, or "Trail of Sauerkraut." I interpreted the discovery as some kind of mystic sign.

Sadly, I had only one day left in the area. As I fondly traced my fingers along the highways and back roads of the brochure's sauerkraut map, on which little anthropomorphic cartoon slices of bacon, heads of cabbage, and links of sausage danced in glee around the towns and villages, I vowed to return someday and make a pilgrimage to the holy temples of sauerkraut.

Many years have passed since I made that vow, but now I count myself doubly blessed. Not only am I on my way back to Alsace to follow the Sauerkraut Trail, but I am traveling with my new girlfriend, a woman who adores sauerkraut. Maybe it was our mutual culinary obsession that made us recognize each other as kindred spirits in the first place. Just as garlic aficionados must look for love among fellow fanciers of the stinking rose, sauerkraut eaters seldom find happiness in romantic attachments with those who turn up their noses at the smell of their favorite food.

We are filled with anticipation as we guide our rental car north toward Strasbourg up the asphalt backbone of the Sauerkraut Route. Scanning the dozens of listings in the little brochure, we decide to start our pilgrimage at a country inn that prides itself on its traditional *choucroute*. The old inn has a bar in the front where the locals are drinking beer and arguing about soccer. We make our way to a pleasant wooden booth in the dining room beyond. The windows offer a wonderful view of a cabbage field, and while we admire the crop, we eagerly order our first platter of *choucroute*.

"The problem is that Americans eat sauerkraut straight from the jar," I rail at my girlfriend as I pour us each a glass of Riesling from a cute little pitcher. "They think of it as something to put on a hot dog and that's it." Here in Alsace, I rant, sauerkraut is cooked in goose fat and Riesling, scented with juniper berries, and treated like the noble dish it really is.

As if on cue, a steaming platter of *choucroute* is set down before us. There are two sausages, a little bacon, and a fatty slice of pork on top. Mustard and horseradish are served on the side. The sauerkraut is tender, but tasteless. One of the sausages is a frankfurter and the other is a knockwurst. The pork is too fatty for my girlfriend's tastes, so she settles for the sausages.

"Yum, hot dogs and sauerkraut," she says with a mischievous grin.

She's right. For all my ranting and raving about the Alsatian mastery of the ingredient, this *choucroute* is not much of an improvement on a Coney Island with kraut. We leave most of it on the platter. I sulk in the car on the way to another restaurant listed in the brochure. The next place turns out to be a pizza joint that also serves a salad of smoked salmon and cold sauerkraut. We sample a few bites and then pluck the salmon off the salad and eat it with bread and butter. After pushing the sauerkraut around on the plate for a while, we leave.

For several days, we visit one after another of the restaurants listed in the brochure. We eat *choucroute* with halibut and cream sauce, *choucroute* with flounder and bacon, and *choucroute* with a giant ham shank. Some of them are pretty good, but pretty good isn't good enough. We came here to climb the peaks of *la haute choucroute*, to savor the sauerkraut of the gods. And this ain't it.

Fanaticism tends to foster ever higher standards of criticism, and sauerkraut lovers are just like any other variety of food fanatics in this regard. The fact that you love barbecue or pizza doesn't mean that you love all barbecue or pizza. On the contrary, you get pickier and pickier as you compare each offering to your ever expanding base of comparison. In short, my grandmother could have cooked any of these guys under the table.

"Maybe these restaurants just pay money to get listed in this brochure because they're hurting for business," my girlfriend observes as we take a seat in another empty dining room during what should be the Saturday lunch rush. I'm afraid she might be right. The brochure lists twenty-nine restaurants. There may be a couple of great ones in the bunch, but we don't have time to take any more chances.

I have put a lot of time and energy into this sauerkraut pilgrimage, and I'm not about to go home in defeat. All I am asking at this point is for one stupendous platter of *choucroute*. We could go back to the tourist favorite, Maison Kammerzell, where I already know the *choucroute* is good, but that seems like a retreat.

"Let's chuck the brochure and get out the guidebooks," I say grimly. We are carrying the Michelin guidebook, the *Gault Millau* guidebook, and Patricia Wells's *Food Lover's Guide to France*. Over a few glasses of Riesling, we spend the next hour cross-checking maps and listings until we have narrowed our search for the ultimate *choucroute* down to one restaurant. It is called Le Cerf in the little town of Marlenheim a half hour northwest of Strasbourg.

Patricia Wells loves it. Michelin has awarded the restaurant two stars and recommends the *choucroute* with suckling pig. *Gault Millau* gives it an 18 out of 20, calling the suckling pig *choucroute* "a minor masterpiece." It's settled, then. We must go there tonight.

My girlfriend goes to the pay phone to make a reservation, but my heart sinks when she comes back to the table with a dejected look. "They're all full," she says with a sigh. I should have known. The odds of getting a reservation for Saturday night at a restaurant this famous on the spur of the moment are slim to none. But we are leaving Alsace tomorrow.

A sad silence fills the car as we drive out of the parking lot and stop at a gas station for fuel. "What are we going to do?" my girlfriend asks innocently. She speaks French. I don't. I know what we have to do, but I'm not sure she's going to like it.

"You have to beg," I tell her.

"What?"

"You have to call the restaurant back. You have to get the chef on the phone. You have to explain that we have traveled all the way from the United States to eat a great *choucroute* and that we have struck out. Tell him we only want one order of his suckling pig *choucroute*.

"But they said they were full," she protests.

"Tell him we'll eat it in the kitchen. Tell him we'll eat it in the bar. Tell him we'll eat it in the parking lot. Tell him we'll take it to go and eat it in our hotel room . . . ."

"In French?" She says with her head in her hands.

"Baby, you know I'd do this if I could. I'm begging you."

The mechanics and motorists hanging around the garage listen in awe as my girlfriend makes her plea over the pay phone, which has no glass doors or dividers to provide privacy. I don't know exactly what she's saying, but judging by the smiles around the gas station, it must be pretty good. She says *"Merci"* at least a hundred times before she hangs up, so I figure we've scored.

"You owe me, big time," she says triumphantly on her way out the door.

"Are we dining in the parking lot?" I ask.

The restaurant's first seating is at eight, she explains. We have to be there at seven o'clock on the dot. We can eat our *choucroute* while they're setting up the dining room, but we have to be out of there in an hour. I kiss her passionately and swear my eternal gratitude.

At seven o'clock, we arrive at Le Cerf, me in a suit and tie and her in a stunning dress. We are quickly seated and, although we are a little sheepish about the imposition of our visit, everyone is very gracious. The menu lists our quarry as *Choucroute à notre façon au cochon de lait de Kochersberg et foie gras fumé*, which translates to "*Choucroute* 'Our Way' with suckling pig from Kochersberg and smoked foie gras." It goes for 185 francs, about $30. Obviously the waiter already knows what we are having, and he suggests an unusual Alsatian wine to go with it. It's a 1993 Klevener de Heligenstein. "It's what we call a curiosity," the waiter says. "It's a blend of Tokay and Riesling, slightly sweet, and a great accompaniment to the *choucroute*." We order a bottle and sip a little while the staff sets tables and polishes silverware. By now we are used to empty dining rooms.

At last, the *choucroute* arrives, and as it is set before us, we are enveloped in its sharp perfume. The sauerkraut is stained in mahogany hues and surrounded by miniature chops of the suckling pig with tiny ribs and loin medallions on either side. An egg-shaped dumpling of liver mousse and a tiny black sausage are tucked into the array, along with a handful of perfectly turned potatoes and crisps of bacon. The regal dish is crowned with smoked foie gras and a plume of fresh sage leaves.

The brown stain on the melt-in-your-mouth sauerkraut proves to be a savory sage-flavored reduction sauce made from the pan juices of the roasted pig. For the next few minutes, my senses are completely focused on the job of keeping the proper rotation of sauerkraut, potatoes, pork, bacon, and liver moving into my mouth. Occasionally, I put down my fork and raise my wine glass in the interest of giving my girlfriend a chance to eat a little of the finest plate of sauerkraut I've ever tasted before I inhale the whole thing.

When Chef Michel Husser comes out of the kitchen and approaches our table, I want to stand and applaud. The handsome young chef inquires humbly what we thought of the *choucroute*. I recite my short litany of clichéd French superlatives, which are completely inadequate to describe the happiness, relief, and gratitude I feel.

I am so euphoric, I don't even mind that our hour is almost up and we will soon have to leave. But before we go, I have a few questions for Michel. First, I ask him about his inspiration for this dish. Michel took over the kitchen at Le Cerf from his father, Robert Husser, not too many years ago, he explains. His father did a traditional *choucroute*, but Michel, who trained under the famous Parisian chef Alain Senderens, wanted to invent a *choucroute* that elevated the traditional flavors to new heights. So instead of pork, he uses the milk-fed baby pig. Instead of liver, he serves the dumpling and foie gras. The bacon is caramelized, the potatoes are hand carved, and the sauce is the kind of intense reduction made popular by the nouvelle cuisine. The whole effect is transcendental, if you happen to be a sauerkraut worshiper.

I have a few more questions. "This combination of fish and sauerkraut that we've been seeing so often, is it some kind of nouvelle innovation?"

"No, it's very traditional in Alsace," Michel assures me. "I serve a dish that combines oysters and sauerkraut in the winter myself."

As long as I have the chef who makes the best *choucroute* in Alsace handy, I have one last question. The Sauerkraut Trail brochure led us to a lot of dead ends, so where should we have gone to eat Alsace's best *choucroute*? Michel gives me the names and locations of some of his favorite spots. As I write them down, I realize that I am back where I started. I am leaving Alsace tomorrow with an intriguing list of restaurants in hand. And once again, I am swearing to myself that someday I will come back here and really eat some serious sauerkraut.

The Best Restaurant on Earth

The kitchen is enormous and, for the moment, very quiet. Huge picture windows all along one side of it frame a flower garden in full bloom on a gray morning. The lush vegetation is reflected in the shiny stainless-steel appliances and tile countertops, suffusing the place in blurry green light. The pointy pink blossoms of a flowering tree seem to jut right through the plate glass.

At 10:45 A.M., the maître d', Jean-Louis Foucqueteau, checks into the silent kitchen. He is reading a computer printout, which he leaves on the tiny table in the corner where I'm sitting. "Véronique Sanson will be here for lunch today," he smiles. Sanson is a popular French singer and evidently one of the waitstaff's favorite customers.

At 11 on the dot, a solemn procession of men in white enters, and the calm suddenly explodes with activity and noise. I am trying to count all the tall white toques flying around the place, but they move so fast I keep having to start over. "There are eighteen chefs in my kitchen," the legendary chef Alfred "Fredy" Girardet tells me. "Today we will prepare forty lunches."

Dominating the center of the tiny village of Crissier, Switzerland, Fredy Girardet's restaurant looks more like a government office than a place to eat. In fact, above the letters spelling *Girardet* on the three-story stone building, an ornate stone inscription reads "Hôtel de Ville," French for "town hall." I was expecting a luxurious chalet in the Alps, but I suppose the stately authoritarian look is more in order. After all, when it comes to food, Restaurant Girardet rules the world.

Girardet has been known for almost a decade as the best restaurant on earth. The designation started in November 1986, when a magazine called *Cuisine & Wines of France* assembled an international jury of forty prominent food and beverage writers. The United States was represented by our premier food commentator, Julia Child, and our foremost wine authority, Robert Parker. The jury was asked to name the world's best chef. They chose Fredy Girardet.

Fredy Girardet sits down to join me at my table in his kitchen. After the *Cuisine & Wines of France* article, he tells me, *Gault Millau*, the highly respected French food guidebook, started calling this the world's best restaurant. Then both Paul Bocuse and Joël Robuchon, the two most famous chefs in France, said the same thing in a French newspaper article.

"So how does it feel to own the best restaurant in the world?" I ask.

"Well, it's nice, but there's really no such thing as the best restaurant in the world," he says rhetorically. "Each culture must have its own tastes."

"Why did you put your restaurant here in the former town hall of this tiny Swiss village?" I want to know.

"My father ran a restaurant in the town hall. When he died, my mother and I took over. We wanted to expand, but the town wasn't interested—so we bought the town hall," Fredy shrugs.

He is looking through the computer printout the maître d' brought earlier. It is a complete list of everyone who will eat lunch at the restaurant today. There is also a complete record of when these guests ate at the restaurant before, including which table they sat at, who waited on them, every dish they ate, and every wine they ordered.

"When I go out to their table to propose a menu, I don't want to recommend something they've had before," Fredy smiles as he makes notes on the list.

I spend a few minutes walking around the kitchen during the prelunch rush to observe each of Girardet's eighteen chefs in action. Girardet's style of cooking has been called "*la cuisine spontanée*," or "spontaneous cuisine." The concept is to prepare almost nothing in advance. Most items on the menu are cooked from the freshest ingredients possible immediately when they are ordered. It's an extremely demanding way to cook, and that's why Girardet needs eighteen chefs to make forty lunches.

Close to my table, a Norwegian salmon is being cleaned and cut into portions; nearby langoustines are being shelled. Two hours ago, Fredy personally selected this seafood just after it arrived by jet in Switzerland.

Around a corner, a group of pastry chefs is slicing fruits, whipping creams, and shaving chocolate curls on the marble countertops. Their freshly made desserts will be put on the cart around one o'clock, so the desserts will be minutes old when they enter the dining room.

From the restaurant's bakery, huge trays of seeded rolls are being loaded into baskets. The bread emerges from the oven at around 11:15, leaving it just enough time to cool properly before it is set on the table in front of each guest.

When the rolls are done, the bakers turn their attention to the special nut breads to be served with the cheese course. And after the cheese bread, they will bake the petits fours to go with the coffee.

While I'm wandering around, a waiter brings me an *amuse bouche*, literally, a "mouth amusement." It is a tiny scallop on an onion puree. Or at least that's what the waiter told me before Fredy took him out into the hall to upbraid him.

"It's not a Coquille St. Jacque [a scallop]; it's a *pétoncle* [a baby scallop]," Fredy is telling the young waiter forcefully out in the hall. It seems like a small matter, but it will be the first of many minute details to inflame the great chef's passion for exactitude in the course of the afternoon. The young man returns to apologize to me for his ghastly mistake.

While I wolf down the succulent little scallop, or *pétoncle*, or whatever it is, Fredy walks through the kitchen looking into saucepans and pointing out little imperfections that catch his eye. I am beginning to realize that here in the French-speaking region of Switzerland, the French passion for food and the Swiss passion for precision have come together in a bizarre sort of way.

Restaurant Girardet has a reputation for being a difficult place to work and, for some, a challenging place to eat. Fredy Girardet greets most patrons personally and consults with them on their choices of food and wine. But if the great Girardet doesn't like the combination of foods or wines you've ordered, he won't serve them to you.

This causes problems sometimes, particularly with affluent foreign customers who expect to be pampered when they pay big money for a meal. Girardet's least expensive lunch menu runs 180 Swiss francs, about $135 without wine; à la carte appetizers go for up to $63. And they don't take any credit cards. At these prices, some people feel like they have the right to dictate how their meal should be cooked. But Fredy doesn't agree. "If you come here, you come to eat *my* cooking, not to tell me what *you* like!" he thunders.

As I watch him make the rounds of the dining room greeting his guests, I am struck by the simplicity of the setting. There is none of the sybaritic opulence of France's grand restaurants here, no ornate fixtures, fancy wall coverings, or plush upholstery. The dining room is all dark wood furniture and neutral colors.

"It's an extreme sensibility," Fredy observes as he leaves the dining room. "There's not a lot of luxury here." Eating Girardet's food in the austere surroundings is meant to be an experience like viewing a painting on the otherwise empty wall of a modern art museum. There are no distractions; there is nothing else to focus on.

Back in the kitchen, Fredy turns his attention to me as a waiter brings something for me to taste. On the menu this appetizer is called *aiguillette de foie gras d'oie en chaud-froid aux noix et raisins, glacée au vieux Madère*, and it sells for 60 Swiss francs, about $44.

It is a slice of cooked foie gras stuffed with nuts and currants that have been soaked in ten-year-old Madeira. The outside of the foie gras is coated with a glistening amber *glacée* made of the Madeira. The whole foie gras creation is cut into perfect slices and presented cold on a plate with salad greens and a walnut vinaigrette. Fredy tells the waiter to bring me a tiny glass of Madeira to drink with the appetizer.

I take one bite and sit back in shock. I thought I knew a lot about foie gras. I've been lucky enough to sample Joël Robuchon's foie gras with lentils, Alain Senderens's foie gras with cabbage, and Gérard Boyer's foie gras with fruit, all of which I judged excellent.

But now all of a sudden, it's like I just tasted foie gras for the first time. As I chew, the woody, faded sweetness of old sherry, the slight crunch of walnuts, and the intensity of currants all melt together into the gamy richness and unctuous creaminess of the rare goose liver. It is without a doubt the most magnificent foie gras I have ever eaten.

Fredy Girardet is smiling at my stunned expression. "It's a beautiful composition, eh?" he says. "That's why I get mad when people mess it up by mismatching it with the wrong wine. Just let me take care of it!"

His face is beaming with genuine pride, and I am beginning to understand. Fredy Girardet is not obsessed with perfection for its own sake; he is obsessed with causing other people to appreciate perfection. He doesn't mean to intimidate his guests when he dictates what they will eat and drink; he is trying to create art, and his canvas just happens to be his patrons' palates.

Girardet will spend the rest of the afternoon supervising the progress of each table's lunch from his command post in the kitchen. Every single plate of food passes before him for inspection, and he often demands changes and improvements.

A young chef is summoned to make repairs. Handling his knife like a surgeon, he carefully replaces a nut that has fallen from its proper place on the side of a dessert. As each dish goes out to the dining room, Fredy makes a note on the huge chart where he keeps track of each table's progress. He is also keeping track of me.

After the foie gras, Fredy sends me another of his favorite creations: *royale de truffes noires à la crème de céleri pistachée*. It is a cream of pistachio sauce studded with chunks of Bresse chicken breast and black truffles. On top of the sauce, there is a creamy foam.

The presentation demands that you treat this as a rare delicacy. The tiny bowl full of chicken and truffles sits atop a stack of four gold-rimmed plates, each slightly smaller than the one underneath. The whole thing looks like a pyramid supporting a ceremonial offering. As I put my spoon into the bowl, Fredy comes at me from across the kitchen. "Wait!" he bellows, waving his arms.

With eighteen chefs looking on, the great Girardet takes the spoon out of my hand and gives me detailed instructions about how to use it. You have to turn the spoon sideways and come down the side of the bowl with it, turning it over at the bottom to get some truffles, he says, demonstrating his technique. Then you raise the spoon through the foam so you get some on top of each bite. He hands me back the spoon and stays to see that I execute the operation correctly.

I am blushing in embarrassment as I fumble at the bowl. Now I know how his intimidated patrons feel when Girardet rejects their order for lunch. But my resentment is soon displaced by the sensation in my mouth. The foamy pistachio cream is awfully good with these black truffles. And the huge smile on Fredy Girardet's face makes it obvious that he didn't go through this soup-spoon lesson out of malice or superiority.

The man is simply obsessed with perfection in his cooking, and he wants everybody who eats at his restaurant to appreciate every nuance of the food that's served there. It may be intimidating to have the world's greatest chef looking over your shoulder while you eat, but obviously, it is Girardet's personal attention that makes the whole experience so intensely rewarding.

There are restaurants more expensive than Girardet. There are restaurants that have even more chefs. And there are certainly more elegant and dramatic settings than this old town hall in a nondescript Swiss village. But there is no other restaurant experience that can compare with that of Restaurant Girardet, because it takes an enormous amount of courage to do what Fredy Girardet does.

No other chef has ever taken his relationship with his audience this far. Girardet is not just a chef, he is a culinary performance artist. He doesn't visit your table and take your order; he sizes up your tastes and temperament and then composes a symphony of flavors for you. If you just sit back and trust his judgment, forgiving him his sometimes obsessive enthusiasm, you will be rewarded with an artistic performance your mouth will never forget.

And that's why Restaurant Girardet is the best on earth.

Q & A

Fredy Girardet

Q: How does it feel to be called the best chef in the world?

A: No one can say anyone is the best chef in the world. Tell me, who is the best musician in the world? Your favorite is the best—right? So, who says chefs are any different from musicians? I'm the best in the world for the people who like my kind of cooking—that's the subjectivity of cuisine.

Q. Well, okay, then who is your favorite chef?

A: Joël Robuchon [Robuchon runs two of the top restaurants in Paris]. He is the most complete chef in modern cooking. There is no better chef in the world.

Q: Have the great chefs of France been an influence on your cooking?

A: The French have given the world the respect for chefs and cuisine that makes great cooking possible. Before Jean Troisgros and Paul Bocuse, you never saw the chef in the restaurant, he was confined to the kitchen.

Q: What do you think of American restaurants?

A: The mentality is different. They have small kitchens and big dining rooms. They try to serve 150 people a night at top restaurants in New York. We serve fifty dinners and we have eighteen to twenty people working in our kitchen.

Q: It's been said that you're not very fond of Americans. How did this reputation get started?

A: I don't understand this reputation. Most Americans who come here are wonderful people. I have American patrons who have been coming here for twenty years.

But yes, sometimes I have problems with people. Americans, Japanese, all kinds of people. They choose two dishes that don't go together; that's very hard for me. Then, when I propose a dinner, they think I'm trying to sell them something.

Like I'm trying to make money on them. People make a special trip here once or twice a year—it's not a meal, it's a cultural event. Money is not the question.

Q: Your cookbook is called *La Cuisine Spontanée*, but your food seems to be getting more elaborate these days. What happened?

A: When I wrote that book, I didn't have such a big staff. I had to be spontaneous in '82; I used to do everything much more quickly. But cooking is a series of mutations, everything is in constant change. I'm thinking about doing a new cookbook now because the old one is getting dated.

Q: What would your new cuisine be called?

A: I can't come up with such a title on the spot.

Q: Well, if it's not spontaneous, in what direction is it moving?

A: [He laughs.] Toward retirement. Maybe I'll call it *Le Cuisine Retirement*.

Fredy's Monkfish Stew with Saffron

With his old dog, Santos, in the back seat of his station wagon, Fredy lead-foots it past the green pastures and bright yellow rapeseed fields of the rural Swiss countryside, pulling up in front of an industrial warehouse. This big cold-storage building is the home of Girardet's fishmonger. Every day the fishmonger flies in fish from all over Europe.

There are hundreds of fish lined up at attention on the floor of this cold locker awaiting the great Girardet's inspection. To me, the jet-flown fish all look fresh and perfect. But to the obsessive perfectionist Fredy Girardet, only a few are worth bothering with.

"You see the blood on this monkfish?" he says pointing to a huge headless fish. "It's too brown. If I find one with blood that's still running red, I'll know it's fresh enough." Fredy turns over monkfish after monkfish

until he finds a few with red blood. The fishmongers
rush to clean these for him before he changes his
mind. When they come back packed in ice for his okay,
only the perfect middle sections of the fish remain. "I
only buy the good parts," he smiles.

Girardet picks up a salmon and looks it in the eyes,
declaring it beautiful. He pretends to kiss it. Today this
fish will receive the ultimate compliment: it will end
up as an entrée at the best restaurant in the world.

If you want to try your hand at cooking fish Girardet
style, you'll have to start the way he does, by finding
the perfect fish. When you've found one worthy, try
following this recipe from the great Girardet.

 3/4 pound boneless monkfish
 1/3 pound boneless salmon
 3 garlic cloves
 4 leaves fresh basil
 1/4 pound little peas in their shells (to yield 2 table-
    spoons shelled)
 1/2 pound fava (or broad) beans in their shells
    (to yield 2 tablespoons shelled)
 1-1/2 tablespoons olive oil
 3 pinches powdered saffron
 3 tablespoons vegetable bouillon
 1/2 cup heavy cream
 1 pinch saffron threads
 1/4 lemon
 Salt and pepper

Preparation

Cut the monkfish once lengthwise and then 5 times
crosswise to make 12 pieces, each about 1-1/2 inches

by 1-1/4 inches. Cut the salmon into 1/2-inch cubes. Mince the garlic. Cut the basil leaves into thin strips. Shell the peas and beans and cook the peas for 10 minutes in boiling salted water. After 8 minutes add the beans. Drain. Remove the skins from the beans.

Finishing

Put 1 tablespoon of the olive oil in a small saucepan over medium heat, add the garlic and 1 pinch of the powdered saffron, and cook 3 minutes. Add the vegetable bouillon, the cream, and the pinch of saffron threads and continue to cook, barely boiling, for 2 minutes. Check the seasoning and squeeze in lemon juice to taste, about 1-1/2 teaspoons. Add the fava beans and the little peas and keep warm over very low heat.

In a nonstick pan, heat the remaining 1/2 tablespoon olive oil over high heat. Season the monkfish and the salmon with salt, pepper, and the 2 pinches of powdered saffron. Sauté the monkfish for 3 minutes. Remove the monkfish to warm plates and sauté the salmon, stirring constantly for 30 seconds.

Presentation

On warm plates, arrange the salmon around the monkfish. Nap the fish with the saffron sauce and sprinkle each serving with some basil strips.

Serves 4.

King Chicken

From the dark shade of the tree line, I'm watching the glowing meadow. The dandelions are yellow smears, their color melting into the lush grass in the bright sun. At the base of the low rock wall I'm sitting on, tiny violets sprout through the clover.

Prancing through the tangle of grass and wildflowers is a regal flock of snow-white chickens. They strut back and forth between the rolling meadow and their palatial half-timbered barn, cocking their huge scarlet combs to one side or the other like jaunty crowns. It is the most majestic pastureful of chickens I have ever seen.

Of course, I have to admit that until I came to the Bresse region of France I'd never seen a pastureful of chickens. Chickens don't eat much grass, so you don't see them out in pastures very often. But then again, I've never seen chickens who live in spacious antique barns and eat gourmet meals of chicken feed, either.

There's only one breed of chicken in the world that lives in such splendor. It is the king of chickens: *poulet de Bresse*. In the meat markets of Europe, *poulet de Bresse* sells for three to five times more than regular commercial chickens. And with their red, white, and blue appellation labels and a metal band affixed to their long blue legs identifying their farm of origin, it's hard to mistake them for ordinary chickens.

Bresse poultry has been the choice of gourmets and aristocrats since the days before the French Revolution. It was a favorite of Brillat-Savarin, the gastronome who said, "Poultry is for the cook what canvas is for the painter."

But it wasn't until 1957 that the poultry of Bresse received a legal appellation, an AOC (*appellation d'origine contrôlée*), like the wine of Bordeaux or the cheese of Roquefort. Even here in the region of Bresse, farmers aren't allowed to raise the famous chickens unless their farms meet the demanding standards of the Interprofessional Committee of Bresse Poultry.

Evelyne Grandjean and her husband, Didier, run the farm I'm visiting in Montagny-près-Louhans, about an hour's drive north of Lyon in the Bourg-en-Bresse. Evelyne is giving me a tour of her picturesque chicken ranch, explaining the strict rules that must be followed in order for her chickens to wear the medallion of *poulet de Bresse*.

"We must provide ten square meters of pasture for each chicken and keep no more than ten chickens per square meter in any one barn," she explains as we stroll down the dirt road that runs through the farm. "Afterwards, we must allow the barn and the pasture to 'rest' for four months before we can raise more chickens."

Dressed for sale, the average *poulet de Bresse* weighs a whopping two kilos, almost four and a half pounds. About 1 million Bresse chickens are sold every year, each with its distinctive blue feet still attached to prove its noble lineage.

What's the point of giving them all that pastureland? I want to know. "Running around in the pasture makes them get bigger," says Evelyne. "And eating all the worms and bugs makes them taste better. Have you ever tasted *poulet de Bresse?*"

Indeed I had. I had eaten *poulet de Bresse* just the evening before. The little inn where I spent the night was called La Croix

Blanche (The White Cross), in the village of Beaurepaire-en-Bresse. It has an excellent restaurant, and when I explained that I was in the area to do a story on Bresse chicken, the chef insisted on preparing me some.

My chicken quarter was served with roasted garlic cloves and pan juices. The skin was brown and crispy, and as I cut into the thigh, the dark meat perfume tantalized my nostrils. The flavor and aroma reminded me of duck. As I sipped a 1991 Givry, a soft-bodied red burgundy that goes splendidly with the poultry, I thought about how funny that was. I'd been eating mass-produced commercial chickens for so long that when confronted with a real chicken, I thought of a duck.

This was my first *poulet de Bresse* in Bresse. I'd been eating it for weeks as I roamed Europe in anticipation of my trip to the chicken farm. It was an expensive item on most restaurant menus, but all the reverence and devotion everyone seemed to have for the bird fascinated me.

In truth, I was disappointed by my first taste. It was a breast in cream sauce; the white meat was dry to my taste. Of course, that probably had more to do with the cooking time than the chicken itself.

The problem of cooking *poulet de Bresse* was best explained by some German chefs I met in Hamburg. We were sitting in a popular little restaurant called Jenna Paradis after it closed one night, drinking German draft beer and talking about French chickens.

"It takes three to four hours to cook a *poulet de Bresse*. Nobody has time to just walk into a restaurant and order one," Sven Bunge, the restaurant's *chef de cuisine*, explained. "And if it's done in advance, the breast is going to dry out while it sits." Bunge, who attended cooking school in France, recounted some of his favorite preparations of *poulet de Bresse*. In the spring, it's good served with morels and asparagus, he said. And in the winter, the breast tastes delicious studded with black truffles.

But if I wanted to see what *poulet de Bresse* was all about, Bunge suggested that I eat a whole roasted bird. "If you like, I'll order one tomorrow," he offered. "Come back in a few days and I'll make you a *poulet de Bresse*."

Three days later, I was back at Jenna Paradis, feeling a little out of place in my cowboy boots and blue jeans among the Hamburg avant-garde in their all-black clothing and countenances of bored hipness. But their expressions suddenly changed when the waiter appeared at our table with a beautifully browned whole *poulet de Bresse* on a platter, its long, blue feet still attached. He carved the breast tableside and spooned a dark sauce over the slices before serving them to us with a vegetable mélange of baby carrots, snow peas, white asparagus, tiny potatoes, and baby onions. After serving the white meat, the waiter took the bird back to the kitchen.

The people at the next table, who had been too cool to notice us a minute before, were suddenly ogling our chicken. Looking back over their menus, they finally asked us, "Is that *poulet de Bresse?*"

"Yes," my dining companion answered coyly, "but it's not on the menu."

This breast meat was succulent, so moist it dripped with juice every time I cut it. It was very good, but actually the difference in flavor between this white meat and that of other chicken wasn't so pronounced. It was the dark meat that was really different.

The leg quarters were served about fifteen minutes later. They were hot, and it suddenly dawned on me that Bunge's secret for serving whole *poulet de Bresse* with moist white meat was to slice the white meat first and then return the dark meat to the oven.

The waiter spooned the same sauce over the legs. It was made with powdered, dry morel mushrooms and red wine that had been reduced with the pan juices from the chicken, and it tasted even better with the rich, gamy flavor of the dark meat.

After dinner, Bunge joined us at our table and we talked about chicken. "All the fowl we buy for our restaurants is French," he said. Besides the famous *poulet de Bresse*, French poultry farmers also sell a black-feathered chicken and a corn-fed chicken.

"The French take great pride in the quality of their poultry," Bunge said. "German farmers are tuned in to the commercial realities of the Common Market. The French love cooking and eating so much that they don't care about the money."

I'm not sure that Evelyne and Didier Grandjean would agree about that, but clearly the people who make the rules for raising *poulet de Bresse* are more concerned with maintaining the poultry's flavor than with economics. A French government committee headed by a master chef sets the criteria for the breeding, diet, and finishing of Bresse chickens, and its decisions are a matter of French law.

As I stand in Evelyne's courtyard admiring the moss-covered roof of her traditional Burgundy farmhouse and the wildflower pasture where the world's happiest chickens are cavorting, the bucolic quiet is suddenly shattered. A Mirage jet screams by, flying very close to the ground. The noise sends a couple of chickens running for cover.

I'm sure if the French government knew that their military maneuvers were disturbing the *poulet de Bresse*, they'd have the flights rerouted.

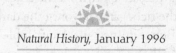

Seeking Le Truffe

Smoke curled invitingly from the chimney of the thirteenth-century farmhouse. I pictured the huge stone hearth inside and wished I were still standing in front of the fire, sipping red wine. But instead I was on my knees in a grove of oak trees a few hundred yards away, my hands stuffed hard in my pockets, trying to ignore the January cold.

We were waiting for a fly. My host—we'll call him Pierre—is one of the owners of this family farm in the Périgord region of France. Pierre volunteered to show me how he finds truffles during the prime midwinter truffle season. "How many truffles have you found so far this winter?" I asked him as we waited. Pierre put his forefinger to his lips.

"We do not talk about such things," my translator, another local farmer, apologized. Neither man would allow his real name to be published. They warned me that disastrous consequences befall farmers foolish enough to speak publicly about truffles around here.

There are some two hundred species of the below-ground fruiting ascomycetes, commonly known as truffles, and gourmets have shown an interest in quite a few of them. We don't know what kind of truffles the Roman culinary genius Apicius used when he created his truffle recipes. Pliny and Juvenal spoke of African truffles, which were probably the desert truffle still found in Libya. But the favorite truffle of French gourmets is the one that Brillat-Savarin called "the black diamond of the kitchen," the black Périgord.

Although these truffles were hunted with muzzled pigs in France as far back as the fifteenth century, it wasn't until the middle of the nineteenth century that black Périgord truffles reached the peak of their glory. According to many reports, they have been in serious decline ever since. In 1991, writing for *Natural History*, Raymond Sokolov speculated on the suspicious nature of this shortage. While truffles have remained among the highest-priced foodstuffs in the world, the harvest figures have fallen from around 1,000 tons at the turn of the century to barely twenty tons a year currently. Sokolov guessed that the French were manipulating the market to keep prices high. And he dreamed of a day when promising new experiments in cultivation would make truffles cheap and plentiful all over the world.

My curiosity piqued, I managed to worm my way into the underground culture of the Périgord *truffiers* (truffle hunters) and returned with some insight into the statistics. Furthermore, I recently received an update on experimental truffle plantations in the United States. So for those still obsessed with the questions, Where have all the truffles gone? and, Where is my next truffle coming from? Here is the truth about *le truffe*.

To understand the reported figures on the modern-day truffle harvest, you have to take into account the secretive traditions of French truffle hunters. Foraging for truffles requires no capital, no land, and no more equipment than a trained dog. Although there are indisputably fewer truffles now than during the heyday of truffle hunting in the nineteenth century, there are still 15,000 to 20,000 *truffiers* in France. While the scrupulous *truffier* might ask the owner of a mansion, farm, or estate for permission to hunt truffles on the grounds for a split of the take, it has always been more profitable for the *truffier* to simply slip into the woods and hunt truffles on the sly.

To my American eye, a Frenchman walking a dog on a country road in the winter twilight is a charming tableau. But to the eye of a Périgord farmer, a winter dog walker is nothing short of nefarious. Dogs long ago replaced pigs as truffle hunters' assistants. To lead the dog to a truffle bed, the truffle hunter scouts groves of oak and filbert trees for the *terre brûlée*, or "scorched earth." Truffles produce natural fungicides that kill grass and other vegetation directly above them.

You can tell when a cattle rustler has struck because your cattle are missing, Pierre told me, but you never know when a truffle rustler has trespassed onto your property with a flashlight and a trained dog in the middle of the night. That's one reason why he won't let me mention where this truffle patch is located or tell me how many truffles he has found here. Suspicious of *truffiers*, Pierre won't even hire them to help with his harvest.

Pierre bragged that he didn't need a *truffier* and his dog to find truffles, anyway. He demonstrated his own technique by walking through the scorched earth, sweeping a leafy branch in front of him, until he caught sight of a fly. He directed us to kneel quietly on the spot and wait for its return. After twenty minutes of shivering, I finally saw the yellow-and-black fly light on a dirt clod and disappear underground. The wasplike truffle fly lays its eggs in mature truffles, and in the process it can lead a patient farmer to the prize.

Pierre dug into the ground with a little wooden tool on the spot where the fly had disappeared. He carefully sniffed each handful of earth as he dug. "As you get closer, the dirt smells more and more like truffles," he said. I started digging dirt out of the hole and sniffing it myself. Ten minutes later we were standing in front of the fireplace with dirt on our noses admiring a ten-gram truffle and drinking wine. That night, I joined them for a dinner that included an immense quantity of goose confit, but no black truffles.

Like the *truffiers*, the farmers regard truffles as a luxury for the rich; they eat only the broken pieces and imperfect truffles that they can't sell. To get a taste of the truffles we hunted, I had to don a coat and tie and visit local restaurants, where I gorged on truffle salads, truffled eggs, and truffled meats. I could easily detect the aroma of truffles in these dishes, but the flavor was a bit of a mystery. Some say that truffles have no flavor at all.

French gastronomes have always insisted that truffles must be eaten in great quantities for the flavor to be really appreciated. So one day, I bought a chestnut-sized specimen for around $20 and carried it with me to a restaurant in Périgueux, where I persuaded the chef to cook it for me whole. I sliced off a few chunks of it and ate it by itself, then I ate more of it with a little bread and cheese. The more I ate, the more the flavor accumulated on my palate. It was a strange amalgam of earthy mushroom, sweet cocoa, and herb flavors, but in the end, it didn't taste like anything else in the world. I have craved black truffles ever since.

That craving proved hard to satisfy once I got home. The wholesale restaurant price for a kilo of black Périgord truffles here currently ranges from the indecent sum of $550 to the astronomical high of $750. Périgord black truffles are native only to Greece, Italy, France, and Spain. For over a century, entrepreneurs have tried various methods of cultivating the precious fungus elsewhere with little success.

In the early 1970s, there appeared to be a breakthrough. An intensive study of truffles by Dr. Gérard Chevalier and his colleagues at the Plant Pathology Station of the French National Institute of Agronomics in Clermont-Ferrand concluded that tree roots could be inoculated with truffle spores. This technique may eventually make large-scale "trufficulture" a reality.

In the late 1980s, inoculated saplings were planted in Italy, New Zealand, and the United States. As Raymond Sokolov reported, an American plantation in Dripping Springs, Texas, was expected to produce truffles by 1991. In anticipation of that harvest, Sokolov fantasized about buying cheap, American-grown black Périgord truffles at his corner convenience store.

Five years after the projected harvest date, there were still no cheap truffles. The Dripping Springs plantation was a failure. I was about to dismiss the whole American truffle-growing business as another get-rich-quick scheme gone awry until I phoned Dr. Jim Trappe, a mycologist at Oregon State University and a leading authority on truffle taxonomy. I asked Trappe if truffles would ever be cultivated in the United States.

Trappe calmly replied with the news that American gourmets have long waited to hear. Truffles are already being grown in the United States.

Last winter, a North Carolina farmer named Franklin Garland harvested a commercial quantity of black Périgord truffles. Dr. Trappe verified the *Tuber melanosporum* specimens personally and visited the truffle orchard. The size of the harvest was modest, only ten pounds. But Garland reports that he sold his truffles for $350 a pound.

Sokolov won't find cheap truffles at the corner store anytime soon. Until the harvest gets a little bigger, I'm afraid we're stuck with French prices. And I can't help but wonder if, along with the prices, American growers will also inherit the secrecy and suspicion of the French truffle culture.

Truffle rustling aside, I knew that there was a more personal reason why the French farmers were so unwilling to discuss their truffle harvests. That reason was taxes. "Tourists go to the truffle markets in Europe expecting to see truffles," scoffed Rosario Safina of Urbani Truffles in Long Island City, New York, the nation's oldest truffle importer. "But all they see are a bunch of guys standing around smoking cigarettes. Nobody's going to put their truffles out on display in a public market."

"Why?" I asked.

"Because then they'd have to pay taxes on them," he laughed. The value-added tax runs as high as 19.5 percent, Safina said, and then there's income tax on top of that. There is no doubt that the French truffle harvest really has declined since the late 1800s and early 1900s as a result of environmental and wartime disruptions. But not coincidentally, the French personal income tax was enacted in 1917. Part of the reason the reported figures have looked so bad ever since is that the underground fungus long ago became a part of the underground economy.

In the abstract, it's easy to fault the French for the legendary skulduggery and apparent price manipulation of this luxury commodity. And it's easy to forget that the ancient trade is still primarily run by small-time foragers who sell their truffles to the rich a basketful at a time. After hanging around with Pierre and the *truffiers*, it's hard for me to believe that Americans would behave much differently under the same circumstances.

We'll soon have a chance to find out. Franklin Garland's North Carolina truffle orchard is a small one, but it's only the tip of the iceberg. Besides selling truffles, Garland and the other orchard owners expect to do a booming business selling inoculated saplings to anybody who wants to buy them.

While cheap truffles at the corner convenience store remain a distant dream, planting your own truffle orchard has now become a possibility. But if, a few years from now, your orchard produced more truffles than you could eat and you sold a few to a restaurant, would you declare the income on your tax form? And how long would it take for you to become suspicious of your dog-walking neighbors?

Part FIVE

Indiana Jones in the Suburbs

Hello, Houston

Abdul picks up the Styrofoam bowl and begins eating the spicy pink yogurt with a plastic spoon, so I follow his lead. The cold yogurt soup has some minced tomato and cucumber in it, along with an intriguing combination of spices. I detect cumin and black pepper, but there are others I can't identify. I am just getting into the soup when Abdul throws me a curveball. He puts the soup bowl back down on the table and starts throwing lettuce, tomatoes, and onions into the yogurt. The soup has suddenly become the salad dressing. He smiles as he swishes the vegetables around in the yogurt and eats them with his fingers. I do what Abdul does.

Abdul Rasheed happened to be first in line at Hobby Airport when I approached the taxi stand. He stood about five foot four, with black hair and dark eyes. He hadn't shaved lately, and he had a strange red stain on his teeth. I asked him where he was from. He said, "Pakistan." I asked him if he knew of a good Pakistani restaurant in Houston. He said, "Oh, yes!" So I offered to buy him lunch.

I've done a lot of whirlwind culinary tours for travel magazines. Since I'm new to Houston, I thought it might be fun to do the same sort of kamikaze dining here. Abdul was the first willing guide I came across.

He drove me to a stretch of Bissonnet west of Highway 59. "This is the center of the Pakistani community," he said. We passed several shopping centers with Pakistani businesses before pulling into the parking lot at Ali Baba's B.B.Q. and Grill, a small freestanding restaurant on a "pad" in front of a shopping strip.

I stood there speechless for a minute as I took in the oddity of the scene. Abdul explained that the location used to be an American breakfast restaurant. The new owners have done very little to change the place, which makes it all the more bizarre. The booths and the Formica counter say Steak 'N Egg Kitchen, but the menu hanging above the grill features brain *masala*. Instead of bacon and coffee, you smell curry and mutton. Abdul likes the quail here, so I order the *batair boti* (grilled quail) special—two for $5.99 (or four for $9.99). We also ask for the barbecue combination plate and an order of *karahi gosht* (stewed beef). The paint on the wall beside the booth where we sit is dappled with sauce stains.

We are the last customers for lunch at around 2 in the afternoon, and the restaurant has grown quiet while we wait for our orders. Abdul is done with his yogurt, and he heads for the washroom. I am idly clucking my tongue on the roof of my mouth, trying to decipher the cryptic spice mix. Since there is no one else around, I get up and stroll into the kitchen. "What are the spices in the yogurt?" I ask a man in an apron. The cook points to a rack that contains some large plastic jars.

"We grind these together to make our own *masala*," he says. Two of the jars on the shelf contain black peppercorns and cumin seeds, as I expected. Another contains cloves, and the fourth holds a pod that looks like a miniature Brazil nut. I fish it out of the jar, scrape it with my thumbnail, and sniff. It's cardamom. In Indian cooking, these four spices, plus cinnamon, are ground together to make the spice mix called *garam masala*.

Shortly after Abdul returns, our food arrives, and after a quick assessment, I zero in on the quail. It looks fabulous. The skin is crispy, brown, and flecked with spices. The bird is very hot, and I burn my fingers pulling it apart. It is really too hot to eat, but I tear off a big rosy piece of juicy breast and pop it in my mouth anyway. I have never before had barbecue with such an exotic aroma. Cumin, cloves, and garlic make quite a grill rub, and they combine stunningly with the slight gaminess of the quail. The birds are basted with *ghee* (clarified butter) to keep them moist. Abdul is watching me eat my little bird with wide eyes and a big smile. I realize I am making a lot of appreciative noises.

He is focusing his own efforts on the little metal hot pot that contains the *karahi gosht*, which turns out to be a sort of Pakistani pot roast. The well-cooked piece of beef falls apart easily under the little plastic knife. The meat is cooked in a spicy tomato sauce that combines the familiar tomato sauce elements of green onions, jalapeños, and garlic with the Far Eastern zing of fresh ginger and aromatic *masala*. Abdul eats his meat and sauce folded in little pieces of nan bread.

The barbecue combination plate is a major disappointment. And it's made worse when I realize that I have made this same mistake many times before. When I hear the word *kabab* I always think of shish kebabs. But *kabab* does not mean skewered meat in India or Pakistan; it means ground meat. When I was told the combination plate consisted of chicken *boti tikah* and *seekh kabab*, I envisioned barbecued chicken and beef grilled on a skewer. What I get is grilled chicken and two ground meat patties. (Now all I need is special sauce and a sesame seed bun.)

The chicken leg quarter has been marinated in *masala* spices and grilled beautifully. It falls off the bone with no resistance. I heap the chicken meat on a piece of nan with some lettuce, tomato, and yogurt and roll it up into a fine taco. Not quite as rich as the quail, but very close. Abdul encourages me to do the same with some of the ground meat, but I complain that the *kabab* is too dry. He yells something in Urdu to the cook.

The cook comes to our table with another Styrofoam bowl. I chuckle as I slather my *kabab* with the brown sauce in the bowl. It has the same sort of sweet-and-sour effect on the meat that barbecue sauce does, except this barbecue sauce is a sort of thin tamarind chutney. I think the *kabab* is made from frozen hamburger patties. In Pakistan, *kabab* is made with goat or mutton.

The ready supply of cheap ground beef in Texas is a delight to Pakistani immigrants. In Pakistan, where goat is the most common meat, ground beef is considered a luxury. The guy sitting at the table beside us is polishing off a plate of *masala kabab*, hamburger meat cooked with *masala* spices and served in a little hot pot with fluffy nan on the side, a Pakistani sloppy joe. You can also get a dish called a bun *kabab*, better known in the rest of Houston as a hamburger on a bun.

Abdul says when it's hot outside and you have eaten a big meal like this one, you should drink a large glass of the sour yogurt drink called *lassi* to prevent heartburn. So I follow his advice. As we leave, he also buys me a strange little package at the kiosk at the front of the restaurant. *Paan*, he calls it. It's a betel nut chew. Pakistanis and Indians are crazy about betel nut. Mine is flavored with anise seeds and sweetened lentils. His is betel nut and tobacco mixed together (*paan parg*). We drive away in silence as I ruminate in the backseat.

What do I really think about Ali Baba's? On a purely culinary level, I can say that the *batair boti* is the best grilled quail for the money I have ever eaten. And at $4.99, the Afghani *boti tikah*—a steaming piece of nan and a skewerload of grilled beef with lettuce, tomato, and sauces in a Styrofoam to-go box—is a hell of a bargain, too. But I can also say with some certainty that the broken chairs and splattered walls here would frighten hygiene-conscious types (like my mother) half to death. Of course, so would most old-fashioned Texas barbecue joints. Authenticity can be a scary thing.

In her authoritative 1973 cookbook, *An Invitation to Indian Cooking*, Madhur Jaffrey told us that the food served at Indian restaurants in New York was a bland, watered-down version of the real thing. In A.D. 2000, restaurants like Ali Baba's have turned the tables on those who complain about a lack of authenticity. The Hart-Cellar Act of 1965, which removed discriminatory "country of origin" quotas from American immigration law, has resulted in a slow, steady surge of immigration from Africa, the Far East, and other corners of the planet that were once underrepresented.

A new style of ghetto has emerged in Houston and Los Angeles, where first-generation mom-and-pop restaurants take over strip center locations in once run-down suburbs. Often a second generation opens another restaurant in newer quarters and offers a partially assimilated version of the cuisine. The evolution of Houston's Kim Son from a humble Vietnamese eatery to a budding chain is a case in point. The beauty of the current situation is that between the extremes of just-like-back-home ethnic food and the inevitable chain version lie enough varying degrees of authenticity to suit everybody's tastes.

Brain *masala*, hamburger *kabab*, and many of the other dishes served at Ali Baba's reflect the preferences of Houston's Pakistani population. These foods are too authentic for most of us. But for exactly that reason, Ali Baba's offers Lonely Planet types a ticket to Pakistan for the price of a five-dollar lunch. I love culinary adventures, and I had a great time eating lunch and arguing politics with Abdul at Ali Baba's. ("India, Pakistan, and Sri Lanka have all had female prime ministers, so where do you Americans get off lecturing us about women's rights?")

If rubbing elbows with the natives while eating a skewer of *masala*-rubbed quail hot off the grill in the Islamabad bazaar is your preferred level of authenticity, Ali Baba's is your kind of place.

The Aroma
of Authenticity

When you walk in the front door of El Hidalguense, the scent of mutton commands your attention. Or is it goat? The restaurant's specialties are *barbacoa de borrego estilo Hidalgo* (Hidalgo-style lamb "barbecued" in maguey leaves) and *chivito asado al pastor* (charcoal-roasted goat).

Whether it's sheep or goat or both, there's always a pungent aroma in the air. There are seven tables occupied at the moment—all by Latinos—two couples, two large families with kids, and three tables of workmen in jeans and boots. A Mexican talk show blares from the TV.

They don't serve the standard Tex-Mex chips and salsa here. But they do bring you a bowl of deep brown hot sauce, made from a combination of hot and mild dried chiles with onion and vinegar, to put on your food. For lunch I order a fabulously decadent dish, something El Hidalguense calls *tulancigueñas*. What comes to the table looks like three thick *flautas*. Inside the fried tortilla rolls are several slices of ham folded around a lot of jalapeños and a little mayonnaise. After being deep-fried, the rolls are sprinkled with cheese and topped with cold avocado slices.

When you bite into one of these taco tubes, the juice—let's not call it grease—practically squirts out the other end. I didn't really mean to order *tulancigueñas*. Actually, I wasn't planning to eat here at all; I had just eaten lunch up the street at Otilia's, which *Zagat's Guide* has rated as the top Mexican restaurant in Houston for two years running. Otilia's likes to boast that it's "100% Mexican, No Tex-Mex!" But the place serves chips with a salsa as meek as gazpacho, and its *chile en nogada* comes in a cream gravy that seems to belong on a chicken-fried steak. I didn't finish it. And now I'm hungry again. So I couldn't resist the urge for jalapeño-and-ham tacos.

At El Hidalguense, they don't make any claims about authenticity.

Have you even been to an authentic American restaurant? I have, and it's quite an illuminating experience. In 1994 I visited the Texas Cafe on Rue de la Sagesse in the French city of Périgueux. The appetizer menu featured buffalo wings, guacamole, New England soup (clam chowder), and tuna fish salad. The entrées included Long Island shrimp (in whiskey tomato sauce), Mississippi chicken (sautéed with bourbon and orange), Texas nuggets (pan-fried chicken bits), chili (*boeuf mijoté aux haricots rouges*), barbecue ribs, and a bunch of steaks. Americans may not recognize some of these dishes. The French feel free to interpret our cuisine however they choose.

But what do you say when a Frenchman asks, "Is this authentic American food?"

I have been to many "interior Mexican" restaurants like Otilia's; they remind me of the Texas Cafe. The menu reads like Mexico's greatest hits: there's *cochinita pibil* from the Yucatán, *arracheras* from Nuevo León, *potosinos* from San Luis, and *chile en nogada* from Puebla. But the menu also expresses some odd notions. Take, for instance, the explanation that begins, "*Mole* is dark gravy with chocolate, peanuts, and spices. . . ." Otilia's may be preparing dishes from many parts of Mexico, but it obviously has its own regional bias. Six out of seven moles in Oaxaca are made without chocolate; same goes for almond mole, *mole de hoja santa*, and guacamole. There are lots of moles in Mexico. *Mole poblano*, the one with the chocolate, peanuts, and spices, is only one of them.

For lunch, I tried Otilia's signature dish, *chile en nogada*. There are all kinds of stuffed peppers in Mexico, but *chile en nogada* is something in particular, "one of the most famous dishes in Mexico," says Diana Kennedy in *The Cuisines of Mexico*.

According to legend, it was first served on August 28, 1821, at a banquet for Don Agustín de Iturbide, the newly proclaimed emperor of Mexico. The dish features a roasted *poblano* pepper stuffed with fruity, highly spiced pork *picadillo* served in a walnut sauce and garnished with red pomegranate seeds. The white sauce, green chile, and red seeds represent the three colors of the Mexican flag.

Otilia's version of *chile en nogada* is a roasted *poblano* stuffed with your choice of beef, chicken, or cheese in cream gravy with about a half teaspoon of ground walnuts and no pomegranates—or any other red things on top. Since the authentic *picadillo* isn't even offered, I ordered the chicken. The meat was boiled and seemed to be unseasoned. The cream sauce had some tomato and cilantro in it, but little, if any, walnuts. The dish bore no resemblance to the *chile en nogada* I had in Mexico City's Osteria San Domingo, which is widely considered to serve the definitive version.

When the co-owner, Otilia's husband, stopped by my table to ask if everything was all right, I asked him if he had ever eaten the *chile en nogada* at Osteria San Domingo. Yes, he said, but he didn't like it. Had he ever seen or tasted a *chile en nogada* anywhere in Mexico that resembles the one on my plate, I wanted to know.

"No," he said proudly. "Ours is different from all the rest. It's our best-selling item!"

"What's different about it?" I asked.

"The others have too many walnuts," he said.

Otilia's, of course, has every right to make the dish any way it sees fit. And if unseasoned fillings and nut-deficient cream gravy are ideally suited to the restaurant's mainly Anglo clientele—well, surprise, surprise. So spare me the authenticity rap. Lots of restaurants list interior Mexican plates on their menus. This one just happens to get a lot of press for it.

I've argued that Mexican restaurants in Houston have been promising "authentic Mexican food" for nearly a hundred years, but what they really deliver is a regional Texan variation.

"Not Otilia's!" shrieked my foodie friends. "It's really authentic!" Otilia's walls are decorated with some of the twenty-six magazine and newspaper stories about the place. The media have taken little interest in other Mexican eateries on Long Point.

You can blame it partly on pack journalism. But food lover Jay Francis takes much of the credit for Otilia's fame. Francis loved the food there, and shortly after it opened, he became friendly with the owners. "I really liked them, and I wanted them to succeed," he says. "So I went on a letter-writing campaign." Food critics got letters from Francis. In them, he described Otilia's as an "undiscovered gem" that serves "authentic Mexican food." About two months later the reviews began to appear.

I asked Jay Francis to join me for dinner at El Hidalguense one night last month. *Hidalguense* means something or someone from Hidalgo, a city in the Huatecan region just south of Mexico City. The restaurant's open kitchen is dominated by a waist-high brick structure with a griddle on one side where the tortillas are cooked, a charcoal grill on the other side where the goat is prepared, and a stainless-steel cauldron in which the *barbacoa* is simmered. On the night we were there, the cook lifted the lid and showed us how he did the *barbacoa*. At the bottom of the cauldron was a broth in which giant maguey leaves stuffed with lamb are partially submerged. I had read about this technique, but this was the first time I had seen it up close.

The *barbacoa* dinner began with a bowl of the lamb broth to which onions, chiles, and garbanzo beans were added. Francis got a bowl of *charro* beans with his order. El Hidalguense didn't have the *chivito al pastor*, so instead it served kid goat cooked in chile sauce. The tender goat meat was brick red and still on the bone. It made for a stunningly spicy meat taco topped with the chopped onions, cilantro, and limes.

Then came my huge serving of steaming lamb *barbacoa*, as soft and stringy as a pot roast, presented on a piece of the maguey leaf with lettuce and tomatoes on the side. I piled lamb meat on a handmade flour tortilla and sprinkled it with onions, the chocolate-colored hot sauce, and cilantro. Then I drizzled a spoonful of broth over the top to keep it juicy. It was the sort of taco that makes you bow down over your plate in complete surrender.

"Well," I asked Francis, "isn't this as authentic as Otilia's?"

"Yeah," he admitted.

"So would you have gone on a letter-writing campaign about this place?" I asked.

"No," he said, "because I don't like goat and mutton. Not to say it isn't authentic."

"And because you knew gringos wouldn't get it. The goat and mutton aroma, nobody speaks English—don't you see some xenophobia at work here?" I asked Francis.

"But I still think Otilia's is very authentic," he said.

"The *chile en nogada* is completely Americanized," I argued.

"Yeah, but I've had the *chile en nogada* at Osteria San Domingo in Mexico City, and I didn't really like it," he said.

"Great, we're in agreement," I responded. "Americans don't want real *chile en nogada*, and that's why Otilia's serves Americanized Mexican food."

"Wait a minute," Francis said. "If you were a Mexican chef and you opened a Mexican restaurant in Holland and you made cheese enchiladas with Gouda cheese, does that mean they couldn't be authentic Mexican?"

"No, they wouldn't be authentic, but they would taste good—especially to Dutch people, and that's what I'm trying to say."

Otilia's is a lovely restaurant, and it's doing a wonderful job of bringing a good approximation of interior Mexican food to a non-Mexican audience. But articles that single it out for serving "authentic Mexican" food seem laughably Anglocentric, considering that there's an Hidalgo-style *barbacoa* pit right down the street.

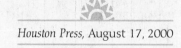

Loco for LOROCO

At a vacant lot at the corner of Hillcroft and Bissonnet a garage sale is in progress. I ask several people standing around the cash table which of the many *pupuserias* around here they would recommend.

"We're all Mexicans," the lady taking the money tells me. "Go down Bissonnet another mile or so; you'll find the Salvadorans."

I get back in my car and follow her instructions. About a mile down the road there is a car wash benefiting Principe de Paz church. I park my car and walk up to the car washers. "Anybody here from El Salvador?" I ask.

A guy named Eric Garcia comes forward. I ask him where the best *pupusas* in Houston might be found.

"Try El Venado," he says.

"Anybody else from El Salvador?" I ask in a loud voice, looking for a consensus. Maybe it's too loud. The laughter and chatter suddenly cease, and a tough-looking kid approaches me warily.

"Are you from the FBI?" he asks.

"No, I'm just trying to get somebody to recommend a place to eat *pupusas*," I plead. He laughs. Everybody relaxes and goes back to washing vehicles.

"You want to talk to Brenda," a woman says. "She's from El Salvador, and she loves *pupusas.*"

"So where is Brenda now?" I ask. The woman checks with a few of the others.

"She went to get *pupusas,*" she says. "At El Campero."

El Campero is right next to the charity car wash on Bissonnet, and its forbidding exterior is not very cheery, let alone inviting. The cinder-block structure sits a little too close to the road, and there are burglar bars on all the windows. I look inside for Brenda, but she must have already left. So I sit and peruse the menu. The orange vinyl chairs and fake-wood Formica tables are pleasant enough. The acoustic ceiling has seen better days. The place may look a little ominous from the outside, but the cook and waitress inside are the exact opposite. They are singing along to the jukebox and smiling at me like a long-lost friend. The waitress recommends the *pupusa* with cheese and *loroco.*

"*¿Que es loroco?*" I ask.

"*Es una hojita del campo,*" she tells me. A little leaf from some kind of wild plant?

"*¿Es una hierba?*" I ask. The cook is leaning over the cash register not far away, and she wiggles into the conversation. No, it's not an herb exactly, she says in Spanish, but I should try it. Everybody from El Salvador loves the stuff. Okay, I'm sold. I order a *pupusa* with cheese and *loroco.*

El Campero has some items stacked on store shelves, and I wander around while my *pupusa* is cooking. I find a bottle of pickled *loroco,* which seems to be a flowering plant whose buds look like capers, except the buds are still connected to the stems. There are also a bunch of tapes for sale, all Christian music in Spanish.

A *pupusa* is sort of like a grilled cheese sandwich made from two fresh tortillas with a filling in the middle. My *pupusa* with cheese and *loroco* is excellent. The *masa* here is very fresh. The *loroco* flavor is difficult to identify: does it taste like a green? The *pupusa* is served with chopped cabbage and carrots and peppers that have been marinated in vinegar. This crunchy slaw, called *cortido de repollo* (chopped cabbage), is the ubiquitous Salvadoran side order; I don't think I've ever seen a *pupusa* served without it. I also try the *tamale de gallina*, which is one of the best tamales I've had in years. It's a warm gelatinous pudding of corn *masa* stuffed with lots of chicken and wrapped in a banana leaf. This is what tamales used to taste like before the Great Lard Panic. I wash down my $2.75 lunch with a Tropical brand *gengibre*, a Salvadoran ginger ale with a nice spicy bite.

As the cook croons along to the latest tune on the jukebox, I hear the word *Jesucristo*, and suddenly the whole scene comes into focus. The posters on the walls are all religious and so is the music. Even the cook's baseball cap says something inspirational. I have evidently chosen to eat lunch at the Jesus-freak *pupuseria*. If my Spanish were better, the whole religious theme probably would be a little more annoying. But in truth, I haven't even noticed it until I'm done eating. And the *pupusa* and tamale are awesome.

I ask the cook, Reina Quintinilla, who is also the owner, where else they make good *pupusas* around here.

"Everybody goes to Pupusadromo," she says in Spanish. "But that's just because they serve beer."

"You don't serve beer?" I ask innocently.

"No, we don't have beer. We're Christians," she says heatedly.

I stand there speechless. The idea that Christianity and beer are mutually exclusive tends to dumbfound persons of Irish ancestry.

If you ever need one of those blue-and-white Salvadoran flags to hang from your rearview mirror, or a poster of San Salvador at dawn, El Venado Taqueria and Pupuseria is the place to go. The booths by the front windows boast some stunning custom-crafted vinyl upholstery—the color is metallic candy-flake turquoise with silver candy-flake trim. A namesake deer head hangs from the wall in the dining room, as do straw sombreros and other rustic bric-a-brac. Wooden tables are surrounded by turquoise-painted ladder-back chairs. It's a tropical hunting-lodge motif with automotive upholstery accents.

But the wacky joint has some great *pupusas*. I had the cheese and *loroco*. At $1.60, it cost ten cents more than El Campero's, but it was really stuffed. The cheese seems to be mozzarella; long, gooey strings of it follow every bite, like I'm eating a homemade tortilla calzone. I get a little more of the *loroco* flavor by pulling out a whole bunch of buds and eating them together. Is there a chocolaty aroma? Does it taste like chocolate chard? What *is* this stuff?

I go to El Pupusadromo No. 1 and have another cheese and *loroco pupusa*. The *pupusas* aren't quite as big, and the stuffing is thinner. Afterward, I go to the kitchen and ask to see the *loroco*. They pull out a bag of frozen greens and hand it to me. The stuff looks like a lot of evergreen buds, and the whole bag of it has a strong chocolate aroma. Xiomara Mendez tells me that in El Salvador people eat it fresh but that here, frozen is the only kind available. Fresh is much better, she says.

In the last few years, I've discovered that the wonder grain called amaranth comes from a weed you see by the side of the road all the time, and that epazote and *chiles pequínes* sprout in vacant lots in much of Texas. Since *loroco* grows wild in Central America, I wonder if it has some North American equivalent. So I start searching the Internet. I see a picture of fresh *loroco* at www.botany.utexas.edu. It doesn't look familiar. I read several restaurant reviews from other cities; food writers refer to it as a flowering plant that is popular in *pupusas*, but I already know that. An academic paper identifies it as a nutritive green that has been eaten with a corn-based diet in parts of Central America for many years. And somebody else trying to track down information on *loroco* has asked about it at the Cornell University nutrition Web site, usually a reliable source of food knowledge. The experts at Cornell incorrectly assume it is fiddlehead fern, but they point the way to better information.

The USDA Nutrient Composition Book of Latin America tells us that *loroco* is commonly called fernaldia in English, or "fiddle shape," after the outline of its flowers. (That must be why the Cornell guys confused it with fiddleheads or fiddlehead ferns, which are the shoots of the ostrich fern, a specialty of New England.) *Loroco*'s scientific name is *Fernaldia pandurata*, and a 100-gram portion contains 32 calories, 2.6 grams of protein, 0.2 grams of fat, and 6.8 grams of carbohydrate, as well as fiber, calcium, phosphorus, iron, vitamin A, and vitamin C. I imagine "Eat your *loroco*" is a phrase that mothers in El Salvador utter often.

Loroco also appears on the list of foods under consideration by the U.S. Department of Agriculture's Commodity and Biological Risk Analysis team, the group that examines fresh agricultural products for import into the United States. I love this list, which reads like a trailer of coming attractions for foodies. *Loroco* is right there with *noni* and maypop from Hawaii, rambutan from Australia, *babáco* from Ecuador, and false coriander from Guatemala.

The good news for Houston *pupusa* lovers is that someday soon, we may be stopping by El Campero or El Venado for a cheese and *loroco pupusa* that will blow our minds. At this very moment, I am imagining the aromatic flower buds, fresh and crunchy, covered with gooey cheese in the middle of some chewy, hot fresh *masa*.

But for the time being, the lack of fresh *loroco* stands between me and the definitive, just-like-downtown–San Salvador total *pupusa* experience. So this is a public appeal: somewhere in this megalopolis, somebody is sitting on a stash of fresh *loroco*. I don't need to know your name, and I don't care how you got it. You can blindfold me and take me to a secret location—just let me have a little taste.

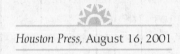

Bagels Rip My Flesh

"What the fuck are you doing taking notes in my business?" seethes Jay Kornhaber, co-owner of New York Coffee Shop, as he grabs my notebook from its hiding place beneath the *New York Times Magazine.* I haven't actually taken any notes yet; I'm working the crossword puzzle while I wait for my order of eggs with lox and onions. But seeing me with a pencil in my hand is enough to cause the veins in Kornhaber's neck to twitch with rage. The lean and muscular young New Yorker sports a mustache and chin patch à la Frank Zappa. He's got Zappa's absurdity down, but he's a little short on the humor this morning.

It is Sunday, the busiest day of the week at his popular coffee shop on Hillcroft near South Braeswood. There was a line when I walked in at 10:30, but Kornhaber's affable partner, Ed Gavrila, waved me to a stool at the counter. The wisecracking waitresses smoke cigarettes and tell jokes back here. But all the joking comes to a halt when Kornhaber flies across the restaurant and seizes my notes.

"Do you want to tell me what you're doing in here with this notebook all the time?" he says, leafing through the pages of my notebook looking for evidence. Luckily my handwriting is illegible even to me.

"Sorry, I can't tell you," I respond.

"You will either tell me what you are doing, or you will be very sorry you didn't," says Kornhaber as he leans forward and gets in my face.

"The ethics of my profession prohibit me from explaining what I am doing," I say.

"What is your profession?" he asks. I figure anybody with a brain should have figured out I'm a restaurant reviewer by now, but Kornhaber is too angry to think. "You are opening your own restaurant and copying my place, aren't you?" he fumes.

Sometimes the hubris of successful restaurant owners is amazing. The interior of New York Coffee Shop is decorated with generic linoleum floors, awful 1970s wallpaper, and Formica-covered booths and tables. And they prepare the same egg dishes, toasted bagels, and deli-style sandwiches that hundreds of delis and coffee shops all over New York City serve. Even the name is generic. What trade secrets could I possibly be copying into my notebook?

I have been buying bagels here for more than a year now. In the coffee shop, I usually order the fish platter for two, which my daughters and I split three ways. It comes with lox or nova (short for Nova Scotia salmon), sable, whitefish chubs, and kippers with bagels and plenty of tomatoes, onions, olives, and all the other necessary condiments. The smoked fish is good, but it's the bagels that draw the crowds. If you think a bagel is a bagel, then try one here.

Whenever I'm in New York, I try to make a pilgrimage to H&H Bagels on the corner of 80th and Broadway. The yeasty aroma and chewy texture of H&H bagels is a breathtaking breakfast experience, but the secret is that H&H is so popular that your bagels are always hot out of the oven. That's why I ignore the sesame, poppy, or onion dilemma at Kornhaber's New York bagel shop and instead order my bagels the way New Yorkers do:

"Give me a dozen of whatever's hottest." And when I'm lucky enough to catch a batch coming right out of the oven, the aroma in the car on the drive home sends me into an Upper West Side reverie straight out of *Seinfeld*.

Come to think of it, Jay Kornhaber could have come straight out of *Seinfeld* himself. He continues to harangue me as my eggs and lox are delivered. I take a bite as he once again demands to know what I'm doing. The eggs are fluffy, and the caramelized onions are sweet and brown. Although I prefer the milder flavor of nova on a bagel, I like the salty lox with the eggs and onions. I get a toasted "everything" bagel with cream cheese with the omelet. The other patrons are staring, and my waitress is so freaked out by Kornhaber's tantrum that her hand shakes as she refills my cup. ·

New York Coffee Shop was recommended to me by former *Houston Press* staffer Bob Burtman, who grew up Jewish in Boston. He preferred this atmosphere to restaurants that ape the appearance of famous East Coast delis. "It's just a coffee shop, but it's right down the street from the Jewish Community Center, and it's a great scene," Burtman told me. "A bunch of old Jewish guys hang out there—you meet some real characters."

Kornhaber and I first met a week ago at about 3 in the afternoon. The coffee shop closes at 3:30, so it's fairly empty at 3. I thought it might be a good time to slip in, quietly eat a Reuben, and jot down some notes. I had recently eaten a Reuben at the Carnegie Deli in New York and at Kenny & Ziggy's. My original intent was to write a review comparing Reubens at all three places. I was copying some information from the menu when Kornhaber descended on me and took it away.

"I am the owner of this place, and I am not going to allow you to sit here and copy my menu," he said.

"I am not allowed to look at the menu?" I asked.

"No, you can't look at the menu, and if you don't like it, get out! Go write your notes in somebody else's restaurant," the belligerent bagel man roared.

Of course my first reaction was anger. But on the way home, I started to reflect about the last time I was thrown out of a restaurant. It was in New York, of course—three of us were eighty-sixed from McSorley's Old Ale House for bringing in a Stromboli's pizza. The waiter screamed at the top of his lungs while he put us out in the rain. The memory made me laugh, and after a while, I started laughing about Kornhaber's tirade too.

And suddenly it dawned on me. At New York Coffee Shop I had encountered the authentic detail that is missing from the other New York–style restaurants in Houston: rudeness. The owner of a New York restaurant should be passionately irrational. He should berate deliverymen. He should swear into the telephone. And he should insult his customers. Everything about him should say: "You want New York ambiance, my friend? I got your fucking New York ambiance right here!"

New York Coffee Shop has it all: ambiance, bagels, and a dainty little Reuben too. Unlike the open-faced monstrosities served at Carnegie Deli in New York and Kenny & Ziggy's on Post Oak, both of which are eaten with a knife and fork, you can actually pick up New York Coffee Shop's Reuben and eat it with your hands. The Carnegie Reuben costs $18.95 and consists of twin three-inch-high mounds of corned beef, sauerkraut, and Swiss cheese completely obscuring a couple of slices of rye bread. Two people can't finish it. (They charge $21.95 if you split it.) The Kenny & Ziggy's version is almost exactly half the size and price, but its undersalted corned beef is not nearly as good as the Carnegie's.

New York Coffee Shop puts a nice solid inch of good corned beef, kraut, and Swiss on a griddle-toasted sandwich for $5.85 and calls it a day. I, for one, applaud this common-sense approach to the Reuben. I'm tired of having to choose between throwing away a pound and a half of corned beef or schlepping around a doggie bag that smells like sauerkraut and Swiss all day.

But my favorite New York Coffee Shop lunch is something the menu calls a luncheon plate. Under this heading the restaurant serves a scoop of tuna salad, chicken salad, egg salad, or chopped liver along with tomatoes, onions, and lettuce with a toasted bagel. I had the chopped liver last time, and it was terrific.

On that visit, I was sitting by myself with the aforementioned notebook when Ed Gavrila walked by. "Hey, guy," he said, noticing that I was sitting alone. "Would you like a newspaper to look at?" What a mensch, I thought, as I thanked him for asking. He made his way through the place kissing women on the cheeks and bantering with little kids.

"Ed's the sweetheart and Jay's the tough guy?" I asked the waitress as she refilled my tea.

"Ed's the PR guy and Jay's the businessman," she replied. "Everybody would rather work with Jay. If something breaks, he can fix it. If a customer tries to send back half a hamburger for a refund, Jay says, 'Forget it.' Ed lets customers walk all over him."

Kornhaber is definitely not letting me walk all over him. In fact, he is now threatening me with permanent exile. If I don't tell him what I'm doing with this notebook, I won't be allowed in the restaurant anymore. So that's what he meant when he said I would be very sorry. No more fresh bagels! What a horrible price to pay. I'm getting a little tired of Kornhaber's face in my breakfast by now.

"Who are you to tell me I can't write in a notebook in a restaurant?" I ask him. "Who are you to read my notebook? That's a pretty serious invasion of privacy, don't you think? And how are you going to stop me from looking at your menu when you've got it pasted on the wall?"

"It's my restaurant, and that's how I'm going to stop you," Kornhaber bellows. I am sure he is deeply committed to civil rights, the First Amendment, and other such abstractions under other circumstances—or then again, maybe not.

"So stop me," I challenge him. "Throw me out! Go ahead!" He stands there shaking in fury, but he doesn't do anything. "Look, either throw me out now, or go away and let me eat my eggs in peace," I say.

"I'll see you in the parking lot," he threatens as he stomps off.

I finish my eggs, pay the bill, tip the poor waitress, and go outside. There I square off with the bellicose bagel brawler, but he backs down.

"I'll settle this my own way," he says. "You just go get in your car." He follows me and copies down my license number. Maybe he'll trace my address and I'll find a horse's head in my bed some morning, or my cat in a pot on the stove. You gotta love the guy. How many restaurant owners are this obsessed with what they do? I admire his passion, even if he does act like a putz.

I probably won't be allowed in anymore, but I still highly recommend New York Coffee Shop for great bagels with a little something on them. And if you're in the mood for a side of good old-fashioned Gotham rudeness, just bring along your notebook.

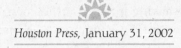

Home of the Squealer

'Bet you a beer the biker is going to get the Squealer. The guy with the Fu Manchu mustache and a blue bandanna on his head is sitting at a table near mine at a roadhouse called Tookie's. He's wearing a Harley-Davidson sweatshirt with the sleeves torn off to showcase his tattoos. His blond girlfriend keeps her sunglasses on as she props her chin up with her hand. Every detail of this man's meticulously selected accoutrements—from his transportation to his choice of companion—is working hard toward a fashion statement. That's why I'm betting he's not going to ruin the whole thing by ordering a fish fillet sandwich.

The Squealer is the hamburger that goes with this look. It exudes attitude. Instead of sporting a pile of bacon that's been fried separately and drained of its grease, this extreme bacon cheeseburger has bacon ground up with the beef. The thick, hand-formed, bacon-slick patty is fried crisp on the griddle, covered with cheese, and served on a bun. The genius of this concept is that the bacon grease bastes the patty while it cooks. The result is a very salty, very greasy, crisp-edged burger that is exceptionally juicy, even when well done.

Tookie's is in Seabrook, a scenic half-hour drive down Texas State Highway 146. All along the route, bayside refineries shimmer in the afternoon sun; the smokestacks stand as straight and tall as palm trees. The aroma of petroleum permeates the air in Pasadena and La Porte. As they say in these parts, "That's the smell of money." Here, in the toxic heart of the oil industry's urban jungle, you forget about alfalfa sprouts and textured tofu. Instead, you long to be a part of all that awe-inspiring machinery and industrial might—and Tookie's Squealer takes you there.

But if you were thinking that this must be the most artery-clogging, cholesterol-elevating, life-threatening hamburger ever devised, you would be wrong. After I got my Squealer, five people sat down at the table beside mine, and one of them ordered a double Squealer. This sent me back to the menu with a furrowed brow. And there I found it: officially known as the Piggyback, this is the double-patty version of the Squealer; it takes the original's excess and squares it. When it was delivered, I admired the double-decker burger with some amazement. It seemed as tall as a cracking tower, and it was dripping grease down both sides. It's a good thing I didn't see it on the menu.

After a solid month of eating healthy, I was craving a wicked overdose of greasy meat—"moderation in all things, including moderation," as the saying goes. But I offset my cholesterol fix by ordering the Squealer "with everything," which includes a healthy portion of lettuce and tomatoes. I got the famous onion rings too. And onion rings are a vegetable; ask any vegan.

There's a large painting of a pixielike, middle-aged woman in a purple dress behind the cash register. They tell me that this is Miss Tookie, the founder of the place. She used to come in early every morning to make the onion rings by hand. Frankly, I'm not all that impressed with the rings. They're kind of chewy, and the batter falls off too easily. But the people at the next table are really in a huff about them. Actually, it's not the rings they're making a scene about; it's the lack of ranch dressing.

"We don't serve salad, so we don't have any dressings," the waitress tries to explain, but the customers don't accept her excuse. Ranch dressing has nothing to do with salad in Texas. Several Texas chefs have told me they've been astonished by the rise in requests for ranch dressing in their restaurants in the last ten years. It's now used as a dip and a sauce more often than as a salad topping. (In West Texas, some restaurant patrons seem to regard it as a beverage.) I suspect it long ago surpassed ketchup and salsa as the number-one condiment in the state. For a major segment of the dining public, onion rings without ranch dressing are unthinkable—so are pizza, biscuits, and canned peaches. They ask the waitress for it again every time she checks on them. "Why don't you go down to the convenience store and buy a bottle?" she finally chides.

The waitresses at Tookie's are no shrinking violets. This one wears dirty blue jeans, a green Tookie's T-shirt, and sneakers. She got straight to the point when I asked her which burger she recommended. "The Champion burger is our biggest seller," she said. "The meat is marinated with Chablis wine and mixed with cheddar cheese and onions. The Squealer is made with bacon. Get the Squealer," she advised. The burger choices also include a bean burger, a barbecue burger, and a chili cheeseburger, along with a pepper-infused burger called Stomp's Ice House Special, which carries the disclaimer "very hot."

I wonder if there really was a Stomp's Ice House around here somewhere and what happened to it. If it once existed, odds are there's some memorabilia from the place hanging in the rafters at Tookie's. The ramshackle premises are decorated with loads of cast-off junk. From my table I can see a pair of hockey skates, several old traffic signals, a Shell station sign, and the feet of a mannequin wearing white high heels and red stockings.

As I get up to leave, the biker's burger is delivered. It's a double Squealer. I'm only half right. So you can buy me half a beer.

My second visit to Tookie's is at night. I'm expecting a Hell's Angels convention, but oddly the place has been transformed into a family hangout. Small children scamper back and forth between their parents' tables and the bathrooms. Moony high school kids on dates occupy several other tables.

I consider the double Squealer for a minute, but then decide to sample another extreme and order the "very hot" burger. The young waitress has trouble discerning the difference between Miller and Miller Lite, but several minutes of remedial menu-reading finally gets me a cold draft in an icy mug. This frosted fire extinguisher proves crucial to the enjoyment of the food.

According to the menu, the Stomp's Ice House Special features "beef topped with Pace picante sauce, chopped jalapeño peppers, and chopped grilled onions with mayonnaise, lettuce, and sliced tomatoes." All of those ingredients are indeed present when the burger arrives. But how many of them will make it into your mouth is something of a crapshoot. A sloppy avalanche slides off the sandwich and onto the plate every time you take a bite. They give you a fork in case you want to eat the excess hot sauce and jalapeños that way.

The heat level isn't excessive for the average Texan. But the jalapeños do add a little fire, and beer is necessary for keeping occasional flare-ups from getting out of hand. But all in all the hot sauce burger isn't nearly as exciting as the Squealer.

It's the ratio of wet stuff to ground meat on this bun that leads me to ponder the logic of Tookie's burger creations. Clearly, what they're doing is coming up with ways to keep well-done hamburger meat tasting moist. And for that they deserve our undying gratitude. Ever since the Jack in the Box hamburger scandal of 1993 and the subsequent changes in FDA cooking temperatures, the liability department of the food service industry has insisted that we eat our ground meat well done. For those of us who like it juicy and medium rare, this change in the American institution of the hamburger has led to a lot of disappointment.

I have always attempted to get around the rules by cooking my own rare burgers at home or begging some patty flipper to take a walk on the wild side. But Tookie's has come up with several innovative ways to raise the moisture level of the sandwich while working within the confines of the new restaurant reality: mixing the ground meat with bacon, marinating the beef with wine and then combining it with cheese, topping the patty with lubricants like beans or hot sauce.

We've come to expect this kind of clever culinary engineering down here in the land of a thousand refineries. After all, this is where used oil pipe was first transformed into that icon of Texas barbecue, the double-chambered steel smoker pit on wheels. So when the modern-day burger is hampered by a soluble grease diffusion problem, it should come as no surprise that Texas oil field ingenuity shines through once again. In Tookie's Squealer, they've got a gusher.

When Jeffrey
Met Thelma

The brisket at Thelma's Bar-B-Que on Live Oak has a tasty black char on the top, but the inside is slick with juice and as tender as the white bread. How Thelma gets it so soft is a head scratcher. She swears she doesn't wrap it in foil. She says she just starts an oak-log fire around 5 P.M., and then lets the meat smoke until the next morning. The buttery brisket comes anointed with dark-brown sauce, and if you order "in and out," you get plenty of black outside pieces along with the inside cuts.

It's not the kind of fanned array of picture-perfect brisket slices that wins barbecue cook-offs. This is a hot and greasy, falling-apart mess o' meat, East Texas style. The first time I tried it, Thelma's barbecue brisket ate better than any I've ever had in the city. That's why I brought Jeffrey Steingarten, the famous *Vogue* food writer and author of *The Man Who Ate Everything*, here for lunch today.

The restaurant is in a little red house just east of the George R. Brown Convention Center in a crusty Third Ward neighborhood composed primarily of littered lots and windowless warehouses. You have to pass through a screened-in porch housing a dilapidated mustard-colored vinyl sofa and a pile of broken chairs before you reach the entrance proper.

Inside the house, there's a cozy little dining room with twelve mismatched tables, a jukebox loaded with blues, Motown, and zydeco discs, and a television that's usually tuned to a soap opera. At dinnertime, the place is practically empty, and the brisket, while still good, isn't as moist as it is early in the day. That's to be expected. As any serious 'cue hound knows, great barbecue joints have peak hours, and Thelma's peaks at noon. Her lunch crowd includes policemen in uniform, truck drivers taking a break, some folks from Thelma's church, and occasionally a couple of barbecue fanatics like us.

Steingarten asks to see the pit and quizzes the proprietor about her methods and cooking times. Thelma fields all questions graciously and takes us around back to see her fabulous little smoker. It's got a firebox outside and a weighted door that opens into the kitchen. In its last incarnation, the building was a bar with a couple of pool tables, but the place obviously started out as a barbecue joint. Judging by the design of the pit, which is nearly identical to the one at Green's on Almeda, I'd guess it was built in the 1950s.

Back at our table, Thelma whips out her pad and we put in our orders. Steingarten attempts to skip the two sides that normally come with a two-meat plate, but Thelma will have none of that nonsense. He settles on potato salad and coleslaw with his brisket and ribs.

"Take off your jacket, honey. Make yourself comfortable," Thelma chides the New Yorker. It's a steamy June afternoon, and Steingarten has arrived from the airport wearing a blue blazer and jeans.

The Harvard Law School graduate and onetime Manhattan legal consultant is known for bringing a rigorous scientific skepticism to food writing. The ultimate in tough customers, he bases his research more on verifiable data than anecdotal opinions. (In this month's Vogue, he sends away to an industrial dairy lab for a vial of butyric acid in order to critique the aroma of butter.) At the moment, he is studying Texas barbecue. And as a regular judge at "Memphis in May," the nation's largest barbecue cook-off, he isn't as clueless about 'cue as your average New Yorker.

Steingarten, along with some seventy-five other food writers and scholars from around the country, is on his way to Central Texas for a barbecue field trip organized by the Southern Foodways Alliance (SFA). I invited him to come down a little early and sample East Texas–style barbecue in Houston before the Central Texas tour got started. Thelma's is our first stop.

Thelma Williams, fifty-two, grew up Creole in rural Louisiana. She never worked in a restaurant before this one; she got her cooking experience doing church dinners at Good Shepherd Baptist on North Wayside. "I just love to feed people," she says. Her father catered parties for a living while she was growing up. "I learned how to barbecue from my daddy," she explains. Thelma's friends and family convinced her to open this restaurant three years ago. But despite the excellent food, her business hasn't really taken off.

Thelma brings me a huge stack of fried catfish fillets. Steingarten was mystified when I ordered fish for lunch, and ordinarily I would consider it pretty strange behavior at a barbecue joint, too. But I'm acting as a guide on one of the tour buses tomorrow, and we're scheduled to visit five barbecue joints in just a few hours. Besides, Thelma's fried catfish may be even more heavenly than her brisket. It's fried to order and served cornmealed and crispy on the outside and piping hot and mild inside. No fork is required; the fillets are rigid so you can pick them up and eat them like candy.

Thelma returns and sets some barbecue down in front of the skeptical gastronome. After a few bites, the movement of his eyebrows indicates that he is having an epiphany. I try to steal a piece of beef off his plate to see what sort of jubilee is taking place in his mouth, but he nearly stabs me with the plastic fork.

Finally, he passes me a little bite. I smile from ear to ear as I chew it: Thelma is having a good day.

The ribs on the two-meat plate are also excellent, but you can get good ribs in many parts of the country. Thelma's wet and winsome extra-smoky brisket is something else altogether.

"This gives me a new perspective on brisket," Steingarten says reverently, still clad in his blazer and regarding the shrinking pile of beef with something approaching awe. "Now I see what people in Texas have been talking about for all these years. I've had only forty or fifty briskets in my entire lifetime, but Thelma's is on an entirely different level." He is also impressed with the crisp, greaseless catfish, and he takes an instant liking to mashed potato salad, which he has never eaten before.

After a quick sampling of the barbecue here, I figured we would visit several other Houston restaurants. But as much as I try to hurry Steingarten up, he won't budge. Evidently, once the New Yorker has empirically ascertained that a given foodstuff is of exceptional quality, he unleashes a wild man's appetite. He grunts contentedly as he eats, and I sit back to watch the soap opera. Might as well relax—nothing is going to separate him from that Styrofoam plate heaped high with Thelma's brisket.

On SFA's Central Texas barbecue tour, Steingarten will see all the celebrated places: the meat markets that appear in the barbecue guides, the smoky temples from the magazine stories, and the quirky haunts that make Jane and Michael Stern's books. But Thelma's supplies a heartwarming illustration of the true beauty of Texas barbecue: in the Lone Star State, you might find the best smoked meat you've ever tasted under a shade tree by the side of the road, at a Baptist church supper, or in a ramshackle little joint nobody has ever heard of smack-dab in the middle of the city.

The Things We Still Carry

The lunch patrons today at Cuisine de L' Orient (Thien Kim) are all Vietnamese or Vietnamese Americans, and every occupied table has a family-style soup bowl called a hot pot on it. I take a table by the window and ask the waiter which hot pot he recommends. He suggests I order the hot-and-sour fish soup. He also favors the hot rice rolls over the cold spring rolls, so I give them a try, too.

The little two-bite rolls, six to an order, are made of sticky rice noodle dough steamed with a filling inside. They're served hot, with cold chopped lettuce, cucumber, and crispy fried onions on top. They come with a bright red dipping sauce, which seems to contain rice vinegar, chile oil, and enough crushed peppers to widen your eyes.

The sign on the corner says "Travis" and, just below that, "*Tu Do,*" the Vietnamese name of the street. In this section of Houston's Midtown, all of the signs are written in Vietnamese and English. I guess there's some kind of festival going on because the streets are decorated with yellow flags with red stripes. I ask the waitress whose flag that is. It's the flag of the former democratic republic of South Vietnam, she says.

The soup is hot and sour, but it's sweet too. I can see that the heat comes from slices of jalapeño; I imagine the sour comes from rice wine vinegar. But I can't quite figure out where the sweetness comes from. After munching on the big pieces of cat-fish, celery slices, and tender whole okra pods that float in the spicy fish broth, I finally bite into a pineapple cube. That ex-plains the source of the mysterious sweetness.

There are a lot of small white bits in the bottom of the bowl, too. I figure it's crushed rice, a popular Vietnamese ingredient.

"You don't like rice?" a waitress named Vickie Huynh asks as she refills my water glass, staring at the partially eaten bowl of rice on my table.

"Sure," I answer, perplexed. "But there's some rice in the soup already."

"No, there isn't. You have to put it in yourself," she says.

"So what's this?" I ask, fishing some of the little white squares out of the soup with my spoon.

"That's garlic!" she laughs. "It's cut into little pieces and fried like that."

I am dumbfounded. There must be three tablespoons of garlic in this bowl. I eat some more. It tastes nutty. The garlic's natural flavor is tempered by frying, I guess, just as it is by roasting.

"Do they use catfish and okra in the fish soup in Vietnam?" I ask Vickie. The ingredients sound Southern to me.

Vickie explains that they have okra in Vietnam, but that cooks there use *dau* or *bong lau* instead of catfish, and a stalky vegetable like *bacha* instead of celery. They would also use smaller, hotter peppers instead of jalapeños.

The nutty garlic, hot jalapeño, sweet pineapple, unboned catfish, and whole okra combine in an unusual way. The Hous-ton version of hot-and-sour fish soup may not taste exactly like the kind in Vietnam, but it has its own appeal. I sheepishly add some rice to mine, which rounds out the flavor.

This is the second day in a row I've eaten lunch at Thien Kim. I had the escargot vermicelli soup yesterday. The chewy snails were so tough, they reminded me of the rubber tires I used to pull off toy trucks and pop in my mouth when I was a kid. Remember that squeaky sound rubber toys made when you bit them? And the sour grimy taste? That was it exactly. Luckily, the soup had a lot of shrimp and nice slices of pork in it, too.

The waiter tried to talk me out of the escargots. "They're an acquired taste," he said, wincing. I took that to mean he wouldn't eat them. To me, the dish sounded like another one of those fabulous French-Vietnamese fusion concoctions, like the Vietnamese baguette sandwiches. So I had to at least try it. The waiter-manager was a college student named John Ngynh. He was sitting with some friends. I imagine they got a kick out of watching me eat the squeaky snails. But that wasn't half as funny as the scene itself.

It was three o'clock in the afternoon, and the only other people in the restaurant were Ngynh and his three Vietnamese American college chums, who were playing cards and eating a Papa John's pizza. I thought it was really hilarious—for a while. The white guy eating Vietnamese food, the Vietnamese American kids eating pizza.

"It does seem kind of ironic now that you mention it," Ngynh said with a smile when I pointed out our respective lunches. "But we get sick of eating Asian food every day—and everybody eats pizza."

Right then, on the oldies station that served as our dining music, Elton John started singing "Goodbye Yellow Brick Road," and the paradox of the situation struck me. The song took me back to my college years and the war in Vietnam. I was the same age as these Vietnamese American kids are now.

My fortune cookie said, "A good laugh and a good cry both cleanse the mind."

Former U.S. senator Bob Kerrey's agonies brought back memories for all of us. Getting teargassed by the police during street protests was about the extent of my combat experience. My father, who fought with the Marines in Korea, thought I was a coward for protesting. I ducked out with a student deferment, and I'm glad I avoided the war. But I have a deep sense of guilt and shame about it, and a feeling of betrayal toward those who fought and died there.

Two summers ago I took my kids to Washington, DC, for a visit. While we were wandering around the Mall, we came upon the Vietnam Veterans Memorial and stopped in for a look. When I walked up to the black wall covered with names, tears started flowing down my cheeks. "Why are you crying, Daddy?" my daughters asked.

"I don't know," I answered truthfully.

In response to the Bob Kerrey flap, the media have been airing the squawkings of the same old Vietnam-era hawks and doves. We've heard these pat answers and easy morals before. And they are as wrong now as they were then.

In Houston, there is a group whose opinions about the war I am much more interested in: the Vietnamese American college students. Which is why I have come back to Thien Kim for lunch today.

Houston has one of the largest Vietnamese communities in the country; current estimates run as high as 46,000 people. The immigrants began arriving after the fall of Saigon in 1975. Some were elite government and business leaders; some, refugees. The college kids hanging around Thien Kim are their children.

There are six students sitting at a round table, five males and one female. Several are members of the Vietnamese International Students Association at the University of Houston (UH). I really want to ask them a question, so I walk to their table and introduce myself.

I explain that thirty years ago, when I was their age, I was asked to go to Vietnam to fight for their country. And I ask them, "If war broke out in Vietnam tomorrow, and it looked like there was a good chance of overthrowing the communist government, would you go fight?"

"No way," they all agree.

"Why not?" I ask. "It's your country."

"It would be brother fighting brother," one student explains.

"Hopefully we've learned something from history," says Andy Chau, a twenty-four-year-old UH student. "Wars don't solve anything."

For these students, who grew up while the communist regimes in the Soviet Union and Eastern Europe were falling, the war in Vietnam must seem anachronistic. Chau's history lesson is direct: governments fail only when people refuse to put up with them anymore. War can't bring that kind of change; it can only cause suffering and death.

The students tell me that the South Vietnamese flags on Travis were put out on April 30, the twenty-sixth anniversary of the fall of Saigon. With the rallies and flags, some members of the local Vietnamese community are trying to keep the memory of a free homeland alive, much like the anti-Castro activists in Miami. But the kids don't seem sympathetic toward the pro-democracy forces. They are pragmatists.

"Vietnam will be communist as long as China is communist," one student bluntly informs me.

"Our student group tries to aid the Vietnamese people directly without getting involved in politics," Chau says. For instance, when floods devastated Vietnam recently, the students raised $26,000 among the local Vietnamese and channeled the money into the waterlogged country through religious groups. "Let the U.S. government deal with the Vietnamese government, and we'll just deal with the people."

"Did the United States do any good in Vietnam?" I ask them.

"No, I think the U.S. was there to pursue its own political interests," says twenty-five-year-old Lucia Tran.

I wonder how their opinions as Vietnamese Americans would differ from those of their purely Vietnamese parents. Like the traditional hot-and-sour fish soup with the Southern catfish and Texas jalapeños in it, Vietnamese culture has undergone an Americanization in Houston. The second generation is proud of their Vietnamese identity, but they are also recognizably American.

But these young people would be inheriting the leadership of South Vietnam if they still lived there. And in the end, their opinion on the war is the one that matters most to me. As I go back to my table to pay my bill and pack up my leftovers, I feel a sense of relief. My fortune cookie says, "Wisdom has kept you far from dangers."

Having one of the largest Vietnamese communities in the nation has added immeasurably to the Houston dining scene. The Vietnamese restaurants here are so good, they make similar eateries in New York and Chicago look laughable. But beyond the exquisite food, these restaurants provide Houstonians with a unique window on Southeast Asian culture. I like the hot pots and the rice rolls at Thien Kim, but it was the fresh perspective on political realities in Southeast Asia that impressed me most.

Part SIX

You Are What You Eat

American Way, November 1, 1996

A Tale of Two Knishes

The television was tuned to WMNB, the twenty-four-hour Russian channel. The news from Moscow had everybody's attention as I took a seat at Cafe Espresso on Brighton Beach Boulevard. The waitress came over and gave me a menu. She was from Odessa, a seaport resort in Ukraine. I asked her for an order of blintzes and a glass of Russian-style tea.

"Meat or cheese?" she asked. I had never heard of a meat blintz, so I ordered one of each. A blintz is a crepe wrapped around a filling and fried. They are usually served with sour cream. The meat filling turned out to be ground chicken. Both the meat and the cheese blintzes were hot, crispy, and delicious.

I'd heard a lot of stories about Brighton Beach, a neighborhood of Russian immigrants out at the end of the "Q" subway line in Brooklyn, so I set aside a day to explore the area on this trip to New York. My grandmother came to this country from Ruthenia, an area in the Carpathian mountains near Ukraine. I grew up eating Russian-style foods, and I thought this might be a good place to get a nostalgia fix. I was right. But I had no idea what an ethnic education I was in for.

After my blintzes, I stopped for coffee at the Brighton Beach Coffee Shop. I asked my waitress, a wisecracking little lady named Shirley, which Russian restaurants she recommended. "I've never eaten in a Russian restaurant," she said. "I'm Jewish."

"But don't they serve the same food?" I asked her. "Blintzes, knishes, borscht?"

"You want a blintz, you should go to the Brighton Beach Dairy Restaurant right across the street," said a guy buying coffee at the counter.

"What's the difference between a Russian blintz and a Jewish blintz?" I wanted to know.

"A Jewish blintz is kosher," he said.

This didn't quite satisfy, so I walked across the street to see for myself. The Brighton Beach Dairy Restaurant, at 410 Brighton Beach Boulevard, is one of the last of New York's kosher dairy restaurants. There I dug into another order of cheese blintzes with another side of sour cream. If there was a difference between Russian cheese blintzes and kosher cheese blintzes, it was lost on me.

When I got up to leave, owner Mayer Brandwein, a handsome wiry guy with a sporty yarmulke, stopped me. "How come you didn't finish your blintzes?" he wanted to know. I confessed that I had already eaten an order of blintzes at the Russian restaurant and told him I was just trying to figure out the difference.

"Ah," Mayer said with a smile. "A Russian blintz is a completely different ballgame."

"How so?" I asked in complete confusion.

"They put all kinds of things in their blintzes," he said. I was beginning to suspect some sort of prejudice, but as Mayer began to explain the differences between Jewish food and Russian food, I suddenly remembered an incident that made the whole thing clear.

Many years ago, when I was first married, I made Ruthenian-style stuffed cabbage for my Jewish wife. She too had been raised on stuffed cabbage. How wonderful that we have this childhood food in common, I thought. But she took only a few bites before pushing away my stuffed cabbage. "What's wrong?" I wanted to know.

"You put sauerkraut in it!" she said with disgust. Of course I put sauerkraut in it. So did my mother and my grandmother and all of my relatives. What would stuffed cabbage be without a little sauerkraut?

The following week, my new wife made me a pot of stuffed cabbage following her grandmother's recipe. It was awful. "What in the world are raisins doing in the stuffed cabbage?" I wanted to know. There was brown sugar in the tomato sauce, too. Sweet and sour stuffed cabbage? Blech. If I had never eaten stuffed cabbage, I would have loved her version. But I knew stuffed cabbage, and this wasn't it.

Comfort food is a funny thing. Eating a dish like Mom used to make may bring on childhood reveries, but when the dish doesn't taste a thing like you remember it, it brings on a completely opposite reaction. It is revolting. It is just plain wrong. If my ex-wife's favorite food had been sushi or tacos or anything else in the world, I would have embraced it. But stuffed cabbage with raisins instead of sauerkraut? Impossible. (Stuffed cabbage was not the only issue in our divorce.)

Being raised in a Slavic household, I thought I knew what this kind of food should taste like. But Brighton Beach was a rude awakening. A kindly Ukrainian man in the coffee shop had explained to me that Russia is a very big place.

"When we say Russia here, we mean Big Russia," he said, explaining that included all the provinces of the former Soviet Union. So the "Russian" food I came to sample in Brighton Beach turned out be food from everywhere from Arctic Siberia to Moslem Uzbekistan.

And, of course, what I called Jewish food was really Russian food too. Before the Russians began to arrive after the fall of the Soviet Union, Brighton Beach was a Jewish neighborhood. And a large percentage of the Jews in Brighton Beach, as in the rest of New York, were Russian Jews.

The foods I had always associated with Jewish cooking, like latkes, blintzes, knishes, and borscht, were actually kosher versions of Russian dishes. Nowadays on Brighton Beach Avenue, you see kosher food side by side with Russian food. And it isn't always easy to tell them apart. In some cases, such as cheese blintzes, the differences are negligible. But in other cases, they are worlds apart.

"I'll show you the difference. This is a Jewish knish," Mayer said, presenting me with a cheese and blueberry version of his famous baked pastry. It was crumbly and dry, like cheesecake with a firm crust. It was also absolutely delicious. "Now go across the street and get a Russian knish," he said.

So I went across the street and bought a knish from the sidewalk vendor in front of the M&I International Foods Store. Mayer was right: the two knishes had nothing in common. The Russian version looked and tasted like a jelly doughnut, except that it was filled with your choice of meat, cabbage, or potatoes. It was tasty, but it bore no resemblance to the square-cut baked knishes at the Dairy Restaurant.

I thought I'd take a look inside the M&I International Foods Store to see what else they sold. My eyes widened and my stomach growled as I took in the universe of Russian food. There were foods I recognized from my childhood: pastries filled with sweetened poppy seeds, coarse breads, and vats of fresh sauerkraut. And there were familiar Jewish deli items, like smoked salmon and whitefish, buckwheat kasha, half-sour pickles, and pickled tomatoes.

And then there were Russians foods that I had never heard of, shelves upon shelves of them. There were sausages of all shapes and sizes (I lost count after thirty). There were stuffed eggplants, stuffed lettuce leaves, and stuffed red peppers. There were piles of latkes, the potato pancakes served at Hanukkah with sour cream and applesauce, only here they were served with pork sausages. And there were piles of different farmer's cheeses.

Still amazed, I walked into Gastronome Jubilee, another Russian food store a few doors down on Brighton Beach Avenue. There I found a long counter of prepared Russian foods that people were buying for lunch: cabbage salads and chopped mushroom spreads and a multilayered, colorful herring salad with striations of dark chopped herring, white chopped potatoes, purple chopped beets, and a topping of chopped eggs.

There were giant sausages called kishkes that were stuffed with a flour and chicken filling. And I came across something that warmed my heart. It was a whole pile of steaming stuffed cabbage. A little old lady with white hair and broad Slavic cheekbones who reminded me of my grandmother was buying two for lunch. She smiled at me as I sidled up beside her.

"*Holupkis,*" I said, using the Slavic word my grandmother had taught me for stuffed cabbage.

The lady clutched her stuffed cabbages and looked at me strangely. "*Golumpshis,*" she corrected me in yet another Slavic dialect. I sighed as I headed for the door. There were probably dozens of varieties of stuffed cabbage in Russia, I realized, and each region probably had its own name for them. I had a lot to learn about Russian food.

I went back to tell Mayer Brandwein about the Russian knishes. And after talking to him awhile, I realized how much respect the Jewish community in Brighton Beach had for the newly arrived Russians.

"They come here with nothing but the shirts on their backs, just like our great-grandparents did," he said. "I gave one Russian guy a job here at my restaurant a few years ago. Now he owns his own restaurant over on the boardwalk."

If I was intolerant of sweet-and-sour stuffed cabbage, I can only imagine the culture shock the Jews of Brighton Beach must have felt when they first encountered Russian knishes and chicken blintzes. I asked a few people at the Dairy Restaurant how they felt about the Russian invasion.

"There was a little animosity at first," a customer admitted. "But you know, twenty years ago, this neighborhood was dying. And look at it now. You can walk down Brighton Beach Avenue at one o'clock in the morning and feel safe. The Russians saved Brighton Beach."

Mayer Brandwein suggested a few outstanding restaurants, and I spent the rest of the afternoon and evening sampling different kinds of Russian food. I walked around with a new appreciation of the lively scene on the avenue. Many of the shopkeepers had run colored pennants from their stores to the elevated train tracks above. Families were strolling down the street and stopping to greet their friends. Street vendors were selling Russian tapes and CDs, Russian videos, and of course, Russian knishes.

If there's anything I learned about Russian food, it's that Mother Russia supplied each of her dozens of ethnicities with its own individual tastes. One man's knish is another man's dough-nut. And though I hate to admit it, there is no right way to make stuffed cabbage.

Grandma's Stuffed Cabbage with Sauerkraut

1 cup rice
1 cup boiling water
1 teaspoon salt
1 large head cabbage
1 medium onion
4 tablespoons fat or cooking oil
1 pound ground beef (or 1/2 pound ground beef
    and 1/2 pound ground pork)
1 egg
Salt and pepper

1 10-ounce can sauerkraut
1 large can tomato juice
Vinegar to taste

Combine the rice, water, and salt in a pan and bring to a boil. Cook for 1 minute. Cover, turn off the heat, and allow to sit until the water is absorbed.

Cut the core out of the cabbage and submerge in a pot of boiling water. Turn the heat off and allow the cabbage to soak.

Cook the onion in the fat until tender. Combine the onion and fat with the meat, rice, and egg. Add salt and pepper to taste.

Remove the cabbage from the pot and gently peel off the soft outer leaves. If the inner leaves are still hard, return the cabbage to the hot water for a while.

When all the large cabbage leaves have been removed, cut up the remaining cabbage core and put it in the bottom of a large pot.

Place a generous dollop of the meat and rice filling in the middle of each softened cabbage leaf and gently roll it up. Layer the cabbage rolls in the pot, and top each layer with sauerkraut. Pour tomato juice over the rolls until they are barely visible. Add a dash of vinegar. Cook in the oven at 350 degrees or simmer on top of the stove for 1-1/2 to 2 hours or until the filling is well cooked. Serve hot.

My Ex-Wife's Stuffed Cabbage with Raisins

Omit the sauerkraut and vinegar. Add 1/2 cup brown sugar, 1 cup raisins, and a dash of lemon juice to the tomato juice.

Chile Duel

It started innocently enough one night in Oaxaca when I tried to explain to a Zapotec named Laurentino Mendez why I was there. I was doing some research on *canario* peppers because Jean Andrews, the chile expert, thought they might be the hottest peppers in North America.

Laurentino thought I was an idiot. He was born in the mountains south of Oaxaca, and the concept of gringo chile experts struck him as nothing short of ludicrous. The next day in Etla, a nearby Indian village, Laurentino picked up a leaf filled with wild *chile pequínes* in the market and said to me, "This is the hottest pepper in the Oaxaca valley."

I looked at him dubiously, "Those are *chile pequínes*," I protested. "I grow those in my backyard in Texas." It didn't take long for Laurentino and me to get into an "Oh, yeah?" contest.

Push came to shove later that evening. Laurentino poured the *chile pequínes* he had bought at the market into a little bowl, set it down on the table between us, and ate one in a silent challenge. I ate one, too. Then he ate another.

We sat down face to face and had a chile duel. We held the leftover stems up in one hand and ate the peppers with the other, adding another stem to the tally each time. When we had both eaten ten of the little devils, I asked Laurentino if he was ready for some really hot peppers.

We dispensed with the *canarios* quickly. Jean Andrews must have gotten a hotter batch than this one. They were not much zestier than the *chile pequínes,* so we moved on to the really hot stuff. If Laurentino believed that the *chile pequíne* was the hottest pepper in the Oaxaca valley before our face-off, I am confident I changed his mind. It was a long, pointy chile of small to medium size called a *paradito* that set the heat record that night. Laurentino and I each ate a whole one, seeds and all.

At first, we both agreed there was nothing special about these chiles, and then, over the course of two or three minutes, we changed our minds. The burn got more and more unbearable. Soon we were both out of our seats and pacing the floors. For the next thirty minutes, we endured our own personal visions of chile hell. Laurentino won the machismo battle for appearing unaffected—mainly because fat gringos sweat profusely.

My hair was drenched as perspiration poured off of my head and face. We both held our mouths open, tongues out, panting to cool the fire. Suddenly I understood why the Mayans used the word *xnipec,* or "dog breathing," to describe the effect of fiery foods.

Laurentino and I declared a truce after that pepper. I may have lost the macho contest, but I had won Laurentino's respect. "I never met a gringo who could really eat chiles," he admitted. It was perhaps the greatest tribute I have ever been paid. Our chile contest served as a sort of Zapotec initiation rite and opened the door to a world I had never glimpsed before.

I had come to Mexico to learn about chiles and their cultural underpinnings. It seemed an amusing way to learn about food; I wasn't prepared for the tragic side of the story. Laurentino broke out his homemade mescal, which we drank long into the night

as he told me about his life—and in the process, revealed Mexico's cultural schizophrenia.

Laurentino showed me a snapshot of his ninety-eight-year-
old grandmother tilling her tiny cornfield in the ancient way
with a planting stick. Other shots showed the dirt roads and
breathtaking beauty of his isolated family village. This was
where Laurentino was raised, a place where the voyages of
Columbus, the Spanish Conquest, and Mexico's modern history
had made little impact on anybody's life. Spanish is a foreign
language there. Everyone speaks Zapotec.

When Laurentino was six, his father was killed by a rival in a
Zapotec blood feud. His mother fled to Los Angeles to earn
enough money to support her family. She sent Laurentino and
his brothers and sisters to live with relatives.

In Mexico City, Laurentino said, he learned what it felt like
to be a "nigger." Fresh from bucolic mountain life, he was suddenly confronted with the urban nightmare of Mexico City and
the scorn Spanish-speaking kids heap on the *pinche indios*, the
"goddamn Indians."

At the age of sixteen he ran away from his relatives and went
to find his mother in Los Angeles. There he learned English, his
third language, and completed an education. In Mexico, education is seldom wasted on orphan Indian kids. But in the United
States, we grudgingly provide an education even to the children
of illegal aliens. There are people who think this is a waste of
taxpayers' money. I wish I could introduce these people to Laurentino.

Today Laurentino has a degree from California State and a
job that no one in his right mind would take. He teaches junior
high in the worst section of downtown L.A. His students are
Hispanic gang members—"net heads," Laurentino calls them
because of their hair nets. The other teachers live in constant
fear of gang violence.

Laurentino just smiles. After a life like his, gang violence seems like child's play. I'm not afraid of Crips and Bloods, he tells his rougher students, because I am a Zapotec, and we're the oldest, biggest, meanest-assed gang on the continent.

Laurentino is also a hell of a good cook. During our days in Oaxaca, he taught me a few Zapotec recipes for chile rellenos, *chilequiles,* and a few other old chile tricks. He also gave me a completely different perspective on the "mestizo" myth of Mexican culture. According to the official propaganda, mestizo culture is a blend of the European and Indian cultures. But from the Indian point of view, there is no such thing as "mestizo" culture. There are Indians, and there are Westerners. There is no middle ground.

Laurentino's ideas and *Conversations with Montezuma,* a book by Dick J. Reavis, explain a lot about Mexico's cultural conflicts. Understanding the country's schizoid personality is the first step to appreciating the strange situation of Mexican cuisine. These are issues you won't find in a cookbook.

"Mexico's staple crop has always been corn, a plant unknown in the Old World at the time of the Conquest," writes Reavis. "Europe's staple, on the other hand, has always been wheat, a plant formerly unknown in the New World. The influence that agriculture exerts on culture is invisible to modern, urban American eyes, and is one of those subjects that need volumes to explain. But because corn is the staple of Mexico, anthropologists contend that Mexico cannot form a part of Western civilization."

Though the local elite likes to call Mexico a mestizo mix of the European and the indigenous, Reavis and Laurentino convinced me that in fact, Mexican culture is not Hispanic at all. "Spain was conquered and ruled by the Arabs for four hundred years. Do we regard it as an Arab nation?" asks Reavis. In spite of the Europeanized elite's suppression of the native culture and in spite of all attempts to modernize Mexico, the indigenous "corn culture" still prevails. But unfortunately, the culture of the people is not the culture of the ruling elite.

Chile peppers are almost entirely absent from the best restaurants of Mexico City. Among the Europeanized elite, chile peppers are considered crude and primitive remnants of the Indian order of things.

That's why we have learned what we know about chile peppers from non-Mexicans like Diana Kennedy and Mark Miller. That's why chile pepper experts are often from the United States. And that's why we need to engage in a form of culinary anthropology to learn about Mexican food. The ancient and largely unpublished recipes of the Zapotecs, the Mayans, and the other Indian peoples represent Mexico's real culinary culture. And that culture is rapidly disappearing.

Salsa Xnipec ("Dog-Breathing Salsa")

This is one of the hottest salsas on the planet.

    4 diced habanero chiles, stems and seeds removed
    Juice of 4 limes
    1 diced onion, red or purple preferred
    1 diced tomato

Soak the diced onion in the lime juice for at least 30 minutes. Add all the other ingredients and mix. Salt to taste and add a little water if desired.

Bread of the Dead

Francisco Marquez and I are sitting at the farmhouse table, drinking hot chocolate and eating sweet *pan de muerto,* the bread of the dead. It is the morning of November First, Día de los Muertos, the Day of the Dead. As we talk, just beyond the dining room's open-air doorway, three baby turkeys peck at the bare dirt in the courtyard. Several radios are playing in other parts of the village, and boys are yelling down by the river. But by far the loudest sound is the frantic mooing of cattle. "They want to eat too," Francisco chuckles.

His wife, Margarita, shows me the kitchen. It is in a shed made of sticks fastened together vertically, so the light on the dirt floor is striped. *Mole negro,* the deep black sauce which is traditional on Día de los Muertos, is cooking in a *cazuela,* a clay pot that sits directly in the coals of the wood fire. Two dead chickens are lying on the dirt floor waiting to be plucked. "Chickens to eat with the *mole,*" Margarita explains. In the poorest houses, the *mole negro* is eaten in a bowl like a soup. To have chicken with the *mole* is a luxury.

In bags throughout the house, there are many more loaves of *pan de muerto.* I ask how many loaves of bread the family bought. The week before Día de los Muertos, she says, it is the custom for the family to buy a ten-kilo sack of flour and take it to the baker along with five dozen eggs and the other ingredients needed for the sweet egg bread. Most families also bring along the papier-mâché decorations that are inserted into each loaf. The papier-mâché ovals have little faces painted on them; when the *pan de muerto* is finished, each loaf of bread represents an individual soul. The baker prepares the family's entire order of *pan de muerto* at one time. The ten-pound sack of flour yielded 130 loaves this year, including the tiny loaves for the *angelitos*.

"The *angelitos* are here now," says Francisco, as he shows me the family *ofrenda*, which dominates an entire wall of the living room. There are tiny cups of hot chocolate and little loaves of bread on the altar. *Angelitos* are the souls of dead infants, including the souls of miscarried and stillborn children.

"Has your family lost many children?" I ask.

"No, not so many," he says. "But that's not important. Some of the spirits don't have families to go to, so we have to put out food and drinks for all of them."

The *ofrenda* is the center of the Day of the Dead celebration. It is an altar that is generally built of three tiers, each smaller than the one beneath it, like a pyramid. The tiers are covered in cloth, and an arch of sugar cane stalks is formed above the altar. It is decorated with the marigold-like flower known as *zempoalxochitl* ("flower of the dead" in the Nahuatl language).

On the top tier, there are often photos of deceased friends and relatives or religious statues and candles. Most of the rest of the altar space is covered with special foods and beverages, especially *pan de muerto*, fruits, and hot chocolate.

"The *angelitos* will leave at noon, and then we will put out the food and drinks for the adult spirits," Francisco says. I am not wearing a watch, and neither is Francisco. I look around the house, but I don't see any clocks. I wonder how he can be so precise about the timing.

It is very warm indoors, so Francisco and I go outside and sit on a porch facing the courtyard. An old woman walks by carrying a bundle of firewood, which she drops outside the kitchen before she enters. "That is my mother," Francisco says. Her name is Vincenta, she is seventy-six, and she has the classic hawk nose and high cheekbones of a full-blooded Zapotec.

Suddenly, the church bells begin ringing and fireworks explode all over the village. A parrot in a cage hanging from the eaves above us begins to shriek. I marvel at how perfectly the village is synchronized. There is never any doubt about when it is precisely noon on November First in the village of San Lorenzo Cacaotepec.

Francisco looks squarely into my eyes. "The *angelitos* are leaving now," he says with a quiet smile. Vincenta and Margarita come out of the kitchen carrying a bowl of black *mole*, a bottle of mescal and glasses, and some *pan de muerto*, which they take into the living room to place on the *ofrenda*. Francisco and I go watch.

"My father was born here on this farm eighty-five years ago," says Francisco. Crispin Marquez worked so hard that people called him El Machin, "the machine." As soon as Francisco was born, people called him El Machin Chico, "the little machine."

Francisco says that he has no photo of his father to mark his altar. But because El Machin loved mescal and *mole negro*, every year the family gives him those things. El Machin Chico pours El Machin Viejo a hefty shot of mescal and places it on the *ofrenda*.

Francisco leads me back to the porch and insists that I join him in a shot of mescal. I understand that I am not just joining El Machin Chico in this mescal; I am also joining El Machin Senior, and to refuse would be an insult. I can also see that by this logic I could become very drunk, very quickly. After a few, I say my good-byes and head off for the village center.

The farm and the countryside are lush and green. By comparison, the village, with its rutted roads and open sewers, is not much to look at, but I spend the rest of the day there gladly. I visit *ofrendas*, give and receive loaves of bread, and eat and drink with the people of the village and all their dead friends and relatives.

I am surprised to see a Día de los Muertos *ofrenda* in the village church. I grew up a Catholic, and I was aware that November First, All Saints' Day, formerly known as Allhallows, had inspired Halloween, or Allhallows Eve. But Halloween is far from an official Christian holiday. In my community some fundamentalist Christians have complained that Halloween decorations should be banned from public schools. And yet, here in Oaxaca, Día de los Muertos is perhaps the most important Catholic holiday of the year.

As it happened, Davíd Carrasco, a professor of comparative religion at Princeton, was in Oaxaca for Day of the Dead. I called him at his hotel, and we discussed the *ofrendas* we had seen that day. Carrasco was particularly interested in the similarity between the modern *ofrenda* and the ancient ceremonial pyramids of Mesoamerica, which were also heaped with fruits and flowers. The holiday predates Catholicism's arrival in Mexico, Carrasco has written, but Catholicism cleverly expanded to include it.

I talked to several other trained observers about the ideas behind Day of the Dead, such as the belief that your life on this earth depends on treating the dead well and that if the dead are not properly worshiped, your own economic security and health could be jeopardized. I heard about villages where people spend all night in the graveyard to welcome the dead back, and I heard about fear of the vengeful ignored dead and of angry spirits with no homes to go to.

In Día de los Muertos, you can find layers upon layers of meaning stretching back into prehistory. But after spending the day with El Machin Chico and his family, I came to a very simple understanding of the holiday. Día de los Muertos is a time for the living to join their dead family and friends in a joyful feast.

That night, I had a dream in which I saw the face of a crying baby. I woke up and thought of my first and only son, who was stillborn. At the suggestion of the grief counselor at the hospital, my ex-wife and I gave the child a name: Andrew, after my grandfather. We had a brief memorial service, and for a few years we lit a candle on his birthday. But since the birth of my two daughters, I had rarely thought of him.

But this year, I plan to celebrate the Day of the Dead. My *ofrenda* will have an old black-and-white picture of my dad and a sonogram of Andrew on the top tier. Underneath that, I'll put out a glass of Scotch and a ham-salad sandwich for Dad and a tiny cup of hot chocolate and a sweet bun for Andrew. Then, on November First, all three generations of us will sit down and enjoy a meal together.

Universal Pizza Truths

The baker slides his long wooden paddle under our pizza and pulls it steaming from the oven. Above his head, the sign in Spanish reads: "El Cuartito, 1934–1994, 60th Anniversary of Great Pizza—Thanks to you, your parents, and your grandparents." The ceiling fans turn slowly over the crowded wooden tables where we're sitting. As the waiter rounds the corner with our pizza, I notice that the terrazzo floor is worn all the way down to the cement along the path he treads.

The El Cuartito Special, topped with tomato sauce, ham, mozzarella, fresh tomato slices, red peppers, and green olives with a sunny-side-up egg baked in the middle, is quite a meal. Although it is piled high with ingredients, the crust is still crisp on the bottom. The patina of history that covers the walls and floors and ancient stand-up counters at El Cuartito not only adds to the flavor of your pizza-eating experience, it also reminds you that pizza is a very old tradition in Buenos Aires, Argentina.

If you ranked the cities of the world according to how hard it is to find a street corner without a pizzeria, Buenos Aires would be right up there with Naples and Brooklyn. And like pizza lovers the world over, *porteños,* as the citizens of Buenos Aires are known, are fiercely loyal to their favorites. They claim their city's pizzerias rank with the best in the world. And as a pizza zealot in my own right, I intend to put their claims to the test.

If a Latin American country with a pizza tradition sounds odd, consider that the Buenos Aires phone book contains more Italian surnames than Spanish ones. With its ubiquitous espresso bars, trattorias, and pizzerias and a language that is supposed to be Spanish but sounds like Italian, Buenos Aires recalls an earlier meaning of the word *Latin*—somebody from Rome.

Rome is easy to picture as my girlfriend, Marion, and I check out the famous pizzerias along Avenida Corrientes, downtown's main drag. At Pizzería Guerrín, Luciano Pavarotti's twin brother is sitting at a table in the dining room washing down his pizza with a quart of beer. An elegantly attired little old lady who must be in her eighties is eating a slice with a knife and fork at the shiny marble counter. The cashier is wrapping up boxes of pizzas to go in elaborate purple paper decorated with gold Guerrín logos. The perfume of pizza is all around us as we trade bites from a garlicky, rich slice with spinach and white sauce and an anchovy slice that tastes like one of Philadelphia's tomato pies.

Farther down Corrientes, we recognize the famous Café de los Inmortales by the huge poster of Carlos Gardel that towers above it. Gardel was the most popular tango singer in Buenos Aires early in the century. I once saw a black-and-white photo of "Los Inmortales" that was dated 1910, and I've been eager to eat in this historic landmark ever since.

"I'll have what Gardel had," I tell the waiter when he comes to our table.

"Gardel never ate here," he says. "This place didn't open until 1950."

"But the old photos—I thought this place was Gardel's hangout," I mumble in miserable Spanish. The original Café de los

Inmortales is long gone, he explains. This place is a modern re-creation. He grows increasingly impatient as we look at the menu. There are pages and pages of pizzas—plain pizzas, combination pizzas, artichoke pizzas, eggplant pizzas, *fugazzas*, *fugazzetas*, and more. We hastily order a Roquefort *fugazzeta*, a tomato and hearts of palm salad, and a bottle of Sangiovese. *Fugazza* is something like Italy's focaccia, but here the flat crusty bread is topped with mozzarella and onions. *Fugazzeta* is a crust with cheese.

"I'll have what Gardel had," Marion mimics cruelly after the waiter leaves. I drink my wine and fume. When the *fugazzeta* arrives, we are overwhelmed. We both like Roquefort, but this is ridiculous—it is melted in a pool that must be half an inch deep.

"It's good, but one slice is all I can eat," I tell Marion. So we sit and drink our wine, write a few postcards, and watch the *porteños* come and go. I nibble at another slice, only because the Roquefort goes so well with the salad and the wine. By the time the wine is gone, I am surprised to realize that we have eaten the whole *fugazzeta*.

After eating another half a dozen pizzas over the course of a week, I am ready to make some judgments. My favorite pizzeria in B.A. is a little neighborhood café called Romario on Calle Cabello, where they bake the pizzas in a brick oven with a roaring wood fire. The olive oil–coated crusts come out of the brick oven with a deep-fried sort of crunchiness, and the wood fire gives the toppings a rustic, smoky flavor.

As I try to express my conclusions, Marion and I get into our usual pizza fight. As good as the crust at Romario is, I say that I don't like the texture as much as, say, the yeasty brick-oven crust at Frank Pepe's in New Haven, Connecticut. Marion accuses me of being hopelessly pizza-centric. If I had grown up in

Buenos Aires, I would call this the best pizza in the world. If I'd grown up in Chicago, the best in the world would surely be a deep dish. But just because I grew up in Connecticut, I have this stupid prejudice in favor of Frank Pepe's. That's why rankings are ridiculous, she says.

And so is the whole food-writer schtick of going around the world rating things, proclaiming this the best chocolate and that the best coffee . . . I shrink a little in my chair. Maybe Marion's right. Maybe ranking foreign foods by hometown American standards really is redneck chauvinism . . . . But then again, she's never been to Pepe's.

On the way home from Buenos Aires, we stop in Punta del Este, a beach resort in Uruguay. In a beautiful little Italian deli called Tutto Sapori, the owner, Franco Cinquegrana, hears our accents and comes over to introduce himself. He speaks great American English.

We talk a little about Italian food around the world. Franco knows Buenos Aires pizza, New York pizza, and Neapolitan pizza too. "I go to Italy four or five times a year, and I used to live in New York," he says. "My son still lives in Connecticut." A smile crosses my face at the mention of my former home state, and I take a chance.

"So where's the best pizza in the world, Franco?"

"I'll tell you what I told them in Italy," he says, waving one finger in the air. "They may have invented pizza in Naples, but the best pizza in the world is Frank Pepe's in New Haven, Connecticut."

Marion is speechless, and I can't stop laughing.

A Ruthenian Christmas Carol

In the two generations since my grandmother emigrated from Eastern Europe, my Slavic heritage had pretty well faded away. I never really noticed its absence—until I had kids. And then something seemed to be wrong, especially during the holiday season. My Jewish wife taught the kids about Hanukkah and Jewish culture, but I had nothing to pass along but generic ditties like "Jingle Bells." For the first time in my life, I felt some sort of tribal loyalty welling up. My mother's first-generation tendency was to ditch her immigrant mother's Old World ways and assimilate into the American mainstream. Now I felt the urge to rediscover my lost culture. I wanted to give my kids their own sense of ethnic identity—especially at Christmas.

In my dim recollections of Christmas past, there was an ethnic celebration we used to have at Grandma's house. I was only five years old at the time, but the faded thirty-five-year-old memories were of hay on the floor, flickering candles, Christmas carolers in strange costumes at the front door, a huge table full of mushrooms and stuffed cabbages, and the unforgettable taste of raw garlic.

We moved away from Grandma's neighborhood when I was six, and unfortunately, no one in my family could recall the details of her Christmas Eve dinner. But fatherly determination eventually set in, and I started following leads. I visited libraries. I called the parish priest of Grandma's Byzantine Catholic Church in western Pennsylvania. And eventually, I took a plane to Chicago to meet a professor who said he could explain the recipes, the customs, and the meanings behind the holiday traditions of my grandmother's homeland, Slovakia.

"Are you sure you're Slovak?" was the first question Dr. Vasyl Markus, a retired professor of political science at Loyola University, asked when I arrived at his office. The Christmas Eve feast I had described to him wasn't a Slovak tradition, he insisted. I assured him that my grandmother came from Slovakia.

Not everybody who lives in Slovakia is Slovak, he informed me. After a brief interrogation, Dr. Markus concluded that my grandmother's Christmas Eve feast, her maiden name (Bender), and the Byzantine Catholic Church she attended all suggested that she was actually from the same ethnic background that he was: Ruthenian. There are currently around 140,000 Ruthenians living in Slovakia, he said.

Ruthenian? I had no idea what a Ruthenian was, but I was sure there was some mistake. Surely my grandmother knew what nationality she was. "Ah, but it was all very complicated back then," Dr. Markus explained. "To identify yourself as a Ruthenian was an act of political defiance in those days."

There are an estimated 1 million Ruthenians (also called Rusyns, Carpatho-Rusyns, and Rusnaks) spread out in the Carpathian Mountains of Poland, Slovakia, Ukraine, Romania, and Hungary. But the ethnic group has been suppressed for so long that it has become unclear exactly what a Ruthenian is. Since the fall of Soviet communism, a lively debate has begun. Some claim that the Ruthenians have a distinct written language, while others argue that the Ruthenian tongue is actually a dialect of Ukrainian. Some Ruthenians consider themselves a separate people; others consider themselves Ukrainians, Poles, or Slovaks.

What constitutes an ethnicity is a difficult question. And not many Ruthenian immigrants of my grandmother's generation were prepared to argue about it. Since there has never been a Ruthenian state in modern history, on arriving in the United States, most of these immigrants simply identified themselves as Ukrainians, Slovaks, or Hungarians. Before World War I, when my grandmother emigrated, the region she grew up in was ruled by Austria-Hungary. Czechoslovakia was created after the war, and its new borders encompassed her former home. (This area became part of Ukraine in 1945.) She always said we were Czechoslovakian, but since there was no Czechoslovakia when she left, that didn't mean much. "If you wish to be sure about your heritage, you should pinpoint the village your grandmother came from," Dr. Markus suggested.

The first pay phone I found, on the street outside the Ukrainian Culture Center, was too noisy. My grandmother, who at eighty-one is a little hard of hearing, couldn't even recognize my voice. Finally I found a quieter one—but she still couldn't understand why in the world I was calling her from downtown Chicago to find out which village she grew up in. Judging by the laughs I got from people passing by, I'd say shouting into a pay phone about Eastern European geography with your slightly deaf grandmother is a great idea for a stand-up comedy routine. Grandma's memory isn't what it used to be. She couldn't shed any light on the Ukrainian-Ruthenian subject, but she did remember that her childhood village was called Jakubiany.

"Jakubiany, Jakubiany," Markus mused when I got back. "That's in my region—they have a very nice church there, I think. . . ." He climbed onto a chair and rummaged in a pile of maps on top of a filing cabinet. Then he climbed down and showed me a map of Slovakia. He'd marked the Ruthenian areas in the Carpathian Mountains with a highlighter.

"There, you see, Jakubiany is a Ruthenian village!" I was dumbfounded as I inspected the little dot of Jakubiany in the

Ruthenian zone. Ruthenian? I had never even heard of a Ruthenian until today. And now, according to the kindly doctor, I was one. I was only looking for a few recipes. Now I had a new nationality.

"Svjata Vecerja, the Christmas Eve feast you're interested in, has become a sociological phenomenon here in the United States," Markus told me as we walked to the Ukrainian Culture Center's dining room for lunch. "Today, the old Christmas traditions are really the strongest among the grandchildren and great-grandchildren of the immigrants. During the decades of communism, Christmas celebrations were all but abandoned in the homeland. Now we Americans are going back over there to help Ruthenians and Ukrainians remember their own customs. People like those here in this room—people like yourself—are the ones who have kept this tradition alive."

I was wide-eyed at the scene in the culture center's huge dining hall—a roomful of people who all looked like they could be my mother's relatives. I was also touched to discover that although it was only October, the table where we were to sit had been set with elaborate Christmas Eve decorations.

A loaf of bread with a candle in the middle was the centerpiece; a flower arrangement contained the ritual shock of wheat. I had expected to taste a couple of holiday dishes, but the ladies of the Ukrainian Culture Center had already prepared a full-scale Christmas Eve dinner.

"The shock of wheat is the symbol of your ancestors, your *didukh*," said Orysia Harasowsky, one of the women who had cooked the feast. As she took my plate, she told me that the dinner consists of twelve vegetarian dishes, which are supposed to contain something from every aspect of nature.

"From the water, fish—when we make gefilte fish, we make a whole stuffed fish, not the little fish balls," she advised. Then there's something from the garden, like stuffed cabbage. As the narrative progressed, my plate got fuller and fuller. There must be something from the fields: wheat bread and dumpling dough. From the forest we have mushroom gravy," Orysia said. "And they have to be wild mushrooms, not those little white ones from the grocery store!" she scolded. "From the orchard, I got fruit compote with dried apples and prunes; and from the sky, honey."

"Honey from the sky?"

"You know," said Orysia, fluttering her fingers, "from the bees."

The hay and wheat are a carryover from antiquity—the feast was celebrated in Slavic lands long before Christianity was introduced, Dr. Markus said. It began as an agricultural festival that celebrated the return of the sun after the winter solstice, when the days began to lengthen. In the tenth century, the agricultural festival was fused with Christmas.

I asked them if they ate raw garlic at their Christmas Eve dinner like my grandmother did. No, we put garlic under the tablecloth, one of the ladies said. Markus explained that the Christmas Eve ceremony varies from village to village throughout the Ruthenian and Ukrainian regions. "In our area, it was the custom to wrap chains around the legs of the dining room table to symbolize holding together the family," he said. Some regions ate different dishes, and some had different symbols, I learned, but I was too delighted with the spirit of the festivities to nitpick about the details. Besides, the food was wonderful.

Orysia proudly handed me a cup of her borscht. It is an excellent version of that famous beet soup, full of big chunky vegetables, with a rich, sharp sour taste that fills your mouth right to the back of your throat. Dr. Markus found me a cookbook that contained all of the recipes I'd been looking for along with a step-by-step description of the ritual festivities, so I stopped taking notes and started wolfing down the stuffed cabbage.

I dug into a couple of cabbage rolls and four or five plump potato-filled dumplings, which resembled crescent-shaped ravioli, all smothered in thick wild-mushroom gravy. As I struggled to mop up all of the sensational gravy made with big, meaty dried mushrooms, Orysia returned with a full plate of cabbage rolls.

"These are hotter," she advised.

I tried not to be a glutton, but it was the food of my child-hood, and I don't come across it very often. It is a cuisine full of simple, earthy flavors. Wheat, cabbage, and potatoes are the central ingredients, and sour is everybody's favorite taste. Vinegar, sauerkraut, and the fermented beet juice called *kvas* are traditional seasonings, and they are used in concentrations that can make the uninitiated pucker and wince.

The sweet gray-haired ladies who fed me looked like my grandmother, and they seemed to take the same joy in watching me eat. As the feeding frenzy wound down, six people approached our table and formed a circle. They burst into a rousing song in Ukrainian—a traditional Christmas carol.

As I looked at their faces I saw the carolers who gathered outside my grandmother's door on the snowy Christmas Eve when I was five years old. In their foreign but familiar words, I heard the sound of my great-grandmother's accent. The smells of poppy seeds and cabbage, mushrooms and fresh-baked bread were all wafting from the table in front of me, and all of my long-lost Christmas memories came flooding back. I choked back a lump in my throat, but it was no use. I was overwhelmed. I wiped away the tears as I listened to my Christmas carols.

Nowadays, my daughters and I start every Christmas season with this ancient celebration from my Ruthenian heritage. The girls don't like the sour flavors much, but I'm willing to bet that someday, when I'm a grandpa, they'll ask me for the recipes.

Grandma's Ruthenian Mushroom Soup

2/3 cup dried wild mushrooms
1 cup chopped white mushrooms

1 small onion, chopped
3 tablespoons oil
1/4 cup carrots, diced
1/4 cup celery, diced
1 tablespoon barley
1/2 cup cooked white beans
1-1/2 tablespoons flour
1/2 teaspoon dried thyme
1/2 teaspoon garlic powder
1/2 teaspoon white pepper
Salt to taste
1/4 cup vinegar or to taste

Wash the wild mushrooms and simmer in 5 cups of hot water for 30 minutes. Strain the mushrooms out, chop them coarsely, and return them to the stock. Cook the onions and white mushrooms in 2 tablespoons of oil over low heat until nicely browned.

Add the onions, white mushrooms, carrots, celery, and barley to the dried mushroom stock and cook until tender. Add the beans. Brown the flour in 1 tablespoon of oil and add the seasonings. Ladle a little of the mushroom broth into the browned flour and stir until dissolved. Add the mixture back to the stock. Correct the seasonings and add salt and vinegar to taste. (Add lots of vinegar if you're a real Ruthenian.) Simmer for 15 minutes. Serve hot.

Yields 4 servings.